# BELIEVE IT

BELIEVE IT

# BELIEVE IT

## JAMIE KERN LIMA

**THORNDIKE PRESS**
A part of Gale, a Cengage Company

**GALE**
A Cengage Company

LIBRARY OF CONGRESS CIP DATA ON FILE.
CATALOGUING IN PUBLICATION FOR THIS BOOK
IS AVAILABLE FROM THE LIBRARY OF CONGRESS.

ISBN-13: 978-1-4328-8711-7 (hardcover alk. paper)

Published in 2021 by arrangement with Gallery Books, a division of Simon & Schuster, Inc.

Printed in Mexico
Print Number: 01          Print Year: 2021

*For the loves of my life: Wonder and Wilder*

*And for each and every person who has helped me to believe . . . in myself, in a mission greater than myself, in God, and in the great potential each of us has to help heal humanity through love.*

# CONTENTS

# INTRODUCTION

The greatest risk any of us will take, is to
be seen as we truly are.
— CINDERELLA

"It's a no. We're going to pass on investing
in your company. If you want the truth, I'm
just not sure women will buy makeup from
someone who looks like you. You know, with
your body and weight." This is what a
potential investor said to me, face-to-face,
on one of the most difficult days in my
journey as an entrepreneur. And as a
woman. Watching his mouth move and
hearing those words come out, I felt flooded
by the pain from a lifetime of battling self-
doubt and body-doubt. It was also a moment when I worried everything was on the
line, and my company's survival was in his
hands. It would be another year before I
could pay myself, when my diet staples
consisted of ramen noodles, $1 hot dogs

from the Costco to-go counter, and frozen yogurt samples from the shop down the street.

Has anyone ever said something so hurtful to you that you had to do everything in your power not to replay it over and over in your head? This was one of many moments when I had to figure out how to handle someone not believing in me, while still figuring out how to believe in myself.

I took a deep breath, looked him in the eye, and listened to his words of rejection graciously. Then I started to see my own fear staring back at me, and knew I needed to figure out how to keep my faith bigger than it. While the logical part of my mind wondered if he was right, deep down inside I felt this overwhelming gut instinct that he was wrong. And I also knew the journey of proving that would hinge first on me learning to truly believe it for myself.

I'm excited to take you on this journey in the pages of this book, and my hope is that through the wild ride, filled with victorious peaks and devastating pits, you'll discover inspirational takeaways that impact how you believe in your own power and dreams. I've read a lot of books where I felt like the advice was coming from a faraway pedestal without including the real, raw, messy human side of it all. I was left wondering what the behind-the-scenes version was. And how I was supposed to connect to it and actually understand how to apply the lessons to my *real* life.

In this book, I hope you feel that the REAL YOU is accepted here. Because I am going to show you the REAL ME. Not just the celebrated person who started a company in her living room with close to no money, sold it for over a billion dollars, became the first female CEO of a brand at the largest cosmetics company in the world, helped change the way the entire beauty industry shows images of women globally, and is now splashed on fancy magazine pages, appears on TV shows, and is on the *Forbes* list, but the real me and real struggles, stories, and lessons behind the headlines. The real me who has struggled with anxiety, self-doubt, body-doubt, and God-doubt. The real me who has cried myself to sleep on countless nights when it felt like no one believed in my ideas. The real me who battles feeling not good enough, not smart enough, or not (fill in the blank) enough.

After seeing the sexy, highlight-reel versions of my story in the press and on social media so many times, usually in the form of a business success story, and then receiving countless letters, emails, and messages from so many people, I realized that in our social-media/headline–driven world, we rarely get to learn the truth. On the outside, the story the press tells about me looks like a fairy tale. Or it looks like it must have come easy. Or that I just got really lucky. Or that I am one of those *other* people or some bionic unicorn. It made me realize how important it is to tell the *real* story behind the flashy headlines, the story that will perhaps let you know you're not alone.

Being vulnerable is hard, but I've learned that sharing our true, flawed, authentic selves is the only way real connection and love can happen. It's the only way to step into our full power and purpose in our lives.

In this part memoir, part manifesto, I'm going to share several of the deeply personal and professional struggles and triumphs, risks and lessons, and failures and victories that have helped me learn *how* to step into my full power. The business lessons in this book have fundamentally changed my personal life in how I parent and love. And the personal lessons I share are the keys to how I turned a dream into a billion-dollar business. This is the story of how it all really happened and how it almost didn't. I hope it leaves you knowing that you have the power inside of you right now to believe in yourself and your dreams too, and then to truly live them! This book is for you if you've ever been underestimated, even if you were the one underestimating yourself.

See, I believe every one of us has a light inside of us — a light that can burn self-doubt to the ground and illuminate your path ahead; a light that gives you the power and confidence to show up authentically and be seen. My hope is that by revealing my journey to find and spark the light of confidence and purpose inside of myself, you are inspired to find the light inside of *you,* even if it's for the first time, or the first time in a long time. Once you are able to illuminate your own path (and celebrate it!), you not only help illuminate the world, you help clear the path for others to do the same by leading the way.

If you picked up this book, I don't believe it's an accident or a coincidence. I believe you and I are meant to be connected in this way. And I believe we all have the power to ignite our light and to know we're worthy and enough exactly as we are. Only by fully embracing this can you align with your true, authentic self and step into the purpose and calling you have for your life. You have everything you need inside of you. It's all in you already. My goal is to create a space with the words and stories shared here for you to embrace that more fully for yourself.

And just a heads-up — the stories in these pages are going to get super personal. So when I imagine you opening up this book right now, it feels like I'm opening the front door of my home to you, reaching my arms out to give you a big hug and inviting you inside, where I have fresh chocolate chip cookies in the oven for your arrival, and there's also some cookie dough still in the bowl, in case, like me, you like eating that even better. I've got a coffee mug with an inspiring or funny saying on it waiting for you, and I can make you coffee, or fill it with wine, like I sometimes fill mine. And I know you won't judge me for greeting you at the door in my favorite comfy sweats. I even have an extra pair if you need some. You are welcome here, and you belong here, and you'll find love here, exactly as you are.

My hope is that these pages become your home for a bit and that you feel like you belong here. Because I believe we are all connected and that we so often share the same feelings, the same doubts, the same hurts, and the same need for love. And what we give to each other, we automatically give to ourselves.

In this book, I share some of the greatest personal and professional lessons I've learned from some really difficult, hurtful lows to some almost unbelievable, fairy-tale-like highs — from how haters stomped me down, to how meeting some of the most incredible and influential women in the world lifted me up. From almost losing everything, hearing *no* more times than I could count, and figuring out how to keep going, to losing a lot of "friends" the day I challenged the entire beauty industry to change. From overcoming the struggles of people-pleasing and perfectionism to learning that being brave is more important than being liked. From being given up for adoption as a baby to figuring out how to believe God made me on purpose. There are powerful lessons I've learned about believing in yourself, following your intuition, and taking risks. Lessons about rising higher than you ever thought you could, because where you come from doesn't determine where you're going; and about connecting with others (like we're doing here!), because life's not meant to do alone.

While this book is a space where I share my stories, my failures, my struggles, and my victories with you, this is your book. While we may not have met yet in person, I am writing this book from a place of pure love, from me to you. My intention is that everything I've experienced, learned, and shared in these pages is, in some way, of service and value to you. One of my favorite prayers is "God use me, love use me." With that said, let's get this love letter started! Here we go . . .

XOXO,
Jamie

p.s. I love you
p.p.s. You're worthy of love

■ ■ ■ ■

# PART ONE:
# BELIEVE

■ ■ ■ ■

# ONE:
# WHEN YOUR INTUITION TALKS TO YOU, *BELIEVE* IT

That thing we call intuition? It's your soul.
You can trust it.

— ANONYMOUS

"Take a breath, my darling, you're doing great," said the QVC host as she grabbed my shaking arm, held it steady, and, like a pro, covered for me on live national television. As I tried hard to appear confident and fought not to tremble, I wondered if the viewers from across the country saw more than just my bright red face and shaking arms. I wondered if they could feel my fear. I was down to under $1,000 in my combined company and personal bank account, which would only cover me for a few more weeks of expenses before I'd have to go out of business. What if going with my gut, instead of what the experts told me to do, in this life-altering moment where everything was on the line, turned out to be wrong?

Before I stood there shaking in my heels on national television, before I ever had the idea to create a makeup and skin care company, I was working as a television news anchor and reporter. I loved my job so much that I thought for sure it was what I'd do for my entire career. My parents worked a lot when I was growing up, and when I was home alone, the daytime talk shows (along with MTV, which I wasn't allowed to watch) kept me company. Oprah, in particular, was a huge influence. The dream on my heart, for as long as I could remember, had always been to host my own daytime talk show where I could do what I loved: interview other people and share their stories with the world.

You know that famous saying, life is what happens to you while you're making other plans? Well, in my late twenties, while working as a morning news anchor, I started developing a skin condition on my face called rosacea. It's hereditary and usually appears in the form of red patches, sometimes bumpy or sandpaper-like in texture and sometimes up to the size of an apple. Strangers at the grocery store would ask me if I had a sunburn or if I was feeling well, all because my cheeks would get super red some days. I became self-conscious. I learned from dermatologists that there wasn't a proven cure, just some ways to try to limit the severity of the flare-ups.

Hoping to cover it up, I started spending my time and money trying every makeup foundation or concealer I could get my hands on. Drugstore brands and, even though they were way out of my price range, I'd save up to buy and try any department store brand I could get my hands on too. The prime-time anchors had professional makeup artists, so I asked for help and tried any solutions or products they'd heard of. Nothing worked. Either a product wouldn't give enough coverage or, if it did, I would look like I was wearing a mask of makeup. There were moments when I was anchoring the news live on TV and I'd hear my producer in my earpiece saying, "There's something on your face. Can you wipe it off?" But I knew there wasn't anything I could wipe off. It was my bright red rosacea starting to appear through the cracks where the makeup was breaking up on my skin under the hot HD lights of television. It was really embarrassing, and it also started to make me feel insecure. That voice of self-doubt in my head would tell me things that

I would never say to another human being. You know, things like, *You're not pretty* or *This is going to hurt your career* or *Viewers might change the channel when they see you* or *Ratings will go down and you'll get fired.* Ahh, that inner critic we all have. Don't you just love her?

I needed to figure out this makeup thing. I realized that it's easy to find makeup that looks good when you really don't have anything to cover, but if you have ultra-sensitive skin, or uneven pigmentation and texture, then it's hard to find anything that works.

I had what Oprah calls an ah-ha moment when it occurred to me that if I was having this struggle, there must be so many other people out there who, like me, couldn't find makeup that worked for them. Or maybe they'd just flat-out given up on it. And it wasn't just about finding the right foundation. I also realized none of the countless beauty companies out there spoke to women like me with real skin challenges, and none used images of women who looked like me to sell their products. They all seemed to use only over-photoshopped, filtered, and altered images of women that were virtually unattainable. Not only were those advertising images of "aspirational" women unrelatable, they weren't even real. When I looked at them, they made me feel like I wasn't beautiful or like I wasn't enough.

As I immersed myself in all of this, it struck me that for most of my life growing up as a girl and now as a woman, I'd wasted so much time feeling insecure about my body, dieting constantly, focusing on being "pretty," and never feeling like I was. The more I realized how much of my life I had lost to this, I started to get *really, really* mad. But I also got really inspired to change it. The blessing in all of this was that it lit a fire in me.

My gut told me that women were sick of seeing airbrushed images of people who didn't look like them promoting products that didn't work.

And that's when the idea for IT Cosmetics was born. I had a vision to create makeup that was good for your skin, worked on all ages, skin types, and skin tones, and gave you coverage if you wanted it but didn't look like a mask. And, unlike practically every other beauty brand in existence at the time, I wanted to use women of all ages, all sizes, all skin tones, and all skin issues as models. I truly believed that not only was there a need for this type of product but that there was an even greater need, on behalf of all women, to shift the culture around the images the beauty industry puts out as "aspirational."

It's one thing to have a dream; it's another thing to do it.

In 2007, I got married to Paulo, who I met my first year of grad school, in statistics class. (Super romantic!) I'll never forget the first moment I saw him. The professor had put a huge, long equation on the board for the whole class to solve with our business calculators (the romance continues . . .), and then I heard this guy blurt out the answer from a few rows behind me. When I turned around to see who it was, our eyes met. His were sparkling brown Brazilian eyes coupled with a very revenge-of-the-nerds-like smart vibe — all that was missing was a pocket pen-protector — and I immediately felt in my gut that he and I had some type of connection.

When he was five years old, Paulo immigrated to the United States from Brazil with his family. He grew up in a town just outside of Manhattan, where he dealt with a lot of discrimination in his early years. Kids would ask him if he lived in trees back home and tell him to go back where he came from. His family eventually moved into the city, which was much more accepting. He was raised around diverse cultures, traveled a lot, and excelled in school.

Before meeting Paulo, I had always gone for the bad-boy type, who always broke my heart, or the athletes, who also always broke my heart. But that first day my eyes met Paulo's in statistics class, I found myself crushing hard on the supersmart guy. I didn't want to wait to see if the crush was mutual, so I asked him if he wanted to study for class together. He said yes, and we set a date and time. That date came and he never showed up. Never called. Nothing.

When I saw him at school the next day, he could tell I was mad. He later apologized and told me that since he's from Brazil, he didn't realize it was a formal commitment and thought it was just a maybe commitment. *Huh? Didn't you move to the States when you were five and live here ever since?* Anyway, to this day he says it was the best mistake he ever made. He's convinced that standing me up got my attention and made me even more interested.

Paulo was unlike anyone I had ever dated. He was oblivious to outward appearances — his and everyone else's. He'd owned only one pair of jeans for over ten years, but (often in those very jeans) he had traveled the world, which was exciting to me. At that point in my life, I hadn't had much opportunity to travel. He had one unibrow-style eyebrow, and he wasn't at all aware of it. What freedom! Today, I celebrate his brows running wild and free, but at the time, not so much. At one point while we were dating, he let me pluck his unibrow into two distinct eyebrows. It felt like such a victory! In hindsight, that may have been his first introduction to the beauty world. He was completely oblivious to fashion or looks, but Paulo was SOOO smart and I learned that I found that SOOOOO hot! I was really, really drawn to him.

Once we'd been dating for a while, though, something got in the way of my feelings for him. Growing up, I'd seen so many examples in my life and in the world of women dimming their own lights to make men happy. Women subsidizing men at the expense of their own power and dreams. Even in graduate school, they made the tired joke of women being there for their MRS degrees. That was not my plan. I grew up believing that men hold women back, and that belief transitioned into the conviction that I didn't want to get married. Many of my friends had been dreaming of their weddings from the time they were little girls, but that wasn't me! I wanted to build an empire.

Paulo and I had been dating for five years. Shortly before he proposed, I asked him not to, and reminded him that I didn't know exactly why but I just wasn't ready for marriage. (I know, I know, this is the most romantic story ever!) Nevertheless (listening to his own gut, I guess), he proposed a week later. His confidence and conviction were inspiring. "I love you with all my heart," he said. And I truly loved him. I prayed about it. When I pray, a small voice that I trust often comes to me in the form of intuition. In my soul, I knew what was right, but in this moment my intuition shocked the heck out of me. It didn't align with my mind, but I set aside my fear and doubt to follow it. Marrying Paulo felt right, and I said yes.

Our wedding was so filled with love, and then (this is the most romantic part), on our honeymoon flight to South Africa, the two of us wrote the business plan for IT Cosmetics. I'd worried so much about a man holding me back from my dreams, but we kicked off our marriage going full speed ahead on one of them. While I learned later that working together isn't always the ideal way to start off a marriage, one of the upsides was easing that fear. It was a gift to have him jumping on board with me.

When we got back home, we both quit our jobs and started the company in our living room. I was sad to give up the dream of hosting a talk show, but I felt an even stronger calling in a different direction. Sometimes knowing when to let go of a dream is as important as knowing when to follow one.

We poured all our waking hours and every penny we had into sourcing chemists and manufacturers, creating the product, assembling the advisory board, and launching the company.

In order to create our first packaging, I begged for help from a friend who had worked with me in TV news doing the on-air graphics — you know, like the maps showing crime scene locations that you see on the news. He agreed, and I paid him hourly to come to our house in the wee hours of the morning, before he had to leave for his day job at 8 A.M. He would take his desktop computer out of the trunk of his car each day and set it up on my living room floor. Then we would sit side by side and create. He had never done packaging before and of course neither had I, but we did the best we could.

Paulo and I didn't know anyone personally from the beauty industry, so we had our work cut out for us. This meant a whole lot of googling, a whole lot of cold-calling people we didn't know, a whole lot of bad advice, and a whole lot of mistakes.

On the fly, while obsessively googling everything I could find and learning through sheer hard knocks, I had to figure out how to work with manufacturers and deal with the issues that emerged. Once, we received a whole batch of makeup brushes where the ferrule (the metal ring connecting the bristles to the handle) was falling off after only one or two uses. They wouldn't give us a refund because we were a small client. And if we fought with the manufacturer, we risked losing them.

I also learned tough lessons with product packaging design. Just because the box artwork might look good zoomed in on a computer doesn't mean customers will be able to read it when they're walking by and see it on a store shelf from six feet away. After that mistake, I always signed off on a full-sized proof that I could test in real life before going into production. And (attention, makeup shoppers!) we learned that there was a fine line when it came to deciding what size container to use. Even if the product would last a year, if the package looked too small, people would say it was overpriced. But if it was too much bigger, they'd complain that it wasn't full. There were countless more lessons — I almost wish I didn't know these things now, because I can't shop in the grocery store without worrying when I see packaging mistakes from baby brands trying to fight for shelf space.

Money was super tight, so any job we could do ourselves we did. Paulo took on the task of building our first website. He bought a big yellow book called *HTML for Dummies.* I just knew that because our mission was so powerful, and, after countless formula iterations, we actually had a product that worked, once we launched our website it was going to be huge! And we were counting on the anticipated online sales to pay the bills. I'll never forget the day of its launch. That morning, I was bursting with excitement and anticipation. Once the website went live . . . nothing happened. No orders. I thought maybe it was just taking a minute for people to find out we had a website. Then on the second day, no orders again. Then the third and fourth and fifth days, no orders. Finally, I went where it's so easy to go when you work with your spouse.

"It's broken. You didn't do it right!" I said to Paulo. Then, after more days, and eventually weeks, went by and still there were no orders, all of a sudden adrenaline rushed through my entire body as I saw our very first order come through! I jumped out of my chair in celebration and ran through the house like a little kid on Christmas morning. "Paulo!!! It's our first order!!!! It just came in!!!!" I was so excited.

Paulo smiled at me and said, "That was me. I just placed that order to prove to you the website isn't broken."

I thought once you turned a great idea into an amazing product, it would just sell, right? Whoa, was I wrong! I knew our product would be life-changing if it got into the hands of real women everywhere, but how exactly was it going to get into their hands? Through stores and online, right? But what if all of the retailers said *no*? What if women didn't even realize that the website existed? Getting into retail stores takes someone believing in you and saying *yes*. Promoting a website takes money. We didn't have either.

Wow, how I didn't know what I didn't know! And the more I learned, the more I learned how much I didn't know! I'd worked hard my entire life, but I had no idea how hard it is to be an entrepreneur, where you can't just clock in and out or leave work at the end of the day. When it's your own business, the pressure, the stress, the unremitting worry is there 24/7. It started dominating everything else in life. For the first time, I found it close to impossible to be in any present moment without having thoughts of the business take over. *How will I make money and stay alive? Will the retailers ever respond to my calls? Why isn't anyone covering the product in the press? Is this all a big mistake? What if my gut was wrong? Am I going to lose our entire savings?*

The first two years of our company would be some of the hardest I'd ever experience. We worked one-hundred-plus-hour weeks, sent our product to every retailer, and heard *no* after *no* from almost everyone. *No* from every department store, *no* from ULTA Beauty and Sephora (the two largest open-sell beauty retailers in the country, where, unlike department stores, the products aren't behind a counter and you don't have to talk to a salesperson to buy them), and *no* from QVC. We had a few yeses, but we didn't sell well with them and never made any profit. Despite my career in television, we even failed to sell well during our brief stint on a TV shopping channel in the US called HSN (which QVC eventually acquired). I didn't understand why our product wasn't flying off the shelves.

My first thought was that we needed more product options. Again, I turned to my own experience for inspiration. As a TV news anchor, I was always getting in trouble for my weight fluctuating. To disguise the changes, I had learned how to contour really well. Contouring is using shading and highlighting on your face and body to enhance its shape and features. So I thought that maybe if we launched face and body contouring palettes, those would sell. The new products were super innovative, and we were the first in the market, but being first isn't always a good thing. They didn't sell. (Note: five years later, contouring became a huge trend, and many much larger brands had success by knocking off some of our early products almost identically.)

Our company was staying alive, barely, because of two things. The first was The Shopping Channel Canada, a live TV shopping network based just outside Toronto. We weren't making much profit on it, but they believed in us and kept bringing us back. The second was word of mouth from our customers. The best part about creating a product that truly works and does what it says is that people *do* spread the word. Real women started posting their own "before" and "after" photos online using our product. While we were getting just two or three orders a day on our website, those early grassroots advocates of the brand truly kept us afloat.

After selling on The Shopping Channel for a while, we got to the point where we could hire our first, true, full-time salaried employee. Until then, we had hired only freelance or part-time help or begged friends to lend a hand. Our first hire was one of my best friends, Jacqueline, who happened to be six months pregnant at the time. We couldn't even afford to give Jacquie benefits, but she took the career risk anyway because she believed in what we were doing. So Jacquie came to work every day, sitting with me and Paulo at IKEA desks in our living room. The three of us covered every role in the company, from packing orders to finance, operations, PR, marketing, social media, IT, product development, packaging, sales, education, customer service, and so much more. Often we had no idea what we were doing, but, as an entrepreneur, when you don't have the money to hire someone who does, you just have to figure it out.

Even in the beginning, in my heart and soul I believed what we were doing was bigger than ourselves!

After countless, and I mean countless, iterations of our product formula, we had finally created a concealer formula that worked for skin like mine. And I believed our messaging and vision were truly needed. I believed women were sick and tired of seeing models who didn't look like them. Our WHY, or mission as a company, was to empower all women to believe they were worthy and beautiful and to shift the culture around inclusivity in the beauty industry, which in turn would shift culture everywhere! That was an ambitious mission for someone who kept hearing that her idea wouldn't work from all of the largest beauty retailers and for someone who was selling only two or three orders a day on her website. But this WHY was something I believed in my soul, and focusing on it was, on many days, literally the only thing that gave me the courage to get out of bed when I truly felt like giving up.

Money was dwindling, and I started hitting "no receipt" every time I got cash from an

ATM because I couldn't stomach seeing the balance. We needed to get a *yes* from someone. I didn't understand why all of these amazing beauty stores that carried hundreds of brands were all saying *no* to us. I sent package after package of our product samples in the mail, not only to every beauty retailer and department store, but to every individual employee I could find online who worked there. And . . . nothing. I would make phone call after phone call. Send email after email to get no reply, no call back. It was *so* hard not to let their lack of interest translate into self-doubt in my head.

As an entrepreneur, you gotta do what you gotta do. We couldn't afford to hire anyone else and could barely manage to pay our advisory board and Jacquie, our one full-time employee. And we still couldn't afford to advertise. When you're scrappy, you have to get creative. We decided that *grit* was our middle name. And speaking of middle names, my real middle name is Marie. So guess what? Marie@ItCosmetics.com got her own email address and became our head of public relations and occasionally customer service. Marie would industriously email every beauty editor and TV show to let them know that our founder, Jamie, was available for interviews. Marie hustled. In hindsight, I'm proud of our grit, but still amazed at how clueless we often were. But turns out sometimes that can be a strength. The unremitting persistence and willingness to do whatever it took actually worked quite often. Many beauty editors agreed to try the product, and then wrote about it. That got the word out and led to more people trying the product, which led to them spreading the word. Anytime an article came out, I emailed every buyer I knew at every beauty retailer. I shared how word was spreading about our products, trying to drum up enough excitement for them to meet with me. And then, at last . . . IT HAPPENED! A buyer at Sephora agreed to meet with me at their headquarters in San Francisco!

I thought, *This is IT! She's going to fall in love with the product and give us a chance in their stores.* I was sure this would be my saving grace! My ability to make payroll. The YES we needed in order to go full speed ahead with our vision. At the time, Sephora had over two hundred stores across the country. Through them, people everywhere could discover our products. A few years earlier, before we ever launched the brand, I had a friend who worked at

Sephora. We'd met at their headquarters once and she showed interest and said my ideas were promising, but to my disappointment she had left the company before we launched our products. In the years after, I'd constantly sent them product samples and emails, but they had always shown zero interest. Until now!

I prepared like crazy for the meeting. I pulled snapshots of "before" and "after" photos that women who used our products had posted on the Web. I put together Power-Point presentations that I had printed out at FedEx, then spiral-bound in presentation books with clear acetate covers. It was a shocking ninety-nine cents per printed color page, which adds up. I thought the graphics my same graphic designer friend from the news station helped me design looked *so* good.

I tore apart my closet to find the cutest outfit that fit. (At this point I was working twenty-hour days from our living room in sweats, so fashion was the last thing on my mind.) Packing up the presentation books and product samples in case they didn't have the ten million I'd already sent, I got on a plane and flew to San Francisco. When I entered the Sephora offices, I felt an internal battle ensue. I wanted to be myself, but at the same time felt like I was walking into the offices of the cool kids' club and had to prove I was worthy of being a member.

I was greeted by a lovely girl at the front desk and asked to take a seat in the lobby. It hit me that I was someone who had started a company, launched great products, and had now been invited to a real live meeting at Sephora. I felt *so* overwhelmed with gratitude just to be there, even in the waiting room, as I took it all in: the beautiful art, the stylish lights, the fun vibe, the chic furniture. I kind of felt like Anne Hathaway's character in *The Devil Wears Prada*, like I was an outsider stepping into this fairy-tale world.

About fifteen minutes later, an assistant led me to the conference room. It quickly filled up with five or six people from Sephora, all kind and smiling and inquisitive. I began my presentation by introducing our Bye Bye Under Eye concealer. From the moment we started talking, I could tell they loved beauty products passionately. But I immediately noticed that the head buyer, the one who made the decisions, wasn't so inquisitive. Her eyes glanced at what I was wearing, then darted back to the product I had set on the table. Everyone else in the meeting seemed to be cheering me on, but not her. Have you ever met someone and just felt like they weren't *for* you? I knew I'd have to figure out how to win her over since her opinion would be the deciding factor.

"I really think your customers will love it and it will sell really well in your stores, and I know it will be life-changing for the customers who get their hands on it, especially people like me with skin issues," I said, pointing out the real-life "before" and "after" photos of women using our products.

Suddenly, the head buyer cut me off. "Women don't buy luxury beauty from images like that. You'll have better luck going to mass." "Mass" meant mass market. She was saying that our products might sell better in drugstores. I tried not to show how much this upset me. I felt like she was saying that women who look real don't have money to spend. Maybe what she was saying about the beauty industry had been true up until that point simply because it had only been done one way for so long. I understood why she was saying it; I just had a vision to do things differently.

We were creating high-quality formulas with clinical testing. Because they cost us a lot of money to make, we had to charge the same price points you'd find in Sephora, ULTA, or a department store. Drugstores typically don't carry high-price-point beauty products, so we had no choice but to sell in stores that would carry our quality and prices.

I told her, "Actually, I believe women *will* buy from images of women who look like them. There's a lot of exciting buzz among beauty editors and real women trying the product."

I'll never forget what happened next. I felt a more dramatic shift of energy in the room, almost as if I was wasting her time and her patience for me had run out. She looked me square in the face and with stern conviction said, "If people were talking about this product, I would be hearing about it, and I'm not."

My heart raced. My face felt flushed and hot. I remember hoping my Spanx had absorbed the sweat I felt just about everywhere on my body. Anxiety knotted my stomach like I'd been punched in the gut. After all my conviction that getting a foot in the door was all I needed to make the sale, Sephora was another *no.* But I wanted and *needed* it to be a *yes* so badly. If it hadn't been for the adrenaline rushing through my body, the kind I imagine UFC fighters get when they refuse to tap out even when they're hurt, I think I would have fainted. I wanted to explain to her that the beauty industry needs to change and that she could be part of the change with me. I wanted to save the meeting and get a *yes,* and I wanted to save my company by getting that *yes.* I was devastated — especially because money was dwindling and with it, my dream.

The meeting ended, and I tried to play it cool while packing up my things and thanking everyone for their time. Then I walked to the elevator to leave. The same elevator that I had just ridden up, filled with the hopeful high of anticipation and dreams of a big break, now felt like a ride down to doom. I was doing everything in my power to hold back tears. I was a CEO, so I felt like I had to be unemotional and professional at all times. And I was surrounded by other people in the elevator who might work at Sephora. When the doors slid open, I ran-walked in my heels straight out the lobby doors onto Market Street and around a corner, then hid up against a wall outside a fast-food restaurant and sobbed my eyes out. I didn't know what I was going to do from there. I dreaded calling Paulo and

Jacquie to tell them it was a *no.* Again.

Back in the office in the weeks to come, it was hard to see how this was all going to work out. Rejection hurts so deeply — especially when you value the opinions of the people rejecting you. One of my best friends, Natasha, said something that helped carry me through this time: "You are putting these people on a pedestal. And the only one you should ever put on a pedestal is God. He's the one who decides what doors open and close and when, and your trust should only be in Him. Not in anyone else." And even though I knew she was right, doing this felt so hard.

Through pure resilience, we kept going. It dawned on me that given my desire to change the beauty industry, I probably shouldn't have been surprised that someone *in* the beauty industry didn't like my vision. Because it was not aligned with hers. Or at least with what she was confident could sell well. It was an important realization, but I still had to figure out how we were going to stay in business.

The hustling continued. And continued. And continued. I sent email after email and left voice mail after voice mail with as much passion and excitement in each message as if it were the very first time I'd contacted that person. I would find people's assistants on LinkedIn or elsewhere online and contact them too. The rejection repeated over and over, for years. From Sephora, and ULTA Beauty, and Nordstrom, and all the major department stores. Then one day, I *FINALLY* got through to Allen Burke's assistant. The then head of beauty at QVC, the largest TV shopping channel in the country, Allen Burke is a legend. He was the guy responsible for transforming that old, often cheesy image of selling products on TV into a new image, and he is credited with convincing luxury beauty companies to partner with QVC. Under his leadership, almost all of the most coveted department store brands started selling their products on QVC and do to this day. Because I thought women were tired of products not working for them, I felt like QVC would be the perfect place to show, live on TV, that our products actually worked on real women. I all but begged his assistant to set up a call with him. She promised me she would relay my message, and that he would give me a call back if QVC had any interest. I followed up by sending (yet another) package of product samples and copies of press articles about our products.

As the weeks went by, I was in a constant

state of suspense, obsessively watching the phone, the way you do when you had the best first date ever but don't want to be the first one to text or call. I couldn't think about anything else. Except I couldn't stop thinking about *everything* else. The mounting expenses and our mounting burnout. My fear of losing not just all of our savings but the small amount of money we'd taken from three investors who were friends and family. And the devastating possibility of having to give up this dream. Then, the phone rang!

"Hi, Jamie, this is Allen Burke from QVC." My heart raced, but I mustered up all of my confidence and enthusiastically said hello. He got right to the point. He said he had reviewed our products and packaging with his team of beauty buyers, and the consensus was that we were "*not* the right fit for QVC or for the QVC customer." Just like that, in a matter of seconds, another gut-wrenching *no.* My heart sank. As I paced the bedroom in our apartment/office, tears streamed down my face. I knew that he couldn't see them, and I hoped he couldn't sense them either. I asked him for feedback and input and put in one more pitch, telling him I really believed their customers would love our products. He thanked me for loving QVC but confirmed again it was a *no*. I thanked him for his time. After the call ended, I got under the covers in bed and cried. And cried. And cried. And prayed. And cried some more. Then, the weirdest feeling came over me: I realized that no matter how hard it got, I wasn't going to quit. I just wasn't going to give up. It didn't make sense in my head, but it did make sense in my gut. My intuition was still telling me to keep going.

One of the best things I've ever done is build a toolbox of things that I can pull from when I get knocked down. A toolbox I can use when staring rejection in the face, when I need to remember who I am and why I'm doing what I'm doing. One that's filled with tools that help me believe in myself, even in moments when it feels like no one else does. It's an imaginary toolbox, but it's filled with real-life stories and messages and quotes and prayers that I can pull from to solve problems. I keep this toolbox in my head, in written form on my computer, and sometimes in the Notes app of my phone. It's free to do, and it's something I've built upon and edited year after year. If this sounds like something you need and don't yet have, an easy way to start is to highlight quotes or stories that deeply impact you, and save them all in one place that you can reference quickly.

This toolbox is part of how I knew in that moment, as I lay there under the covers crying over the painful rejection from Allen Burke at QVC, that I wasn't going to give up. I read quote after quote that inspired me and reminded me that almost all great things come with opposition. I read stories I had saved for times like this one, of underdogs who overcame rejection to triumph. I prayed and asked for clarity over whether I should keep going, despite all the rejection. And I really focused on my WHY. See, a lot of people set goals, and even have a goal-setting journal, but I've learned that for me that isn't enough. I believe you have to attach a WHY to any goal, and that WHY has to be so meaningful to you that no matter how hard things get, your belief in your WHY is powerful enough to withstand the hard times when things don't go your way.

Lying there under my covers, I remembered the deep pain I had felt as a little girl when I saw images of beauty that made me feel like I wasn't good enough. I was determined to change this, for other little girls out there who were about to start learning to doubt themselves, and for every grown woman who still does. I was determined to use up every ounce of myself, and every ounce of fight I had inside myself, before tapping out of accomplishing that mission. Before falling asleep that night, I wrote these words and texted them to myself, vowing to read them each day until I didn't need the reminder anymore: *Know your why, then fly, girl, fly.*

The CEW awards show was coming up, and I signed up to demonstrate our product at it. CEW, which stands for Cosmetic Executive Women, is an organization with more than ten thousand members — membership is open to anybody in the beauty industry, from assistants to decision-makers, who sponsor the events, most of whom happen to be women. Once a year, hundreds of products are displayed and demonstrated to all of them. Imagine a huge expo with makeup and skin care products. I was hoping that maybe if other women in the industry tried our Bye Bye Under Eye concealer, they would see how great it was and vote for us to win one of their coveted newcomer awards.

I was assigned to a three-foot demonstration table, and when the doors of the expo opened, I was quickly consumed by countless women in the industry streaming by, pausing to test each product. I was excitedly showing our concealer and explaining why it was special when I noticed a huge QVC booth far in the background. *Oh wow. QVC is here,* I thought. Whenever there was a lull in foot traffic, I would sneak over to the QVC booth, hoping to meet a buyer. We weren't supposed to leave our demonstration tables, so when I saw that the QVC buyers were swarmed, I would rush back to my table and keep working it. Then another brand founder stopped by to say hello. When I told her how excited I was that QVC was there, she pointed her buyer out to me and advised me to meet her. Over and over, I snuck away from my table to scope out the QVC booth until finally that buyer was free and alone. I went right up to her and introduced myself. She was super kind, said she recognized my products, and gave me her card. I told her I would love to share more. She agreed to set up a future meeting, but I couldn't tell if she was just being courteous. With my heart in my throat and my head in the clouds, I went back to my three-foot table and continued to demonstrate our concealer to the thousands of women who stopped by.

Then, almost two hours into the event, a woman introduced herself to me. Little did

I know she would change my life forever. She said she was a show host at QVC and that she had talked with me earlier in the evening. I couldn't believe I hadn't recognized her when she spoke to me earlier. Anyway, she was so impressed with our concealer that she said, "I think our QVC customers would love this concealer! And I want you to know I just spoke to the buyer over at the booth and told her about it!"

"It truly means the world to me that you did this," I said, tears immediately welling up in my eyes. My tears took the host by surprise and she quickly said, "Now, sugar, I don't have any say on if they take a product or not; I just wanted to tell you this is a great one." I thanked her and tried to pull myself together.

I followed up with the QVC buyer, and we got a meeting! The QVC headquarters are about thirty minutes outside Philadelphia. The meeting room was down a long hallway wide enough to drive a car through with several identical doors along both sides. In between the doors were framed images of their successful brands and photos of QVC distribution centers all over the US and the world. I wanted to believe I belonged there in that hallway and up there on the wall, but it was hard when all I'd ever heard was *no.* The meeting room was small. I thought, *Oh no, is the small room a bad sign?* Paulo and I pulled out the presentations filled with those ninety-nine-cent color pages that we'd bound at FedEx with their acetate covers.

I felt passionate but numb. The numbness was probably a defense shield to protect me from feeling and exposing my own doubt. I didn't want them to sense the discouragement I'd walked through. Buyers need to believe you're going to make them a lot of money. And I didn't have data to support any sales promise. I knew my shot at selling would have to be based on my contagious energy and conviction, not data. In the past it hadn't been enough. I didn't want the buyer to ask why we weren't in any stores. If she did, I'd have to be honest and tell her it was because they'd all said *no.* Also, I hadn't forgotten the call from Allen Burke less than a year prior telling me that the *consensus* was that we weren't right for QVC's customers. I tried to drown out that memory as best I could. When I finished, there was a pause, almost a lull in the meeting. I braced myself for some tough questions, but that's not what happened. She smiled and said, "Great, we'd like to give you a shot."

WE GOT A *YES!* A *YES!* I'd spent years waiting to hear that word and so far in this book I haven't really had a chance to write it, so, just to write it again, we got a *YES!*

If you're a stress eater like me, I advise grabbing a snack and taking a quick break, because it's all about to go down in the most stressful way.

What I didn't realize was that *YES* and how we handled it would lead to one of the greatest business and life lessons I've ever had. And it comes down to believing in the power of your own intuition.

Here's the deal: the *YES* meant that QVC was giving us the chance of a lifetime — one single live airing on their channel. It was slated to last ten minutes. During that time, we needed to sell over six thousand units of our concealer. Six thousand units in just ten minutes! It was a consignment deal, which meant we had to pay to make the concealer and ship it to QVC, and we would only get paid afterward for however many units sold. Whatever didn't sell, we would have to take back home . . . without getting paid for it. Remember, at this point we were doing only two to three orders a day off our website.

We were down to less than $1,000 in our company bank account, which was also my and Paulo's personal bank account. *Note to entrepreneurs:* one of the most critical business best practices is NEVER accept a purchase order you can't afford to lose! And this was a purchase order we absolutely couldn't afford to lose. But after years of hearing *NO,* we decided to take the risk. We spent all the money we had, plus borrowed some more, to make the concealers and pay for all the clinical testing and legal requirements for QVC. Every bank rejected our loan applications except for the very last one, a small independent bank in California, which granted us an SBA loan just large enough to cover our expenses to get our shot on QVC. Once we had the product, it all came down to what would happen in those ten minutes of live TV. If this single show on QVC didn't work out, I had no idea how we were going to pay Jacquie. And at that point, almost three years into the company, Paulo and I still hadn't paid ourselves yet, despite working hundred-hour weeks without a break and living on the verge of burnout. To top it all off, if it went really badly and we had to take back the inventory, we'd go out of business. I was about to face one of the biggest decisions of my life as it pertains to trusting my gut.

To prepare for the best shot at success in that ten-minute spot, we met with a few different third-party experts. These consultants made a living counseling companies on how to successfully sell on TV. One by one, they all gave me the same advice. They told me that the only way to do well was to use a select group of models to show our product. Models who were in their early twenties and had flawless skin. I asked these consultants questions like, "Okay, but what's the point of showing a concealer on someone with flawless skin?" or "What if someone watching has skin challenges like I do — how are they going to know if this product will work for them?" or "If I am sitting at home, seventy years old, and I see this product on a twenty-year-old, how do I know it will work for me?"

I wanted to show the products on diverse models so that viewers might identify with their age, skin tone, and/or skin type. I told the consultants I'd even be willing to go on live TV without makeup, baring my bright red rosacea-covered face, to demonstrate how effective the concealer was and how passionate I was about it. They strongly advised against this, arguing that the only recipe for success that had ever worked was what they were telling me to do. I didn't have the luxury of trying it both ways. My company's survival was on the line. I had only ten minutes and one shot!

In the weeks leading up to our show, I felt sick over the decision I had to make. I couldn't sleep. The experts told me my vision of how to showcase the product would never work. But my gut told me women deserve better than to see only unattainable images of beauty that don't look like them. I flew out to QVC one week before our show, and I drove to the QVC parking lot in my rental car, parked thirty yards from the front door, and just sat there alone each day, for hours. I stared at the front door and the huge QVC sign stationed in front of it, watching people walk in and out. I knew that the next time I walked through those doors I was going to succeed or literally go out of business. During those hours I planned out what I was hoping to do and say in those ten minutes, and I envisioned success. The way an Olympic athlete visualizes landing a triple axel or standing on the podium with a gold medal, I envisioned the SOLD OUT sign going up on air. But every day that week, sitting there in that rental car in the parking lot staring at the front of the building at the QVC headquarters, I also felt the mounting pressure of everything being on the line.

I remembered a story Oprah had told on her show about how she wanted to be part of the movie *The Color Purple* so badly that it practically consumed her. One day, she ran around a track singing the song "I Surrender All" while praying for God to take the obsession from her because it was too much for her to carry. Well, that's what I did in that car. The weight of what was at stake truly felt too heavy for me, so I prayed, asking God to take it from me. I asked Him to let me know what to do. Should I follow the experts' advice on how to have the best chance of success? After all, they were experts for a reason. Or should I follow my gut and take my shot at changing the industry and redefining the images women see as "beautiful"? Some of us call it intuition or gut; for others, it's God or the Universe. But in that rental car, after days of praying and trying to listen for the answer, it became clear as day to me.

I made my decision. I was going to go live on QVC with ten minutes and one shot and expose my barefaced "before" shot and show how our product worked for all types of women. Women who looked like my mother and grandmother, like my sisters and friends, women who looked like Jane at the coffee shop and Jennifer at the post office. Real women. Even if it failed and I lost my chance to succeed at QVC, I was not going to throw away my shot at standing for something, my shot at showing women that I truly believe they are beautiful and deserve to feel beautiful. I was going to use my one shot to show them that "beautiful models" should be every woman. I was going to take my shot, with everything on the line. I mean, seriously, if the only images women and girls see over and over are of models who don't look like them, then how is anyone ever supposed to see herself as beautiful? I decided that no matter what happened, I had one single goal for everyone watching. I wanted every woman to feel beautiful. I want every person to feel beautiful. Even if it's for the first time, or for the first time in a long time.

I was minutes away from what felt like the biggest moment of my life. I put on my best dress, said a prayer with Paulo, got my microphone on, and headed down the long hallway to the live studio. I walked onto the set and saw the cameras all around, and I watched the seconds run down on the on-air countdown. In a few seconds we would be live on air, broadcast to over 100 million homes across the country. My heart was in my throat. I had to drown out those voices of experts telling me I was crazy, that I was making a huge mistake. I had to put aside the potential for my company to go out of business. And I had to let go of comparatively small things like how the dress I was about to wear on national television felt a little snug. Instead, I focused on fighting for the women all across the country who deserved to see a *new* definition of what was aspirational. Women who, like me, have been told they're not enough. They're not thin enough and they're not pretty enough. Which, if you think about it, is just about every single woman. Women who, just like me, have reminded themselves of those words so many times that they believe them, creating a prison in our own minds. Women like me who have *wasted* SO much energy, every day of our lives, having this crazy false sense that if we could just look like someone else, we would be happy. I was not wasting my chance. The red ON-AIR light went on, the live camera zoomed into my face, the clock started at 10:00 minutes, and as the host opened her mouth to say her first word, I saw my time flashing before my eyes . . . 9:59, 9:58, 9:57 . . . WE ARE LIVE . . .

# HERE WE GOOOOOOO . . .

The first minute or so I felt out of my body, almost unaware of what was going on and in disbelief that it was all really happening. I had a demonstration prepared to show that our concealer didn't crease or crack. On my wrist, I would apply our concealer next to two of the best-selling concealers on the market. I had practiced this demo in the bathroom mirror hundreds of times leading up to the show. I'd stand in front of the mirror, then bend my wrist back and forth. Within ten to twenty seconds, the other two concealers would crack like desert clay. Ours would stay smooth. This was a big deal. When concealers create cracks and lines you don't even have, they're doing the opposite of what they're supposed to do. And magnify what you're trying to cover instead of making it look like real skin. My demo showed exactly what we'd achieved, and I was excited to do it.

Once we were live, the concealers did their part, but my body didn't. I wasn't nervous to be on TV. I was stressed because of what was at stake. So stressed that my arm and hand were shaking! Not shaking like I was a little nervous; shaking like Scooby-Doo the cartoon dog when he saw a ghost. I was supposed to be the expert, not shaking in my boots. It was so bad that mid-demonstration the host whispered, "Take a breath, my darling, you're doing great," and then grabbed my arm, held it steady, and, like a pro, covered for me and talked about how much she loved the product. Then I pivoted to the moment that would change my life forever: my bright red, barefaced "before" shot went up on the TV screen.

Ever since my battle with rosacea began in my twenties, I had rarely left the house without makeup. It was the only way to avoid the countless people who would ask me if I was feeling ill, how I got my sunburn, if I had windburn, if I was okay, or simply, "What's that on your face?" Growing up a perfectionist, I had spent my entire life in a mental prison of what I thought I should look like. I even sought out opportunities that rewarded me in big part for my appearance, like being cast in an episode of the TV show *Baywatch* (yep, I ran in slow motion in a red swimsuit), or winning Miss Washington USA and competing in the Miss USA pageant, both of which were pretty incredible experiences, and the first in my life where I would ask myself, *Is this really happening?* In college I had fallen in love with a Major League Baseball pitcher who always told me how "hot" I was. (By the way, what a *disaster* that relationship was.) I had been dieting in unhealthy ways since I was fourteen and to this day *still* struggle with emotional eating. And, as happens to so many of us, the thinner I got, the more compliments I got, especially from many of the well-meaning, good-hearted women in my life. Everywhere I went were messages that love and approval were tied to appearance, so getting rosacea was confidence-killing. When I learned there was no cure for it, my thoughts immediately turned to questions I'm embarrassed to admit, like, "Will guys find me attractive?," "Will this hurt my TV news career?," and "Will I ever feel pretty again?" I had been in that beauty mental prison my whole life, and my thoughts weren't able to expand beyond the cage I had created. But in that moment on QVC, I took the plunge and went from being a girl who wouldn't leave the house without covering her face with layers of makeup to a girl who showed her naked, rosacea-filled, bright red face on national television.

Life can change in a moment. And mine did. What I had been taught were my "flaws" were blown up to *big-screen TV size* in people's living rooms everywhere. I have two words for you: *High Definition.* If I allowed myself to think about it, I would have gotten in my head. But what I believed and would later know for sure is this: you can't fake authenticity. If I said every woman was beautiful but was focused on my own insecurities, people wouldn't connect with me and I would fail. But I knew it wasn't about me; it was truly about something so much bigger. And because it wasn't about me, I became free.

While my "before" and "after" shots were live on national television, I was talking, but I couldn't feel my body. It was as if I were standing on air in the sky. Then I brought out my models: real women with real skin challenges. The clock was flying, and it felt like a scene in a movie where everything is happening in fast and slow motion at the same time. Then I saw that the countdown clock was already down to just a few minutes. Instead of some emotional movie score playing, it was me talking without a script, without a teleprompter, just live and from my heart. This was the biggest risk I had ever taken, at one of the most important moments in my life. And I had no idea how it was going. All of a sudden I heard the host say, "We began with sixty-two hundred and the 'medium shade' is now gone. In the 'light,' there are nine hundred remaining. In the 'deep' there are two hundred remaining, and in the 'tan,' only two hundred left!" I felt like my dreams were coming true right before my eyes. My heart was pounding. My adrenaline was flying.

I needed to keep getting my message out, but the host had just said shades were selling out! That meant more to me than that my company was going to survive. It meant real women were using their voices, their time, and their hard-earned money to tell me, QVC, and the world that they didn't want or need to see unattainable images of beauty to buy products. They're telling the world, *We're over it. We want products that are designed for us to be shown on women who look like us, so we know they actually work for us.* Before I could take a breath, the clock was down to a few seconds and the sold out sign went up across the screen. The host turned to me and said, "Bring it in, sister," and gave me a huge hug. The camera cut to something else, and then, at last, I cried.

As mascara ran down my face (how did I forget to use waterproof mascara?), I heard the producer in my earpiece ask if I was okay. Another producer came rushing through the double doors into the studio with a concerned look on her face and said she could help me walk back to the greenroom. I was confused. Apparently, the people in the control room were worried I was going to faint, something that's happened before during people's first time on air. There's just so much pressure. In the world of TV shopping, every minute counts. Having to bring home all that unsold inventory isn't the only risk. If you don't hit a certain sales target, known there as "dollars per minute," you aren't invited back for another chance. In the board game of cosmetics sales, that's when you go broke without passing Go or collecting $200. I glanced over and saw that Jacquie had tears streaming down her face too, and just then Paulo came rushing through the double doors into the studio. I'll never forget the look on his face. We hugged and he proclaimed, "We're not going bankrupt!"

Not only did we sell the six thousand units of concealer in ten minutes, the demand was so great that more than three thousand additional orders went on a wait list. We were invited to QVC again. And again. And I showed my bare face on national TV each time. I put out casting calls the modeling agencies weren't used to, asking for women of all ages, shapes, and sizes, with acne or other skin issues, who were willing to show their bare faces with me. We hired models of varying skin tones and ages, like Helen, who is in her seventies; Alisha, who has acne-prone skin; Sheila, who has hyperpigmentation like the majority of us do; and Desiree, who has hereditary dark circles, has battled acne her whole life, and would never leave the house without makeup when I met her. Jacquie, our one and only employee, went on air to show how, in addition to hiding the hyperpigmentation on her skin, our concealer covered her giant arm tattoo saying "DJ Jacquie Jack." (She'd been a disc jockey in a former life.) In fact, she did her tattoo demonstration so many times, we would later joke that the tattoo had become a diva and was demanding a raise and its own greenroom. Standing as a group, we didn't look like anything the beauty industry had ever seen. Together, we all showed our bare faces and how the product worked live. Together, we were models for a beauty company. Together, we authentically believed every woman is beautiful.

We did 5 live show airings that first year, in 2010. And then over 100 live airings in 2011. Then over 150 in 2012. We grew and grew, and every year since, we've done over 200 live segments and shows on QVC. IT Cosmetics grew to be the number one makeup brand on QVC, then the number one beauty brand across all categories. Today, as I write this, we're the largest beauty brand in the history of QVC.

QVC said *no* for many years. Then when we finally got a *yes,* all the experts said my vision would never work. If I'd taken those years of rejection from QVC to heart, I wouldn't have had the confidence to keep trying for a *yes.* When the opinions and words from the best experts didn't align with what my gut was telling me, the safest and most tempting thing to do would have been to listen to their experience and track records. One of the great lessons I learned was, when you have a truly new idea, product, or vision, it shouldn't be surprising that experts won't believe it will succeed. There's simply no proof that it will. How could there be? *It's never been done before.* Often experts who mean well haven't actually created or built anything themselves. And, though they may believe they are visionaries, they often aren't able to imagine the success of something they haven't seen before. Had I known this earlier as an entrepreneur, I would have saved myself so many nights crying myself to sleep.

To venture into unmapped territory, sometimes we have to take the experts off the pedestal we've created in our minds for them, and put our intuition onto one. We have to be still and listen to that small, clear voice inside of us telling us what to do. And then have the confidence and courage to do it. These are the moments that define us. Had I listened to the experts, we might have hit a sales goal. We might even have been one of the very few brands that gets invited back. But we would be doing what everyone else does, instead of sticking to our authentic mission, which was much bigger than sales. Playing it safe would have meant putting fear on a pedestal, instead of love. And like everything in life, when we let fear, or other people's opinions, govern our decisions, it often comes at the price of everything that actually matters.

As our business grew on QVC, I continued to pursue all the other beauty retailers that had told us *no* up to that point. One by one, we eventually got a *yes* from each of them. Three years after our first QVC show, the first came from ULTA Beauty, who enthusiastically launched our products in their stores nationwide with great passion and partnership. They saw the vision and went full speed ahead with us. We even partnered on a co-branded makeup brush line together. Between the brushes and our makeup products we grew to become the number one, top-selling luxury brand in their stores nationwide. How crazy, right? From *no's* to their top-selling brand! Then, ready for this? Six years after the meeting where they turned me down, we finally got a *yes* from Sephora!

Imagine: I was crushing it on QVC, but there were many more grueling years of hearing *no* from Sephora, even after showing proof of sales. If this were a dude, your friends would be like, "He does not deserve you. And you need to let it go. He's just not that into you." And those would be words they'd use on a nice day. When your spirit feels rejection it can be soul-depleting. Especially if the rejection feels like it must be personal. But you can't take it personally when it's business. Not if you want a *yes,* and to win in the long run. This is a mistake a lot of entrepreneurs make. But you have to keep your head in the game. It's hard. But when the victory happened for us, it was all worth it. And Sephora is truly an amazing partner. That head buyer who wasn't so nice to me had long since left the company and the beauty industry. The buyers and team we work with there today are world-class — supportive, kind, and smart, and they help cultivate and launch new beauty entrepreneurs often. As I share this story with you, we are one of the top brands in the skin care division of Sephora nationwide. We went from years of *no* to eventually becoming a top brand and having a fun, successful partnership at the same time. Wherever you may be stuck right now, that doesn't indicate where you're going in the future. Don't let anyone else's doubts about you or your dream turn into doubt in your own head. And also, don't become resentful of their disbelief and *no's*. This is super important. Our human nature is to get resentful when someone hurts us or doesn't believe in us. But if I'd held grudges against anyone who once rejected me, I'd never have turned those *NO's* into glorious *YESes!*

Making the decision to trust my gut when literally everything was on the line opened every other door afterward. That single moment was in big part responsible for turning a dream that I started in my living room into a billion-dollar company. I truly believe our own gut instinct is one of our greatest superpowers. And we all have it! You have it right now! But one of the greatest challenges we often face is when our gut is telling us something completely different from what our head/heart/other people/the experts/the trolls on social media/friends/family/partners/coworkers are telling us — and we have to decide which to listen to. The key is being aware of the things that prevent us from listening to our intuition: past mistakes, self-doubt, other people's opinions. These can cloud our instincts, but when you're aware of them you're able to take your power back. Every one of us has intuition, and the better we get at tuning in to it, the more we're able to step into our authentic selves and our full power.

And it's important to be patient with ourselves. Sometimes learning to develop and then trust our own gut can be a journey. It may require us nurturing ourselves while looking at where we came from, just how far we've come, and how strong we had to be to get where we are right now. Rejection, failures, and even the times our gut turns out to be wrong, are all gifts along life's journey. Don't waste them — they are all valuable lessons. We can use them to refine our instincts and intuition. This is key in training our gut to know the difference between sound advice and the sound of opposition. Then when our doubters see obstacles, our gut will lead us to solutions. The more we do this, the better we get at hearing and leaning into our intuition when it whispers to us. This builds a confidence and eventually a knowing that your intuition is more powerful than anyone else's advice.

*The moment the SOLD OUT sign came up in our QVC debut. The host, Lisa Mason, held my hand and then my back (I think everyone was worried I was going to faint) just as tears started to stream down my face.*

# Two:
## *Believe* Where You Come from Doesn't Determine Where You're Going

> You didn't come this far to
> only come this far.
>
> — ANONYMOUS

Have you ever been completely blindsided or had the rug pulled out from under you in a way that had you questioning everything you believed to be true? Maybe it was about a relationship you found out was filled with lies, or family beliefs or stories you learned weren't true. Well, that's what happened to me the day a secret was revealed by accident. A secret that had lasted nearly three decades in my family. The struggle that followed taught me that when the rug is pulled out from under you, how you handle the uncertainty that follows can singlehandedly change the course of your life.

As a little girl, I learned to fend for myself and daydream to fill the time. My parents divorced when I was six years old. My dad,

Mike, was a kind, charismatic, struggling alcoholic and up until that point had worked as a chef his whole career. A restaurant environment where alcohol was all around and accountability wasn't didn't make for a good mix. After his shift ended, he would often stay out for hours drinking, and many times wouldn't come home at all. By overhearing things I wasn't supposed to growing up, I learned that my dad cheated on my mom with a lot, and I mean *a lot,* of women.

I have so many good and not-so-good memories of him. As a little girl, on days when he was supposed to watch me, he would often sleep in past noon. Today, I understand that it was because of his drinking. But all I knew at the time was that I would sit on the floor next to his bed for hours as he slept, watching the clock slowly flip its black tiles with big white numbers and imagining all the things I hoped we'd do when he woke up. My job was to have a can of beer ready for him when he woke up because I knew it would make him happy. This was a plan we had together, one that I never told my mom. When the minute and hour tiles finally flipped to the number on the clock when he said I could get him up, at say 10:00, I would get so excited, with his beer in hand, ready to play. Many times I would whisper, "Daddy, Daddy, it's time to wake up," and he would then revise the plan, telling me I now needed to wait until the numbers said 11:00 or 12:00. So I would sit there, by his side, watching those tiles flip the minutes away.

When he was awake and sober, my dad was the kindest and funniest guy. He wasn't ever mean and never really disciplined me. Within the limits of his capacity as an alcoholic, he loved me as much as anyone could. We collected baseball cards together and I loved sitting on his lap watching his favorite football team, the San Francisco 49ers, win multiple Super Bowls in the 1980s. He taught me how to ride a bike, how to blow up an inflatable boat, and how to swim back to shore when the inflatable boat got a hole in it while in the middle of a pond. Without intending to, he also instilled in me the deep belief that women are stronger than men, that men hold women back, and that women need to be super-women and do it all on their own.

My mom, Nina, was exactly that: a super-woman. She got up early every day to get me to day care or school so she could go to work, manage the bills, do all the errands, and take care of all the family responsibilities. She did this while somehow holding it together, as my dad disappointed her and broke promises to her over and over. After almost twenty years of marriage, she had had enough and finally ended it.

After the divorce, my dad worked in a manual-labor union job at a glass factory, inspecting glass jars and wine bottles on an assembly line. He worked rotating shifts that changed each week. One week he would work 7 A.M. to 3 P.M., the next week 3 P.M. to midnight, the week after that midnight to 7 A.M., and then it would start all over again. He never got great sleep and was always tired. Remarkably, instead of going out drinking each night and prioritizing his nightlife, he did a full 180 and became a hermit, rarely leaving the house.

The storm of divorce is never easy, but God definitely brought me many rainbows in the form of my stepfamilies. My dad married my stepmom, Laura, who was kind, sensitive, and loving, and she took on the role of superwoman in their household. I grew very close with her and years later, when I was sixteen, she and my dad had a daughter together, my sister Karly, who would become one of the loves of my life. My dad adored Karly too, and one benefit of him becoming a hermit is that he was a far more present father to her than he was to me.

From day one, my stepmom Laura and her entire family loved me as if I were their own. And in their minds, I was. And still am to this day. Laura's parents, my grandma Betty and grandpa Dick, embraced me with the kind of unconditional love that makes a granddaughter feel special and chosen. When I was fifteen, Laura's sister, my aunt Terri, taught me to drive on her stick-shift silver 1980s-model Mazda 626. I ground the gears, sacrificing her car's transmission, while she patiently instructed me. Throughout college, the whole family sent me care packages filled with Kraft Mac & Cheese and whatever items were on sale from Walmart. One of Laura's other sisters, my aunt Karen, lent me her station wagon during my first TV news job when I couldn't afford to buy or rent a car. Laura's family is the kind that welcomes you in with a hug, a cup of coffee, and a muffin from Costco, no matter who you are or how your day is going. They invite you to join in the card game around the table and love you fully even if you don't feel like playing. They're salt-of-the-earth people who love with their whole hearts. They couldn't have had any idea that I would one day achieve any type of monetary success and when I did, none of them changed one bit. Because their definition of wealth is love. And they are some of the richest people I know.

My mom also remarried shortly after the divorce, and I lived with her and my step-dad, Dennis, who truly loved me like his own daughter from day one. They say God gives you double for your trouble, and for all of the pain the divorce caused, God definitely gave me more than double in the form of my stepfamilies on both sides. He also gave my mom double, as Dennis is rock-solid in his loyalty, love, and intentions. They were so in love, they made a habit of wearing matching sweatshirts and do to this day. Of course, as a little girl I found this mortifyingly embarrassing. But now, I find it so freakin' cute!

Growing up, my mom and stepdad, who I lived with, worked a lot. And by a lot, I mean *a lot*. When I was seven years old, they started an escrow business together. (All of my childhood friends would ask, "Escort business?" "No, not escort, escrow. As in the people that hold the escrow money while it changes hands between home mortgage lenders and people buying or selling homes." "Ooohhh," they would say.)

Right from the start, their small independent escrow business had them working seven days a week to stay afloat. (Sound familiar? It was a pretty intense work ethic I would later find myself replicating in my own business). It felt like from that day forward, my entire life was dictated by the real estate market. When it was a down market, my parents would have to lay off employees and work even harder and longer hours to stay in business, and when it was a booming market, they would have to hire more people and yet, still, work many more hours to keep up with the demand. They were always working hard and incessantly so that they could afford for me to participate in activities like gymnastics and go to camp. But it also meant I was alone a lot as a child, sometimes seven days a week, and often lonely. I became a huge fan of TV, especially MTV, and I would sneak friends, and then later boys, over to reenact the dance moves in the music videos in my living room. I also became obsessed with World Vision commercials that showed kids all over the world who didn't have enough to eat. I begged my parents to adopt a child who needed a family, and when my begging didn't work, I wrote stories and plans for how one day I was going to adopt these kids. When I learned about the one-child policy in China, I told my parents that the baby girls needed us *now*! While they said no to adopting, they told me that I could surely do it one day. They always instilled in me a power to believe I could do anything I set my mind to. They made me feel like nothing was impossible, and that if I dreamed it up and worked hard enough, I could achieve it. Even as a little girl growing up, I thought that one day I would for sure adopt.

During those years, I was frequently the last kid at gymnastics practice late at night, sitting in the gym with the coach long after all the other kids and parents had left, waiting for my parents to finally leave the office and come pick me up. Often this would be well past 9 P.M. They couldn't be there to watch me at practice like the other parents. They almost always had to work. Some years we would go on a family vacation, but many more they weren't able to get away from the office for us to take one. But they did the best they could, and I never doubted that they truly loved me. And I certainly got my work ethic from them.

In my early years in high school, I was part of an all-girls rap and singing group called SOB+1, which stood for "Sisters of

Blackness plus One," and, yes, I was the "plus One." We performed at the school talent show and even went into the recording studio. (Shout-out to SOB+1!) I rapped in the group and danced, and even cowrote a song called "Show Me a Man" (which I swear could have been a huge hit had we had any money or connections at the time, but I digress).

I had always been pretty boy-crazy growing up and had some pretty great boyfriends in high school. The funny thing is that even then, I never fantasized about my wedding day or marrying any of them. I pretty much only fantasized about things that weren't man-dependent or even man-relevant, like building an empire, how to get SOB+1 on MTV, or solving the crisis of abandoned children I saw in those commercials. The only exception I can remember was when one of my high school boyfriends, Eric, and I had been dating for quite a while. See, Eric's last name had me thinking about marriage all the time. This seems so ridiculous now, but I remember worrying what would happen if we got married, because his last name was Lard. Yep, Lard. In my not-yet-fully-developed teenage brain, this was a worry. *Jamie Lard,* I used to think to myself; it was the only time I can remember actually daydreaming about what it would be like being married. Could I confidently rock that last name? Would my kids get teased? *Lard* on its own isn't the most attractive of words, but Eric was super hot. So at least we'd make supercute babies!

At its core, *Lard* triggered my already mounting insecurities about my body that were reinforced daily in the messages all around us, that somehow our self-worth should be tied to how we look. When I started dating Eric, I was already a few years into taking every diet pill I could get my hands on, with the false conviction of youthful invincibility. I brought diet shakes to school, hid them in my bag, then drank them in the bathroom during lunchtime with a few of my friends who were doing the same. The older sister of one of my friends would supply us with these bottles of energy pills for weight loss from the gas station that you had to be eighteen to buy. I always noticed the health warnings on the bottle, and always ignored them. And the thinner I got, the more praise I got. Which made me mad, even at that age. But praise can feel like love. And so I chose to hurt my health to get more of what felt like love. And speaking of love, after a year or so of dating, the romance with Eric fizzled out, as did my worry about his last name. And I actually then began dating my next boyfriend, Ethan Hornbecker. Yep, true story.

High school years can be such a time of shaky self-esteem and newfound inclusion and exclusion — dealing with labels and perceived differences, and often struggling to decide if fitting in is worth all the effort. I loved beauty products even then, but at the time, for me it meant Bioré pore strips and tinted Clearasil — you know, the acne fluid that leaves a pink line of demarcation all around your jaw when you try to use it as your foundation.

I was friends with many different groups in high school, not just one, and around the age of fifteen I was both boy-crazy and starting to set big career goals and feel crazy ambitious. But . . . not when it came to schoolwork. Even though my imagination ran wild with big dreams, I went through a long bout of procrastination in my high school years, and began missing deadlines and turning work in late. I was even voted "Biggest Procrastinator" in my high school yearbook. At the time I wished I'd been voted "Most Likely to Succeed" or "Most Beautiful" or "Best Smile" or "Best Spirit," but instead the only accolade I got was

"Biggest Procrastinator." It took me many years to get over being super ashamed of that (and, believe me, it wasn't procrastination that made it take so long). Of course I understood why it happened. But it did disappoint me. And it also stirred something up in me: a deep conviction to change.

I made the decision that I wouldn't allow that label to stick to me and take root in my mind. In life, we aren't who people say we are, we're who we believe we are. We don't have to accept the labels that other people put on us. We're also not our family, for better or worse, or our past mistakes. We're not a nickname someone gave us, or a regrettable incident we miscalculated. It's easy to carry around old labels and mistake them for permanent ones. But they come with a light Post-it adhesive, so don't let yourself believe they're attached with superglue! They're removable! Sure, sometimes there is some truth to those hurtful labels, like procrastination for me at the time, but we have the power to shake off old labels and make new choices as we grow. We can change our minds and change our decisions about who we are and how we show up for ourselves, for others, and for the world at any moment going forward. Where we come from doesn't have to determine who we are, or where we're going in the future.

Speaking of going places, as far back as I can remember, I was itching to get my own car and drive wherever I wanted to go. I knew my parents weren't going to buy me one and that I would have to figure out how to get one on my own. I had been earning money from side jobs since I was eleven years old, and by the time I was fifteen I was ready for a real, paying job. I started coaching gymnastics a few nights a week, and then took on two weekend jobs. I worked at a popcorn concession stand at the local swap meet on weekend mornings, then took a bus to another town to work at Safeway, a grocery store. I bagged groceries and pushed shopping carts in from the parking lot. That summer, I also talked my parents into hiring me as a forty-hour-a-week receptionist at their escrow company. Not escort, escrow. I had four jobs at once and was practically always working. But by the end of that summer, I had $2,500 in my bank account and bought my first car! Not the car I had dreamed of, but it drove. It was a bright blue Geo Metro with blacked-out windows. It was a stick shift, and in the rain, it often couldn't make it up the hills of Seattle or the suburbs around it where I was raised. Since it was only a three-cylinder, the wheels would start spinning on the wet pavement. I would have to wait until all the other cars passed me, then reverse-roll back down the hill and find a different route to get where I was going. But I didn't care. I had a car! I also had my first taste of the upside of being a workaholic. It would take me many more years to understand the downsides.

In my late teens and early twenties, I did a complete 180 from the procrastination days and started to become obsessed with achievement. With entering competitions to win awards and gain recognition. With getting great grades and being honored. At age twenty-two, I won the Miss Washington USA competition, and my parents were there and were so proud. I worked my butt off waiting tables at Denny's Diner and took a second job at another grocery store, slicing meat and cheese in the deli department to pay my college tuition at Washington State University. I graduated valedictorian with a 4.0 GPA. At graduation, where I was class speaker, I was draped with honor cords and medals of achievement and ribbons all around my neck, the way one of my childhood idols, Mr. T, wore chains. When I spoke in front of the packed stadium at the university-wide commencement, my parents were there, beaming with pride and tears in their eyes. I later did the same thing in graduate school.

What I know now is that I felt like I had to achieve things to be worthy of love. I chased recognition to feel worthy of my parents showing up, to make them proud, and to show the world that I mattered. Sometimes, we express our need for love and belonging in the opposite way — for example, by acting out or through self-destructive behaviors. For me, one of the forms it took was simply not feeling worthy of love just as I was. And then when I did achieve something, and got recognition for it, it was never enough. I still never felt like I was enough. So I was on to the next big achievement. This need to achieve, and to prove my worth, is something I continue to struggle with. It feels like a cage I created in my own head, that I am still working to break free from, even to this day.

It would also take me years to understand that because I spent so much time alone, I learned to depend on myself. If there was one person who was going to show up for me, it was me. When I did form attachments, I didn't want to let them go. This would later play out in my relationships (and even in my decisions as a boss at IT Cosmetics). I didn't want anyone to feel alone or abandoned, even if they did me wrong. That took its form in many ways. I stayed in toxic relationships far longer than I should have. I stayed with boyfriends who didn't treat me well. I stayed friends with people who weren't good for me, all because they made me feel included. I would later learn that one of my greatest deficiencies as a boss was that I wouldn't fire people soon enough. Other company founders shared one of the greatest lessons they'd learned: When you know an employee is toxic to your culture, get rid of them right away. Otherwise, that toxicity will spread in your culture and take over, infecting others. Despite believing that to be true, I always had the hardest time firing people. Even now, having grown a company with over one thousand employees, I still wait too long.

The work-addiction and overachiever and abandonment issues would all play key roles in a lot of my choices in my twenties, as I wasn't yet fully aware of their power over me. And then something happened that would shift my perspective on everything I knew about myself and who I was.

On Christmas Eve 2004, my dad and stepmom were getting a divorce, and my dad had just moved out of their house and into an apartment. While setting up his new place, he couldn't find the baby pictures of me and my sister Jodie. I haven't told you about Jodie yet. For as long as I could remember, I had known that a year or so before I was born, my mom and dad had a baby girl named Jodie. At just nine days old, she died from a hole in her heart. They had me a year and a half later. Growing up, my parents in both households always had my baby picture and Jodie's in two separate, small frames on their bedroom dressers. Now, twenty-seven years later, my dad couldn't find his photos of Jodie and asked me to see if my mom had any extras he could have.

Paulo and I were engaged and spending the holiday with my family. The plan was to spend Christmas Eve with my dad and sister Karly, and Christmas Day with my mom and Dennis. I called my mom to let her know I would be stopping by her place that day to pick up any extra photos she had of me and Jodie so that I could take them to my dad's that evening. When Paulo and I arrived at my mom's house, he stayed in the living room to play with the dog while I walked into her bedroom with her to get the photos. My mom handed me two baby photos, duplicates of the ones of me and Jodie that I had seen in frames on her dresser all my life. We were sitting on the end of the bed chatting, when I glanced at the two photos and idly turned them over to see the backs. Mine said July 1977, which was the month I was born. Jodie's said March 1977. My brain quickly did the math: that was only four months apart. But I knew Jodie had only lived nine days. Four months wasn't enough time to get pregnant and have me. Maybe someone had written Jodie's date wrong and it should have said 1976 instead of 1977?

"Mom, why does Jodie's photo say March 1977 on the back?" I asked. "That's only four months before my birthday."

A look that I had never seen before came over my mom's face. After a long pause, she said, "There's something I've wanted to tell you for a long time." She turned to me. "Maybe you've suspected this, but you're adopted."

WHAT??? *Maybe I've suspected this?* Ummm . . . no, I hadn't ever suspected this. My world came to a screeching halt. Who was I? Was everything I knew a lie?

"What? Are you being serious?" I said calmly, but in complete shock.

"Yes," she said. "I thought maybe you knew."

"How could I have possibly known?" I asked. When I say I had no idea, I mean literally. No. Idea. I even look like Mike, the father I grew up thinking was my birth father. And remember, growing up, I had always begged my parents to adopt other kids. And I made sure when we got engaged that Paulo knew that I had my heart set on adopting one day and that he supported it. It was always on my heart, even as a little girl, to one day adopt, but how could I have known *I* was adopted?! My mom had named me Jamie after the character Jaime Sommers, the Bionic Woman in the hit TV show. Sure, the Bionic Woman had superhuman powers, but did my mother really think I had real-life superhuman powers too, enabling me to just *know* something like this?

"I'm so sorry to have kept this from you," she said. "We got you just a day or so after you were born, and your dad never wanted you to know."

I was in total shock. I was sitting there with the person I was closest to in my entire world, my mom, and she had just told me something monumental that made me question everything I knew to be true. I couldn't believe she had kept this from me.

She went on to tell me that when Jodie died, she went back to her doctor for a follow-up visit. The doctor forgot what had happened to Jodie and asked my mom how breastfeeding was going. My mom starting sobbing in front of him and reminded him that her baby had died. After the doctor's major blunder, he called my mom later that day and asked if she would be interested in adoption. (Note: this is how God's miracles can work in our lives.) He had a young patient he was caring for who was hiding her pregnancy and planned to give her baby up for adoption. My mom and dad hadn't even considered adoption before, but they said yes. They never met my birth mother. They had no idea if she had used her real name on any of the paperwork and they never heard from her in all the years that they raised me. All they knew was that she wanted to keep the pregnancy and adoption a secret. There wasn't really anything my mom could tell me about who my birth parents were except for what was listed on the paperwork.

You know how when you are hiding a secret, the longer you keep it, the harder it is to share? My mother had been hiding this from me for twenty-seven years. Her shame from that quickly filled the room like a heavy blanket as she told me the story. Her eyes were filled with tears of fear over how I was feeling. I was completely stunned but couldn't help but empathize with how she was feeling. My instinct was to comfort her. Tears started streaming down my face. "Mommy, it's going to be okay," I said as I reached over and hugged her.

She then walked to her closet and pulled out a fireproof file box filled with paperwork. Through tears, I looked through the items she handed me. I shuffled through the papers, at first glance not even sure what I was looking at. I saw my birth certificate, and then the nonidentifying background information forms. There were some legal documents that listed a name for my birth mother and said the birth father was never told about the pregnancy. And then my mom handed me a handwritten note and a gold necklace with a Virgin Mary medallion on it. I opened the note and noticed it wasn't signed. It was a note my birth mother had written for me to see one day. It read: "I am content knowing that my baby is with such wonderful people. Although the baby and I will never know each other, I wanted her to have something that is very special to me. My own parents gave this medal of the Blessed Virgin Mary to me when I was a little girl. Perhaps you could give this to her when she has become older and explain everything and tell her I love her very much. God Bless you both."

In that moment I looked into the eyes of the person I loved and trusted most in my life, my mom who raised me, and all of a sudden I felt this painful confusion over everything I knew to be true about who I was. The foundation of trust I had stood upon my whole life had fallen out from beneath me. I felt hurt, betrayed, and so overwhelmed. I was torn between wanting to comfort and reassure my mom, while at the same time wondering what else I had taken as truth that wasn't. I felt shattered and alone. All sense of peace left me. My mind took me to the dark shadows of mistrust and loneliness that you feel when someone you're so close with pulls the rug out from beneath you.

In life it's not our experiences that make us unique, it's our response to those experiences. And to the uncertainty they immerse us in. Where you come from doesn't have to determine where you're going, but it definitely shapes the foundation you have to build on. When something hard happens, once you're able to process it emotionally, you're then left with choices. Do you victim-up or do you warrior-up? Do you give up or do you level up and believe? The *up* is up to you.

Learning that where I came from was a lie was like being thrust into one of those machines from *The Jetsons* cartoon, where you enter and moments later come out a different person with an entirely new outfit on. I felt like I walked into my mom's bedroom that day wearing comfy sweats and filled with the nostalgic cozy Christmas spirit, and walked out in tears and fully blindsided, yet knowing I was now in the midst of the biggest game of uncertainty I had ever played in. Wondering if my parents were truly on my team, and why they kept the ball from me all these years. Who was I? Who was my birth mom? If I found her, would she even want to be on my team? What if she saw me as an opponent? How we react to times of uncertainty, and whether we make decisions based in love or fear, can change the course of our life. Champions aren't made when the game is easy. In any area of life. I couldn't let fear or pain decide my outcome.

I knew in that moment that maybe my birth mom never planned to know me, but I needed to know her. I needed to find her. And I needed to find out who I was and where I really came from. And then I felt this strong sense of knowing come over me that in order to ever feel peace again, I would need to find all of the missing pieces.

# Three:
## *Believe* in the Power of Embracing Your Truth

Make peace with your broken pieces.
— R. H. SIN

I was on a full-out, obsessive mission to find my birth mom. I spent the next few days and weeks scouring the paperwork that my mother had saved for any information and clues I could extract. Since I was working as a journalist at the time, I was familiar with researching and finding people. Most of the paperwork was very vague, but it did have a first and last name listed for my birth mom, *Rosemary Ryan,* although I didn't yet know if it was real or not. There were some nonidentifying background details she had to fill out by state law at the time. They included some personal information like how many siblings she had and her parents' level of education. There was very little about my birth father. The paperwork said that the two of them had attended the same

98

college, the University of California, Santa Barbara, and that she had never told him about the pregnancy. There were doctors' names on some of the medical records and my birth certificate. The biggest challenge was that in 1977 all of the records were on paper, and now, twenty-seven years later, many of the doctors and lawyers listed were long since retired or had passed away.

I organized everything I had, and then I hit the ground running, full speed ahead. I was arriving at work by 4 A.M. to anchor the morning news, and then heading out to the live locations of the daily news stories and reporting after the morning show, usually leaving work around midafternoon unless there was breaking news. I devoted every free minute I had to my mission of finding my birth mom. I researched and tried to contact the real-life person behind every single doctor, lawyer, and caseworker named in the documents, but those who were still alive had no idea about or memory of my case and weren't able to help me. I felt like it all came down to the name of my birth mom. But I had no idea if that name was actually real. Rosemary Ryan.

I spent all of my waking hours outside of work calling every Rosemary Ryan, and Rose Ryan, and then any combination of a woman's name that included Rosemary or Rose or Mary. Every time I dialed a new person, I felt the anticipation of knowing that the woman who answered might be her.

"Hi, is this Rosemary?"

"Who is this?"

"My name is Jamie. I'm actually looking for a family member of mine named Rosemary." Each time a woman I spoke to hung up on me as if I were a scammer or a telemarketer, in a small way it felt like it could have been my birth mother rejecting me. And it happened about half the time. I understood, and knew I might react the same way if I received a call like that. But I had no choice other than to keep taking the punches and keep getting back up. I was determined to find her.

I spent the next *five years* calling every Rosemary, or variation of the name I could find, across the country. I eventually also started calling any woman with the last name Ryan. I called thousands and thousands of people. I searched every online database for names. And I drove to the University of California campus in Santa Barbara to scour through all their yearbooks looking for her, only to learn that in the 1970s at UCSB just a small fraction of the students got their yearbook photo taken. This tenacity (er . . . obsessive all-in commitment) would later prove very useful in business.

As the months and years went by, I couldn't stop obsessing over this. While I had begun my TV career at a station in Tri-Cities, Washington, I had now moved to a larger TV market, to a local news station in Portland, Oregon. I anchored the weekend morning news and reported during the weekdays. I got into work around midnight, would help write and edit stories, then went live at 5 A.M. for my weekend show. I was also planning my wedding to Paulo, orchestrating everything from the simple details, like invitations and flowers, to the more complicated things like the guest list and budget. Even though it was a season with a lot more than normal on my plate, I still found myself obsessively researching any ancestry site, UCSB alumni social pages, and anything I could think of that might lead to another clue bringing me closer to finding my birth mom. Working overnight shifts, along with my futile quest to find her, started to take a toll on me. I wasn't able to get any deep sleep; I was always tired and never felt truly alive. I started to feel like it was more serious than just exhaustion.

Something felt off.

I began seeing a therapist. I was really, really sad and just didn't feel like myself. I started to have panic attacks. If you've ever had a panic attack, you know how scary they can be. My heart rate would skyrocket, I would feel like I might pass out at any moment, and even if I knew in my head it was just a panic attack, it still felt like there was a real chance I could die. I wasn't sure if it was the crazy schedule and stress of my job, or having to report at crime scenes (one time as a reporter, I had to stand on a street filled with blood and splattered brains after a shooting and report live while standing in the middle of the red-coated pavement, no joke), or my anxiety over marriage, or my seemingly never-ending battle with weight and perfectionism, or my futile search for my birth mom; I really had no idea what was causing my issues. I was too embarrassed to share this with any of my friends or family members at the time. But there is still such a stigma around mental health in our society that I feel it's important to share this part of my story with you. There's no shame in seeking professional help, and I can't wait for the day that saying you're heading to your therapy appointment is seen as no different from saying you're going to get your nails done (except ideally it's a more profound experience). My good friend Miles Adcox, CEO of Onsite Workshops, sums it up brilliantly. He says focusing on mental health and emotional wellness, including seeking help and going to therapy, "isn't what's wrong with you, it's what's right with you."

My therapist — I'll call her Dr. Z — was a godsend. She came into my life at just the right time. At our first meeting, she shared with me the only personal thing about herself that she would ever end up sharing. She said, "I need to let you know that I only take appointments Mondays, Wednesdays, and Fridays. And if you're going to cancel you need to give me twenty-four hours' notice. Also, I'm a lesbian." She said it so matter-of-factly that it made me think those three points must have been consistently important to her patients. To me, her sexual orientation was completely irrelevant, but I wondered if she disclosed this because a patient-therapist relationship can be a deeply personal one and some details matter, or because some people might discriminate. I hoped for the former but feared in reality it might be the latter, yet another reminder that as a society, we still have a long way to evolve.

Dr. Z was in her midfifties, and one of the best listeners I had ever met. Growing up, when tough things happened, my family would just process them the best way they could, without seeking any professional help. So this was my very first time seeing a therapist. With Dr. Z, I felt safe enough to share out loud how I truly felt, and what I was truly insecure about. I highly, highly recommend therapy for anyone who has the blessing to be able to access it. Dr. Z helped me resolve my panic attacks and helped me get through my depression. I opened up to her about everything. Even deep and super-private topics like how I was starting to doubt that God existed. The more I traveled, lived in different places, and saw the world, the more I was exposed to science-based arguments around whether or not God was real. The more I was around people who live their life and form their beliefs based on proof, not faith, the more doubt about my Christian faith started creeping in. I explained to her how so many of the science-based arguments made sense. And how I could see the logic in only believing things that you can actually see, touch, hear, and *prove,* for which, of course, no faith is required. And I shared with her how between not knowing where I came from, and now starting to doubt what I believed, I felt lost. She shared something with me during one of these conversations that would change my life and forever shift my thinking. She said, "If you doubt God exists, tell Him. And tell Him to prove you wrong."

I said, "What? What do you mean?"

Now, keep in mind that to this day I have no idea if Dr. Z believes in God, or practices any particular faith, or even identifies as spiritual. She never shared with me anything about that part of her life. But on that day, her words made so much sense to me. She went on to say, "If God created the entire universe, what makes you think He can't handle doubt? Tell Him you doubt Him, and ask Him to prove you wrong. Ask Him to show you that He does in fact exist. And then see what happens." So I did. For the next few days, then weeks, then months and years, when I prayed, I would also tell God I was doubting His existence. And I asked Him to show me that He does exist, and to let me know for sure. There are more stories than can fit in this book about how He did.

Dr. Z helped me to heal in so many ways. Yet though I had transitioned out of a season of depression, the missing puzzle pieces surrounding my birth family were always still weighing on me, no matter how hard I tried to ignore them, especially since I knew it was possible that I would never get answers.

After launching IT Cosmetics and starting those hundred-hour workweeks, I didn't have as much time to look for my birth mom. But whenever I could, I still searched obsessively. If you've ever gone down a rabbit hole on any social media platform, then you'll understand what I mean when I say I totally dove headfirst down the endless vortex of personal information and search portals and ancestry sites. Sometimes I ended up staying up all night searching. Paulo often got worried about me and when he'd get up to use the bathroom in the middle of the night, he'd usually catch me awake searching online. "Sweetie, you need to go to bed," he would always say, but I couldn't stop. I also started recording those adoption shows where they reunite birth parents and kids. The ones where they run to each other in wheat fields in slow motion, while emotional music plays, then dive into each other's arms and live happily ever after. And I daydreamed about this happening to me. I wondered what my parents looked like. Did I have any brothers and sisters? Some days I got lost in the realization that I had never actually met anyone I was related to. That was a super weird and lonely feeling. I was also growing more and more sure that Rosemary Ryan, the name my birth mom listed on my paperwork, wasn't her real name. After calling thousands and thousands of people and spending years searching the databases, I just didn't see how it was possible anymore that she hadn't used a false name. And this meant that just about anyone could be my mom. Anytime I would see an actress or any woman on TV who had features like mine, I would google her and read her bio, wondering if she could be my mom. It was overwhelming.

One of the adoption TV shows encouraged people to submit their own stories for a chance at being on the show. The idea was that their expert locators could help you find your family. Paulo asked my permission to write in to the show about my story, on the one-in-a-million chance they could help. This was so unlike him, as we have totally opposite taste when it comes to TV shows, so I was surprised he had even seen this show I was recording, but I agreed to let him do it and didn't pay it much mind. Then we got a call that they hadn't selected me for the show, but that, for a fee, their location company could be hired to help me find my birth mom. I totally thought it was a scam and just a way for them to make money. But after years making no headway, we paid the fee, a few hundred dollars that we couldn't really afford to lose at the time, and took the chance.

On New Year's Day, 2010, I was working in our IT Cosmetics office, aka my living room in Studio City, California, when my cell phone rang. And my life was about to change forever. (By the way, what is it with me and major things happening on holidays?) I answered the call and it was the adoption search agency. The woman on the phone said, "I believe we've found your birth mother."

"Really? How? Are you sure?" I exclaimed.

"I'm pretty sure. Check your email." I opened up my email to find a link to a Realtor website showing their real estate agents and their photos. There was a picture of an agent named Rosemary (whose last name was not Ryan). When I saw her photo, my mouth fell open.

"Oh my goodness! She looks *so* much like me," I said.

"Yes, she definitely does," the woman replied. She went on to tell me that while my birth mom had not given her real last name on the paperwork, she did accurately answer her sibling birth order (how many brothers and sisters she had and the order in which they were born). Rosemary was her real first name, and she did in fact attend UCSB. It was enough information for them to find her. I thanked the woman, hung up the phone, and was in the same state of total shock as I was when I found out I was adopted in the first place. I sat with Paulo, unable to process it fully, just freaking out. Happy New Year. OMG.

Within the hour, I had done a Google search and found her phone number, her home address, and a Google Earth image of her house. I continued and discovered she was married and had two sons. (I had brothers!!!) I examined all of the photos on her Facebook page, figuring out everything I could about her siblings and their kids, and I put together a spreadsheet where I pasted in everyone's photos and information. She lived in Northern California, and when I was through, I had enough information to be able to hop in my car, drive six hours, and be at her doorstep. We could be reunited at last!

Then it hit me. After five years of waiting

and dreaming, my self-doubt kicked in. I couldn't help but think, *What if she truly doesn't want me to find her?* I had to slow down and really think about this hard. Should I call her? Should I send a letter or an email? Should I really just show up at her door?

This was too much for me to handle, so I prayed for God to show up for me in that moment. And I felt this overwhelming intuition that first I needed to send her an email. So I did. I told her my story, and that I believed I was her daughter. I told her that while I didn't have any of the answers yet as to why she gave me up, I wanted her to know that no matter what, I loved her. I spent the rest of my New Year's Day writing this email. And I prayed, and I hit send.

The next morning, I woke up and rushed to check my email to see if she had responded. Nothing. Then, I didn't know I was strong enough to stomach what happened next. Suddenly, her Facebook profile disappeared. I knew what this meant. She was removing her online presence so that I couldn't see it. My heart sank. In that moment, I knew in my gut and heart that she didn't want me to find her. It crushed me.

It was like she was choosing to give me up again.

One week later, she actually sent me an email reply that confirmed this. She said that, yes, she did believe I was her daughter. And to please respect that she didn't wish for us to meet.

I was devastated. This wasn't like the TV shows I had seen. No one was running toward me, embracing me, telling me how much she loved me and that she had been desperately searching for me her whole life. That giving me up was her greatest regret. I was so disappointed and so deeply hurt. I truly felt like my love was being rejected. *I* was being rejected.

All I could do at that point was pray for her, and ask God to take this pain away. From both of us. I was tempted to get in my car and drive to her home so many times. It was only a six-hour drive, and even though she didn't want to meet me, I couldn't stand it. I now knew who she was but still had never met her, and it was so difficult to just be okay with that. It felt at times like too much pain for me to bear. I knew in my heart God had better plans for me than I could ever imagine for myself, and I had to trust that. But some days I felt so hurt that I would think to myself, *She doesn't deserve to meet me. She was the mom, and she was supposed to love me and take care of me.* I felt like I was this little girl who she gave up, this little girl who had spent years trying to find her, and now I was standing there right smack-dab in front of her and asking her to love me. And she was saying *no.* I tried to guess why she reacted the way she did, and I tried to tell myself there must be a reason that would one day make sense. But I still didn't know what that reason was. And I also knew it was possible that maybe there wasn't one.

Five months passed, and then one day out of the blue, I got another email from her. This time, she said she would be open to meeting. It took me aback. I was still deeply hurt from her initial reaction and had started to feel angry about it.

Nonetheless, I couldn't resist the desire to know where I came from. I had an upcoming meeting at Sephora in San Francisco. (Yep, there was about to be another meeting with Sephora where they would again say *no* to carrying IT Cosmetics, but I had hope at the time that maybe *this* Sephora meeting would be a *yes.*) I decided to agree to meet my birth mom while I was in town for that Sephora meeting. She set up a reservation for lunch at the Palace Hotel.

We had a time and a place to meet. I couldn't believe this was going to finally happen.

I arrived at lunch early and sat in the lobby of the Palace Hotel waiting for her. Fifteen minutes past the time we were supposed to meet for lunch, she still wasn't there. Thoughts started to flood my mind.

*Will she show up? What will she look like in person? What does her voice sound like? Is she kind? How does she treat other people? What will she think about me? Will she think I look like her? Will she think I'm overweight? What if we don't hit it off? What if we're nothing alike? Will she love me?*

And then I saw her. She began walking toward me with this warm, beautiful smile on her face and eyes sparkling with excitement mixed with worry or fear. She had such a loving energy about her, but I felt, almost instantly, that she was carrying a heavy story that I didn't yet know.

We had lunch together, but I could barely eat. Same for her. We talked for five hours straight. She brought me a small photo wallet that she'd filled with some family pictures of her wedding day, with my brothers and her siblings and parents. When she gave me those photos, for the very first time I felt acknowledged as part of her life. She showed me photos of all the family members I had never met, and the one that stood out the most was the picture of her mother, who had passed away a few years before. Leontia was her name. She was my grandma, and she and I looked identical. Literally, absolutely identical. Rosemary shared with me that her mother, my grandma, who they all called Nana, was the only person who ever held me when I was born. Rosemary never held me. She said it would have been too painful. But my grandma Nana held me. She was the only one. Before I was given away.

Those words would echo in my mind for years. But in that moment, I just kept listening and asking questions. I learned that Rosemary and my birth father, whose name she didn't remember, were together only once. They hung out at a college party, then went back to his place and slept together. And in that single encounter, I was conceived. She hid the pregnancy from almost everyone, including him. She hid it from all of her siblings and friends. The only two people who knew were her parents.

In the final months of the pregnancy when she started to show, she went into hiding in an apartment in Novato, California, a city not too far from San Francisco. Her siblings all thought she was still at school in Santa Barbara and just staying longer into the summer. She said none of them suspected anything was off. She hid in that apartment until she gave birth to me, and then she resumed her life. Shortly after college she married her husband, Pat, and they both built successful careers and had been together ever since. I learned that she had never told him about me either. And of course had never told her two sons. So when I first emailed her and she disappeared, then later told me she didn't want to meet, it was because she had been carrying this secret ever since. She had lived over thirty-two years at that point without telling anyone. Not her husband, not any of her friends, not any of her siblings, with whom she was super close. And she needed some time to figure out how to process it all and what to do.

Learning this helped me understand why she had disappeared when I first reached out. I could only imagine how traumatizing it must have been for her to hold on to this secret for thirty-two years. And when I contacted her, how worried she must have been about how all of the people important to her would react. I mean, how do you tell a husband that thirty-two years ago you had a kid and never told him? How do you tell your two grown sons that they have a sister you've kept secret? Rosemary had built a beautiful life in the same town where she and her siblings grew up, and even married a man she had met in her grade-school years. And not a single one of them had any idea that she was carrying this secret.

Rosemary and I had to start from scratch. We had to build trust from scratch. And we had to get to know each other from scratch. That first year we met, I introduced her to Paulo, and she introduced me to her husband, Pat. Then a few years later, I met my two brothers, Steve and Patrick. Our relationship grew slowly, in part because I was so consumed with building IT Cosmetics. But it grew. I invited them to some of my family events and holidays and they invited us to some of theirs. And as I write this book, we're still in the process of meeting everyone in each other's families. I've been so blessed, though, that literally everyone I've met on her side, including her husband, my brothers, and all of my aunts, uncles, and cousins, are so welcoming. So loving. So open to including me in the family.

They're funny, and smart, and quirky, and beautifully kind.

One of the first times I had dinner with Rosemary, her husband Pat, and their entire family at a restaurant, I went to pay the bill. Pat stopped me, and when his kind eyes met mine he said, "No kid of mine is allowed to pay." I teared up instantly. He quashed my worry over whether he would fully accept me into his life. In that moment, in front of the entire table, he was claiming me. Not just as Rosemary's daughter, but as his too.

Throughout all of this, I worried how the family that raised me would handle this addition of new people to my life. Mike, my adoptive father, had passed away from colon cancer and never got the chance to meet any of my birth family. My stepdad, Dennis, and mom, Nina, have been more supportive and open-hearted than I ever could have imagined. I worried initially that Nina might feel threatened or jealous, but instead, when she met Rosemary for the first time, she thanked her for giving me to her. Nina told Rosemary that I was the best thing that had ever happened to her, and together the three of us cried. When Rosemary and my mom Nina met for the first time, Rosemary brought a set of three gold bangles that had belonged to her mother. She gave one to my mom Nina, one to me, and kept one for herself. All three of us put them on our wrists that day and joined hands. That was one of the most special, love-filled moments I have ever had.

I never had that moment I had always dreamed of where I ran across the wheat fields . . . but together Rosemary and I grew to have that same powerful love-filled hug each time we're together. We say we love each other on the phone and we both mean it. We're building a relationship one step at a time.

Everyone has their unique struggles they're walking through on the journey to owning and reconciling their story. While Rosemary's initial reaction when I found her hurt me deeply, I also know that we can't ever judge another person, because it's never possible to truly understand the pain and obstacles they've navigated on their own unique path of life. The years of persistent searching, and keeping an open heart even after she rejected me again, helped us both get to a point where we owned our own stories fully. The truth has set me free from my search and set Rosemary free from her secret. And we are now able to heal together, with open hearts, and an open door to a beautiful story that continues to unfold.

Little did I know that my search for my birth family would also become my search for my identity. My quest for where I came from led to discovering what I'm made of. And that prepared me to see through a whole new lens while building IT Cosmetics, and to help millions of women as they struggled to embrace their own identities and be reminded for themselves what they're made of too. I learned that where you come from matters less than what you're made of. Pay attention to your

*My birth mom, Rosemary, and my mom Nina on the day they met for the first time.*

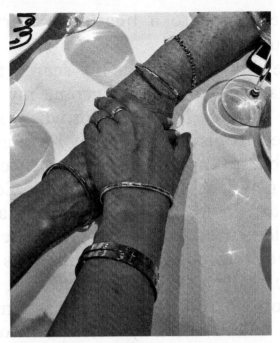

*Me, my mom Nina, and Rosemary
joining our hands together, wearing
the matching bangles that belonged
to Rosemary's mother.*

struggles, as they can become your super-power. They're often the parts of our story we want to erase or forget because they're painful. But when you consider them as moments you've been strong enough to experience and endure and triumphantly emerge from, they can also become part of your greater purpose in life. And part of your highest expression of what you have to give to others while you're here.

Believe in the power of embracing your

story, including the messy parts that ultimately can make it even more beautiful. And believe in loving others on their own journey to do the same.

When I look at these hands joined together, I see three women's superpowers uniting. And while this was all happening, I was about to learn that I would have to muster enough superhero-like strength to face villains in a whole other part of my life.

# Four:
## Believe You're Stronger Than Your Opposition (Including Mean Girls)

You can't sit with us.
— *MEAN GIRLS,* THE MOVIE

"You shouldn't come in here. Just trust me." These words felt like a warning, as a grown woman closed the door of the room I was about to enter right in my face. If this were elementary school, I would have rushed to the bathroom to hide, and cry. But it wasn't school . . . it was the big leagues of the QVC *communal* greenrooms, and I had just a few minutes before I had to sell more than $100,000 of product. I couldn't afford to hide, or cry. After the huge success of our debut launch, I was the rookie regularly getting a shot alongside the starting lineup of beauty company founders who were trusted to hit the big sales targets of QVC's prime-time shows.

As I got booked for more and more airings, the pressure didn't get any easier. I

122

knew that each time I went live on QVC, I still had to hit the sales goal, or risk not being invited back. And each time I hit it, I never felt joy, I really only felt relief. Like we were still in the game. The iron was still hot! And I felt this unremitting fear that at any moment that could change. I kept going on air, showing my own bare face live, showing real women, and it kept working. Over and over. As I kept batting 1,000, QVC gave us more and more airtime and started allowing us to launch new products on the air. We began growing rapidly and soon had three core products that were selling extremely well. While we still had a very junior assistant buyer handling our account at QVC, we were getting a bit more attention. And when it came to the competition, I was about to learn that when you're small and flying under the radar, you're usually underestimated and not a threat to anyone, so they're usually nice to you or, at worst, indifferent. But when you start to do really well, not everyone is going to like it.

The more airings we were given, the more I noticed that two of the founders and one on-air spokesperson of competing beauty brands were distancing themselves from me in the greenroom. I empathized, figuring we were all under the same pressure. And it was only three women. So I tried to spend my time around the many, many other amazing women and men, including other beauty-brand founders, who were supportive. But as time went on, these women went from distancing themselves to all-out attempts to isolate me or mess with me. At first, I just thought maybe they were using competitive tactics to throw me off my game. But it eventually turned into full-blown bullying.

There was a row of several communal dressing rooms. During any given show, someone might briefly close the door if they needed to change clothes in private, but for the most part, the doors were open and the rooms were bustling with people in and out, all sharing the mirror and makeup lights for touch-ups and prepping to go on air. During a prime-time airing one night, these three women were in a dressing room together. One of them closed the door just as I approached. It was borderline rude, and I thought I caught a glare from another, but I told myself I had to be wrong. They wouldn't shut me out of a dressing room! I went to get my stuff, assuming one of them must have needed to change clothes. As I walked back toward the room to use it quickly, two of them were heading off to the show set and only one was left inside. I started to slip in to get ready, but that third woman met me at the door. That's when she said, "You shouldn't come in here. Just trust me," and closed the door in my face.

*What?* What did that even mean? Was it a threat, a warning, or a piece of helpful advice? I thought to myself, *I am a grown woman in my thirties. Am I getting bullied by other grown women? Seriously? Is this really happening?* And it was.

Anyway, another dressing room packed with far more people finally became less crowded and I used it to get ready. It felt like I was in school and not part of the mean girls' club. And even though I wouldn't want to be part of any mean girls' club, rejection in almost any form really hurts. And I felt rejected. I knew in my heart that the only reason this could be happening was because I was gaining a lot of success. Their three brands were much, much larger than mine. It was possible that they were threatened that I was going to catch up to them and that my success was taking away from their airtime (translation, money). But they knew that QVC dictates who gets airtime and it's all based objectively on who is selling the most. It's all earned. So my success could have inspired them to work harder and up their own games, not try to crush mine.

One person's success doesn't take away from another's. And even though airtime at QVC is limited, in the beauty world and beyond there is space for everyone to succeed in big ways. On a side note, but one that I'm passionate about, when women compete with each other, there is a deeper issue at play. Here's what I mean: men grow up competing, but typically they don't have a scarcity mindset when it comes to what's possible for them to achieve. As women, on the other hand, we often grow up thinking — and seeing — that there's one seat at the table. That only one woman can win the coveted spot. We see boardrooms in movies, and in real life, with only one woman at the table. One female VP, or one token woman on the leadership committee. The message is so ingrained in women's minds that often instead of thinking, *Let me bring another woman to the table,* they think, *Another woman at the table means a threat to my seat.* It seems so antiquated, but unfortunately it still exists. This is starting to change, and plenty of women aspire to make their own seat at the table, or make their own table altogether, and, even more than this, to literally bring other women to the tables where they sit, but it's still not happening as quickly as it should and needs to happen. So this form of basically self-imposed gender suppression continues to persist, as women continue to believe there are only limited possibilities and see each other as direct competition.

Whatever was behind the situation in the QVC greenroom, the hard part was that there was no way for me to avoid these women. We were often booked for the same shows. At QVC there was a prime-time show called *Friday Night Beauty,* which was one of the highest-sales-volume programs. It was on every Friday evening at the same time, and the show always opened the same way. There was a live group shot of the brand founders and presenters who were going to appear in the lineup that night, all standing around in an onstage salon, socializing and having fun, as if we were at a party together. I'd always enjoyed that opening of the show, broadcasting live to more than 100 million homes, until now. Whenever I was in the same show with these three women, they would form a tight circle to talk with one another and wouldn't let me join. Imagine a party where three people are talking in a circle and you try to join, or even inch or wedge your way in, but they make it clear you're not wanted. That's what they would do to me. If I was lucky, there were other people in the staged show opening and I'd talk to them. But one night their circle was the only option, and I had no idea what to do. They used their bodies to physically shut me out. So as we went live on national television, I stood all alone, pretending to be happy and excited for the show, while fidgeting and holding back tears.

Afterward, I had to go out for my airing. I pulled myself together the way I imagine boxers do before a fight, when they are about to go into the ring and realize self-doubt is entering their head. I shook it off, put my big-girl panties on, and went out onstage. I had a massive sales goal I had to hit. But, honestly, the sales didn't drive me. And proving something to those mean girls definitely didn't drive me. I wasn't there for them to like me. What got me out of my own head was the idea of something bigger than myself. I was there to let every woman watching at home know that she mattered. Know that I saw her. Know that I *was* her. Know that I related to her pain of feeling like she wasn't enough. I imagined real women across the country. I wanted the single mom in Nebraska watching as she folded laundry to know that she too was beautiful. Whatever was going on in her life, whatever gave her self-doubt, whoever was judging her or treating her unfairly or leaving her out, maybe my message would carry beyond makeup. I wanted to include all women, and in that moment, I felt it more strongly than ever. I didn't even care if each woman watching ordered or not. All I cared about was that when she turned her TV on and saw me, she somehow felt like she mattered, and she was beautiful, and she was seen, and she was enough! That was my WHY. Focusing on it was the only chance I had not to lose my power. So I went out there on that set and took my makeup off to expose my bright red cheeks and showed my favorite models. And together we lived that WHY.

When the airing was over, I left the QVC building, took a deep breath, and . . . you would think that the glow of accomplishment would have taken away the sting of rejection, but, BOOM, all of a sudden the pain from earlier in the night hit me again. I sobbed in my car in the parking lot of QVC until I cried off all my makeup. I went to that place of "what did I do wrong?" or "why am I not lovable?" even though I knew in my gut this was a counterproductive way to think. It was as if I had regressed to my childhood and was feeling like kids on the playground didn't like me. I had to get it together because the next morning, like every morning, I needed to walk into an office and be an inspirational leader to everyone who was working so hard to build this company with me. We had started to hire several awesome, talented people who had left very established beauty brands to take a chance on us because they believed in our mission. I couldn't let them see me defeated. But inside, I was really torn up.

I didn't want to share that this bullying was happening with any of the other vendors or brand founders, as I didn't want to make it bigger, or risk it spreading through the rumor mill, and mostly because I was embarrassed and just wanted it to go away. Even though I knew QVC would never condone this, I decided not to complain to them. At the time, the only person we were supposed to liaise with was the junior assistant buyer in charge of our account. While she was fifteen years their junior, I knew these women who were bullying me included her in social events outside of QVC — perhaps because she was a decision-maker, perhaps because they had a real friendship. Either way, I didn't trust that this junior assistant buyer would handle it properly if I did tell her. So instead, I sat and cried. It hurts so much when people treat us like we don't belong. Even though I knew in my head that I only wanted friends who valued me, it still bothered me to feel left out, or rejected, or unappreciated. And no matter how I explained it to myself in my head, it still hurt my heart.

It was one of my real friends who helped me find my way out of the pain. Sitting in the parking lot, I called my ride-or-die friend Natasha. My closest friends are all very different. They have different backgrounds and different faiths. They vote differently and love differently. Natasha is one of my strongest prayer-warrior friends. She actually taught me how to pray. She's also my most conservative friend and rarely, if ever, swears. (I can't say the same for myself ☺) And she's the laugh-out-loud, not-give-a-flying-f-what-people-think kind of funny. She once bought me a furry kangaroo Halloween costume for my birthday present in July and somehow convinced me to put it on. (Note to self: pouches are not flattering . . . especially when it's a pouch on top of a pouch, lol.) She's the friend who reminds me not to take myself too seriously.

When I told Natasha about the mean girls, I assumed she was going to start praying right there on the phone. Instead, she said, "Girl, you've got big balls, just like that picture of the squirrel with big balls, and every time you walk into that building at QVC and pass those mean girls you need to swing 'em with pride!"

Let me give you some context. A few years before these mean girls were bullying me, Natasha came to visit me while I was in graduate school in New York City. We were in a gift shop and all of a sudden I heard her howling with laughter. I glanced over and she was holding up this poster-sized photo of a squirrel with giant balls. She yelled across the store, "This is us! Jamie, this is us. We're like this squirrel. Fearless. We've got big balls like this squirrel!" Remember, this is my most conservative friend.

Since that day in the gift shop, this squirrel has been our alter ego. When Natasha was up for her own network TV show on CNN's HLN with her name on it, I reminded her to channel the squirrel ahead of her interview. She got the show. When I was nervous prior to the QVC launch, she reminded me to channel the squirrel. And that day, again, as I sat in the QVC parking lot crying, she reminded me to "swing 'em." She reminded me never to let other people dim my light. She got me out of my woe-is-me state and right into pure laughter.

Natasha was right. We shouldn't ever let anyone stop us from "swinging 'em." To this day, I often pump myself up by imagining myself as a giant squirrel "swinging 'em" right into the boardroom, or right into a retail meeting, or right into a party I am not feeling cool enough to attend. If you're looking for more tools to add to your toolbox of confidence, I've got one true time-tested business-backed lesson for you: SWING 'EM!!!

This fearless squirrel is my and Natasha's alter ego, but here's the thing: it's an abundant squirrel. Remember, the scarcity thing is antiquated! The squirrel can be *your* alter ego too! If you need to channel the fearless squirrel, do it! And I know it has big balls, but those might just be external ovaries. It can be anywhere on the gender spectrum you want it to be. And it doesn't matter, because either way, SWING 'EM! You can decide what the fearless squirrel is for you. But if it helps you, BE THE SQUIRREL!

Natasha cheered me up, and when I got home, I told Paulo what had happened. He

*Be the squirrel when you need to, and SWING 'EM!*

could see I had cried my makeup off, so he closed his laptop to give me his full attention. "I just don't understand why they're excluding me like this," I wondered.

His response was genuine confusion. "Why would you even care? Why does it matter if they like you?"

He wasn't saying that to be comforting. He legitimately didn't understand why I was so hurt, as in his view it was crystal clear that they were just jealous of my rising success. Besides, Paulo literally doesn't care what people think about him. To truly not care at all must be so liberating!

I wished I were the same, but, especially at the time, I wasn't. The people-pleaser side of me just wanted to be liked — but I could see that he was right. I spent my life championing other women, so why would I care so much about women who did the opposite? These women had shown me who they were, and it wasn't kind, so why was I giving them my power? If I let those women take any more of my energy, they would also be taking my energy away from my mission. I wanted to tell them one thing I knew in my gut for sure: *You might be tempted to underestimate me, but let me save you some time . . . don't.*

But instead of telling them anything, hoping they might change, I found comfort in the knowledge that being underestimated can be a superpower. Because they never see you coming. And I knew that while they might have been upset because I was starting to have success, they had no idea just how much *will to win* and *faith that it's possible* is inside of me. I wasn't there to compete with them. I was there to compete with what God made me capable of. That day, I vowed to myself that one day I would grow my company so large that the thought of competing with me wouldn't even cross their minds. And I believed it.

Michelle Obama has since famously said, "When they go low, we go high." But before I had a chance to prove to myself or the mean girls that I could rise above their treatment of me, things took a really bad turn that I could never have anticipated. I was about to find out what it felt like to be attacked not by individuals but by a giant competitor.

One afternoon, I opened a mass email blast that QVC sends to all of its customers showing sneak peeks of new items about to launch, and I saw what looked EXACTLY like one of our products, but with another brand's logo on the packaging. WHAT???

No. This couldn't be.

My heart shot into my throat and my body went into a state of shock. I instantly felt like I was going to get sick. See, we owned our product formulas, and the manufacturers we partnered with legally couldn't give them to anyone else. In addition, I was obsessive when it came to perfecting formulas, to the point where we often tested hundreds of iterations before reaching our final formula. My perfectionism drove our chemists crazy, but it also meant the odds of someone just happening to create something identical were virtually nonexistent.

So how had this happened? Something wasn't right. I sure hoped I was wrong, but I suspected this brand was playing dirty.

I called our manufacturer here in the US and showed them a picture of the product. I felt anxiety and anger that would soon be replaced by an insurmountable sense of powerlessness. At first the manufacturer denied any involvement in our competition's product, but I pressed my contact, and eventually he admitted that they had sold a "very similar" version of the formula WE OWNED to this much larger brand. Apparently when one brand is much larger than another, the formulation manufacturer and mixing facility is incentivized to sell them a "very similar" version of the smaller client's successful invention, changing it just enough to claim it's different. This is not exactly legal, but it's what our manufacturer had done. They knew they'd make way more money off this larger brand than they would off us, so they sold us out.

This brand had knocked off our product. We were tiny compared to them, and QVC was our only major account. They already got far more airtime than us on QVC. They were also in all of the big retail stores and department stores. And they were about to launch a complete knockoff of our product across all of these platforms. All I could think about was how they were about to use their vast exposure to tell the world that this innovative product was their creation, and they had the reach and distribution to launch it everywhere. They could get it out there quickly, even in advertisements in magazines. This was our blood, sweat, and tears, and I worried that, *boom,* just like that, they would not just get credit for the innovation; more devastatingly, they would destroy our business in the process. What if one day it ended up looking like *we* were the ones who copied *them*? Every worst-case scenario ran through my mind. I felt like we were under attack. And at war.

Here we go back down the rabbit hole of how hard it is to be a small company. We could have sued our manufacturer, but we didn't have the money to, and worse, they were still the ones making most of our key formulas. Suing them would likely mean they would halt manufacturing our products. When you're a new business there are so many roads that are ideal or just, but if you go down them there's a high chance it will hurt more than help, or worse, you'll go out of business.

The next option was to call QVC and alert them to this knockoff product, made with a formula that WE OWNED, about to launch on their channel. I knew QVC had placed their orders with no idea the formula was similar, but maybe if I proved to them it was, they would prevent it from launching.

I called Allen Burke to ask him what to do. Yes, the same Allen Burke who had once told me *no* and that our products weren't the right fit for QVC (which led me to sobbing all night, crying myself to sleep, then waking up multiple mornings in a row and sobbing some more as I didn't know how we were going to stay alive as a company).

Well, after we launched on QVC, Allen ended up becoming one of my greatest mentors and dear friends. He was a huge champion of our brand's authenticity and mission, and of how real women everywhere were responding to it. Even after he had retired from QVC, he remained one of the smartest and most valuable mentors in my life. He gave us advice that day that probably saved our business. He said we could do what I wanted, which was to call QVC and ask that they pull the product, but ultimately it would hurt QVC if we did. They'd allocated airtime to the product and their forecasted sales goals were tied to the launch. A last-minute substitution would likely fail to hit projected sales. It helped that he explained there was no way QVC could have known it was a knockoff when they placed the order with the other brand. He reminded me that this other brand had a totally different positioning than ours, and that the product wasn't a good fit for that brand's marketing story. He was right. For example, it was as if a brand that sold glitter- and sugar-infused fun makeup all of a sudden offered an organic antiaging discovery from the depths of the ocean because it was trendy. It was that drastic, and our product just didn't seem authentic to who they were as a brand. They were likely just knocking it off and launching it because they saw this small, under-the-radar brand (us) having great success with it. I knew it was a mistake to hop on something off-brand just because it was trendy and/or successful, because it would dilute customer trust. But that didn't change that they were doing it. It felt like a David vs. Goliath story, and this giant brand was a Goliath that could destroy us.

In the weeks leading up to this other brand's launch of OUR product, I felt sick beyond words. Have you ever gotten really bad news and then in the morning when you woke up, you hoped it was all a dream, and then you got horribly sick to your stomach when you realized it wasn't? Well, that was happening to me daily. Paulo decided to channel the TV show *Survivor,* and he started putting up paper signs all over our office (aka the living room) saying things like "Outwit," "Outplay," and "Outlast." He also made me "Super JJ" T-shirts. He had decided I needed to be reminded of the superhero I am, so he drew an *S* and two *J*s in a Superman-style logo with black marker. I wore those shirts. A lot.

We chose to follow Allen's advice. We didn't notify QVC about what the other brand had done. We didn't want to hurt them by trying to have them pull something from their airtime lineup. Plus, QVC was still our main distribution partner. We couldn't risk damaging that relationship. And we definitely couldn't afford to get caught up in a legal battle with the Goliath competitor.

The day arrived. The major brand launched the knockoff product on QVC and in retail stores in every corner of the US and across the globe. It was positioned with a slightly different story from ours but looked and performed almost identically. I watched the sales counter as the product was presented on QVC. To my surprise, using my own sales goals as reference, it wasn't moving fast. It wasn't selling what it should! And when I saw it in retail stores, the shelves were full. The knockoff of our product sold just okay! *What?* Wait, really? Yep, it sold just *okay.* It barely made its sales goal. This MUCH larger brand did worse than we did, with virtually the same product. *Why?* I thought back to something Allen Burke had told me on our phone call: "You can't fake authenticity." I knew and believed that, but here was proof of it right before my eyes. The knockoff product (aka *our* product) got great reviews! The people who bought it loved it. But even with great reviews, since their product wasn't authentic to their brand DNA, not enough customers connected with it emotionally to buy it for the first time. But guess what? It kept selling INCREDIBLY well for us! Because it was core to who we were, what we wanted for our customers, and what we believed. To this day, now with hundreds of products in our portfolio, it is still one of our most beloved and best-selling products.

One day, many years later, we grew to become much larger than the brand that did this to us. And a few years after that, when crossing paths with the founder of that brand who knocked us off, I decided it was about time for us to have a conversation. We were in a big open area at QVC, part of the large greenroom. There were a few dozen founders there, all of us in various stages of prepping for shows. I saw the founder, sitting alone, and decided I was going to talk to this person. I didn't know if it was going to turn into a disagreement or a repair, if they would freak out, take ownership, or even apologize.

"Do you have a second to chat?" I asked.

"Yes," they said. We walked over to the wide, carpeted stairs that lead from the vendor space up to the control room and sat on the steps, about twenty feet from everyone else. The moment was super intense. My heart was pounding. If we spoke the truth, maybe we could move past this.

I reminded them of the product launch, and our shared manufacturer, and explained how devastating it had been for me. "You were so much bigger than we were," I said. "What you did could have put us out of business. It really, really sucked."

I was in a one-in-a-billion position where I was David, talking to Goliath in person. For such a long time that opposition felt huge, overpowering, insurmountable. But by then I'd summited peaks far greater than this. And learned time and time again that God is more powerful than any opposition.

The other founder denied doing it. I explained that I had proof, even from my own manufacturer, that it had happened. This other founder explained that they changed a few ingredients and the way they positioned the product and that they never knocked me off. I looked them in the eyes, and wasn't afraid to say what I thought, and that I hoped they would never do it to anyone else. Regardless of how this person chose to respond, I felt no pain anymore. No resentment anymore. Honestly, I just felt victorious. Because I had survived and thrived. I had relearned the lesson of the power of authenticity. And I was a stronger businesswoman, and human being, because of the experience.

Oh, and as for the manufacturer that sold our "very similar" formula to the larger brand, well, we've now grown to be their largest customer. By a lot. And now *we're* the ones they're scared of losing.

One day the people who never believed in you will talk about how they met you.
— ANONYMOUS

144

As for the three women who bullied me for a bit? I fulfilled the vow I had made to myself on one of my lowest nights at QVC. My company eventually grew to be so big that those three mean girls gave up hating on me. Two of them eventually became pleasant, courteous, and mostly indifferent toward me, and the third ended up making a bid toward a friendship with me. The closest I was comfortable with is the relationship she and I have today, one I would call supportive acquaintances.

My experience with them made me even more grateful for all the other brand founders, many of them women, who did support me along the entire journey at QVC. Many of them I consider great friends to this day. We have a bond of deep respect for each other, knowing how hard the journey of entrepreneurship is. Even though we're competitors, we support one another and speak positivity into each other's lives. And we get competitive by upping our own games, not tearing down someone else's.

To this day, anytime I ever see another woman standing or sitting all alone, whether it's at a party, a work event, or anywhere else, if I can, I make it a point to be inclusive. I go up to her, say hello, and ask her how she's doing. And my closest friends are people who do this also. So thank you to those three women, for teaching me how much simply doing this could mean for someone else who feels all alone.

One more thing. I mentioned earlier in this chapter how I called Allen Burke for advice. Well, when he retired from QVC, we hired him in a paid position on the IT Cosmetics advisory board. Allen Burke, the beauty industry legend who was head of and transformed all of QVC beauty, joined our advisory board. The guy who once REJECTED ME was now WORKING FOR ME!! What?!

As our business grew, I also realized that Allen was actually right when he said *no*. See, sometimes even though the *no's* hurt, they're actually gifts. Here's what I mean. Had QVC said *yes* any earlier, we would not have succeeded. At that point, there was no way we could have handled the back end of the business to meet the volume, timing, and inventory flow demand that's required to be successful in an account that large. Simply put, we didn't have a big enough team, infrastructure, or operational relationships and we would have failed miserably. Allen had actually been right all along; we just didn't know what we didn't know at the time. Sometimes those *no's* are actually serendipitous grace, wrapped in a package labeled *painful rejection.* And just as the mean girls made me appreciate even more those who are supportive, the *no's* make the *yeses,* when they happen, that much sweeter!

Here's what I learned, and what I believe is true in life when you live your truth, work extremely hard, and do right by others: When it comes to the mean people, the ruthless competitors, the naysayers, and the critics, they might not believe in you now, but one day they'll call you for advice. They might call you *unqualified* today, but one day they'll tell people how they know you. They might call you *meek,* but one day they'll call you *mogul.* They might call you *uncool,* but one day they'll call you *friend.* They might call you *smaller,* but one day they'll call you *baller.* They might call you *crazy,* but one day they'll call you *genius.* They might call you *unworthy,* but one day they'll call you *legend.* They might watch you *cry,* but one day they'll watch you *SWING 'EM.* They might call you on the

phone to *reject you,* but one day they just
might end up calling you *boss.*

148

# FIVE:
## *BELIEVE* IN THE
## POWER OF YOUR MICROPHONE

What counts is not necessarily the size of
the dog in the fight; it's the size of the
fight in the dog.
— DWIGHT D. EISENHOWER

I've grown so much from my days of letting
mean girls like the ones I encountered at
QVC hurt me, and I've truly learned that
the power of your inner circle is one of the
greatest secrets to success both in business
and in life.

When you look at my six closest friends,
they have really diverse personalities, pretty
fantastic careers, and some of the biggest
hearts of anyone I know. If you only knew
them by seeing them in photos on social
media, it might look like they have the kind
of glamorous and success-filled lives that
only happen to *other* people. But, like mine,
the stories behind their stories are far from
picture-perfect. I asked their permission to

share some parts of their stories with you that aren't what you see at first glance on social media, in their professional lives, or in person.

Take a look at the faces in this picture of the seven of us. I think my friends are all so beautiful and so for me, this sure makes for a perfect picture! But the seven of us are brave, and messy, and triumphant, and definitely not perfect!

*Left to right: Natasha, Dana, Me, Denise, Lia, Desiree, Jacquie*

Here's the real-life truth behind these beautiful smiling faces:

Between the seven of us,

1 of us was homeless growing up.

1 of us was a foster kid.

2 of us are adopted.

1 of us had a mother with extreme mental illness.

1 of us had a father who committed suicide when she was just fifteen.

2 of us don't know who our father is.

1 of us has a learning challenge.

1 of us became pregnant at age fifteen and raised her baby as a single mom.

1 of us was diagnosed with breast cancer.

We've each also had some fairy-tale-like VICTORIES, many born out of pure grit:

4 of us are entrepreneurs, founders, and CEOs.

1 of us has had her own network TV news

show named after her on CNN's HLN (that's Natasha, whom you met in the last chapter).

1 of us recently came out and shared with her friends/family that she identifies as bisexual/fluid.

1 of us is known as the female Jerry McGuire and has an A-list celeb playing her in an upcoming TV series.

1 of us is on the *Forbes* Richest Self-Made Women List.

1 of us has had more than one major role on a prime-time network TV drama.

1 of us is breaking free from the insecurity of a physical deformity.

On paper, we're a mismatched group of puzzle pieces that don't look like they fit together. We don't all share the same religion, politics, or socioeconomic status, yet none of this is relevant to our friendship. All of us cry together, dream of changing culture together, champion women and amazing causes together, and ALL of us are VICTORS, not VICTIMS, despite our pasts, despite our challenges, despite our shortcomings. All of us believe in living a life in service, of service!

These are my closest friends because they show up for their lives, bravely and authentically. They show up for me fully, and I show up for them. They sharpen me. They remind me that I'm enough, both on the good days that make my highlight reel and the bad days when I can't get out of bed. We see each other in our full vulnerability and truth. And love each other without judgment.

I'm sharing these women's stories and our friendship as an example of how, despite our pasts or the parts of our stories we've been ashamed to share, if we're brave enough to share them, we often discover that we're not alone.

Dana has been my close friend for over twenty years. She is the one who recently discovered and shared that she identifies her sexual orientation as bisexual/fluid. She told me, "I feel like my relationships with friends and family absolutely suffered when I didn't share that I was fluid. I felt more alone than *ever*. My life started unfolding in the most glorious ways when I started to share my truth." When Dana confided in me I cried tears of joy, because I've never seen her happier. She asked that I share with you the impact and freedom she felt when she finally embraced her truth and decided to share it with the people she loves most. And while they haven't unanimously supported her the way she'd prayed they would, she now feels freer than she's ever felt.

In author Brené Brown's research, she finds that owning our truth and sharing it, even when it's hard, is the only way to truly connect with another human being. And authentic connection is the key to love.

When you hide important parts of who you are, you can't ever have authentic relationships. Because that other person is loving someone who isn't exactly you. We hesitate — what if they won't love us as we truly are? But then we have to ask ourselves what's worse — losing that person or losing the chance for true, authentic love the rest of our lives? We are born with the need for human connection. So, if you've been scared to show up fully and authentically as the real, true you, then you are robbing yourself of that real human connection.

My friend Desiree found out she was pregnant when she was fifteen years old.

"Just after I found out, my boyfriend disappeared on me. I was scared, alone, and overcome with fear. As an uneducated single teen mom, I was torn between giving my baby boy up for adoption or raising him when I knew the odds would be against me . . . and him. At the last minute I just knew I couldn't part with him, but on the day he was born, as the nurses were placing him in my arms, I became so paralyzed with fear that I refused to look at my own baby. I didn't want him to see my face and have his first memory of his mom be eyes of fear. As I lay there with him in my arms, staring up at the ceiling with tears cresting over my lashes, I couldn't help but have thoughts like *Am I strong enough to do this at such a young age? Why is God trusting me with this gift? Will I ruin this innocent baby's chance at a normal life?*"

Then just like that, Desiree's Momma Bear–like instinct took over. And she made the decision that she was going to be guided by love, not fear. And in that decision, her whole life changed. "I looked into my baby boy's eyes for the very first time and flooded him with every ounce of love in my being. And in that moment, I knew for sure that this was exactly where and who I was supposed to be: a mommy. *His* mommy."

Fifteen years later, Desiree and I met for the first time, when she was modeling for us on air at QVC. She had dealt with severe acne-prone skin and shared with me how IT Cosmetics had changed her skin and her confidence. One day, she and I ended up having lunch and talking for hours. I saw this light inside of her that day. I could feel her heart and raw vulnerability. "How would you feel about sharing your heart and your authentic story with millions of women across the country?" I asked Desiree. I needed to hire some additional people to represent IT Cosmetics on QVC — not just to model but to be IT Cosmetics present-ers, introducing our products on air. Unlike most brands, which hire seasoned TV sales professionals to promote their products, I wanted to find people whose lives were authentically changed by our products, and whose hearts were aligned with our mission, and *then* teach them the TV and sales part.

When I first asked Desiree if she'd be up for this new role, she looked at me like a deer in headlights. Later, after many days of struggling with self-doubt, she called me up and said yes.

I'll never forget her debut on QVC. Like the producers who once had worried for me, I worried Des might faint that day. Off set, she was teary-eyed and filled with fear. But when the cameras went live, I watched the look in her eyes shift from fear for herself to love for the women watching at home. She poured her heart out in that debut airing and in the countless airings she's done since. I took a huge risk for my company by hiring authenticity over experience. And she took a huge risk by trusting me, showing up, and leading with love over fear.

Our trust has grown over the years into a beautiful friendship. Desiree reminds me that there is strength and power in being vulnerable. And whenever I'm tempted to let fear take over or play it small without realizing it, Des is the first to remind me to walk toward love, never toward fear.

Think about how good it feels when you're being your true self. You don't have to try. It just happens. And it feels effortless. If you work in a creative field, or have a creative hobby, you know that when you're in that state called "flow," where you're engaged and energized by what you're doing, creativity and your best work just emerge. The same thing happens when you're in a state of flow in everyday life. And the only way to experience that is to be your authentic self fully. The good parts, the quirky parts, the awkward parts, the kind parts, the scared parts, the *true* parts. When you hide parts of yourself, dim your own light, or change to try to meet someone else's expectations, you risk missing out on becoming the person you were born to be, and developing the types of relationships that will fill your soul.

So many of us waste *so* much of our lives shrinking who we are and how we show up because we're worried what other people think.

One of the biggest fears that holds us back from showing up as our true self is the fear that people won't like us. Here's the thing: We're going to encounter mean girls, underminers, gossips, ruthless competitors, and even misguided supporters. Not everyone is going to like each of us all of the time no matter what. So why not accept it and show up as yourself?! Otherwise you're going to have haters and critics judging someone you're actually *not,* on top of it all. Maybe it's less painful, or you think if you shrink down or hide, you'll encounter less negativity. But at the end of the day, when you reclaim your power and show up in your life as your authentic self, you literally gain your whole life back.

A key to believing in ourselves is surrounding ourselves with people who not only believe in us and love us for who we are but also sharpen us. It's been said many times that you are the culmination of the five or so people you spend the most time with. Think about that for a moment. Aside from your kiddos, of course, if you're a parent, who are the five or so people you see or talk to most often? Do they sharpen you and help you reach your full potential and live your best life? Do they love you well and inspire you to love greater? Do they remind you of your talents, strengths, and beauty? Do they call you out on your BS? Do they help lift you out of self-doubt?

If the five people you spend the most time with aren't sharpening you and inspiring you to be the best version of yourself, it might be worth spending some time taking inventory of who you surround yourself with. Because it's easy to keep people in our lives who are actually hurting us or lowering our energy/vibration. And we often keep them around because it's comfortable or convenient. Or because we've been friends with them forever. Or because we fear that it will be too hard to make new friends. It's easy to lower our bar and get sucked into gossip even when it doesn't feel good in our soul. It's easy to hang around people who actually encourage our bad habits and the worst sides of ourselves to take root. It's even easy to excitedly tell people our fresh ideas or biggest dreams, even when we suspect they're not going to share our excitement or belief. Reshma Saujani, in her book *Brave, Not Perfect,* writes, "We've become conditioned to compromise and shrink ourselves in order to be liked. The problem is, when you work so hard to get everyone to like you, you very often end up *not* liking yourself so much."

Maybe you feel like you don't have a choice, and like you're stuck with the people around you? And what if some of the people who you spend the most time with aren't supportive of the kind of life and dreams you want to accomplish — and happen to be your actual family members? Even your partner? I mean, you can't just be like "peace out, Mom" or get rid of family members that easily, right? I learned a powerful lesson from my brilliant friend and mentor, author and speaker Bob Goff. He shared this idea in a small group conversation once, and I asked his permission to share it with you, because it's been so helpful to me.

Bob taught me that we all have a microphone that we control in our lives. And we get to choose the people we hand that microphone to. We decide who speaks into it and at what volume. When we're able to decide who to let speak into our lives, or who we hand our microphone to, it can change everything.

During and after high school, one of my many jobs was as a receptionist in a health club, where I worked my way up to sales, and quickly became a manager. At the time, my father was working as an inspector on the assembly line in a glass factory. As I advanced in my job at the health club, I was receiving commission on membership sales in addition to my salary and began making more than $50,000 a year — and it was a lot more than my dad was earning. When I told him that I'd been accepted to Washington State University and was planning to go to college, he said, "No! Why would you think of doing that? You're making so much money. You've got a great thing going and you need to keep at it." He meant well, and he was giving his best advice, but it was through the lens of his own limited experiences.

I wanted to get out of the town I was raised in and travel and go to college and meet people who'd had different life experiences than me and, most of all, I wanted to see the world! In that moment, I knew he loved me the best way he knew how, but I also knew I had to take the microphone back from my dad on that topic.

It's so empowering when you master the art of deciding who to turn up or turn down the volume on. Maybe you have a friend who you love working out with, but you don't like that they often have a victim mentality. You can be kind and loving while in the gym but choose not to give them a microphone in your life in any other capacity. Maybe you have a family member or partner that you love, but you know that when you share your goals or dreams with them, they turn negative or cynical, and it depletes you and sucks your soul dry. You don't need to abandon them altogether, but you can change the topics in your life that you let them speak into your microphone about. You have the power to turn down their volume whenever you want. Some days, you might end up listening only when they talk to you about the weather, or what's for dinner, or who is really there for the right reasons on the TV show *The Bachelor,* but you choose not to seek their input on ideas you're excited about. You can save that conversation for someone who is high-volume microphone worthy for the specific topic! Someone who inspires you to be the best version of yourself and to fly higher in that area of your life!

When something doesn't sit right with you in your gut, imagine yourself taking your microphone back from that person, as quickly as a reporter takes it back from an out-of-control witness on live TV. When we launched IT Cosmetics, Paulo and I consistently received doubt-filled comments and questions, even from many of our friends, family members, and colleagues at the time. "What do you know about makeup?," "Paulo, makeup isn't very macho!," "Why would you give up a secure job with benefits?," and "Are you sure you're ready to do this?" Had we seen the prospects of our dream through their lens of doubt, where would we be now? Similarly, when you sense people are only telling you what you want to hear because they want to please you, you need to turn down the volume on that too, because it's not real.

If your intuition tells you that a friend, partner, or family member doesn't see your goals and dreams with the helpful perspective you need, don't actively seek their advice. Don't hand them the microphone on that topic. Love them from a new, healthier boundary. Share, but focus on the areas where you best connect. Energy is contagious, and even though you can't control how other people show up, you can control who you let impact yours.

If your circle isn't supporting you, then consider if maybe it's not a circle but more of a cage! When we surround ourselves with negative or toxic people, we often start to mirror their negativity. Think about the people in your life who bring you down. Would you want to catch their contagious negative energy and take it on as your own? You might be doing that already without even realizing it. It's so easy to let happen.

If you aren't surrounded by the kind of support you need, be open to adding some new people to your circle who can help you strive to be the best version of yourself. And who you can do the same for. When someone operates at a higher vibration than you, you can feel it, and they're a good person to ask to speak into your microphone when you need good advice in that area.

One friend in my inner circle, Lia, exudes the most joyful energy of anyone I know. She's like sunshine in the form of a human being. Lia is the friend in my list above who grew up homeless, then later in the projects in Philadelphia. She was surrounded by people who never encouraged her to dream big and never dreamed big themselves. But even as a little girl, Lia felt like God had big plans for her life. And even though she grew up in an environment plagued by fear, she decided to choose joy instead. She taught herself at a young age how to turn down the volume on the people around her, and, through her own sheer grit, one by one, she brought people into her own circle who lifted her up, the way she does others. And similarly, when people in her circle, like her mom, told her to shine her light, she knew to turn up the volume on those words that felt true. Lia eventually started filling her circle with people who knew more than her in business, and then Lia started her own business, a jewelry line called Valencia Key, that she recently launched on QVC. The girl who grew up *homeless* was now live on TV in 100 million *homes,* sharing her dream and her joy. In the many years she's been my close friend, she's the person I go to anytime someone online says something super hurtful, or I find out an employee betrayed my trust, or a competitor tried to hurt me personally. Lia sharpens me real quick and snaps me right out of it! She reminds me not to give them my power and not to let them steal my joy.

And remember to give yourself grace. It

can take time to build a strong circle of really great people around you. Sometimes one of them will hurt your trust and turn out not to be who you thought they were. And it might even feel impossible to find the kind of people you're looking for, but I believe when you're a true friend to other people, you will attract true, honest, like-minded friends. Don't settle when it comes to who you surround yourself with.

When you form authentic connections, they help you believe in yourself and your dreams, and ultimately help make them come true. Lia inspires me to elevate my joy. Denise inspires me not to take crap from anyone. Natasha inspires me to be the fearless squirrel. Dana inspires me to speak my truth. Desiree inspires me to embrace my vulnerability. Jacquie inspires me to be strong and brave. The people I surround myself with and let speak into my life have been critical to my success. They are kind and nonjudgmental. They see the best in me and remind me of it. They don't let me lower my bar or talk myself back into a bad habit. They challenge me. They keep their word. They embrace my weirdness and love me for me. And I try to do all of this for them. Having a strong circle like this has been critical to my ability to endure the failures and heartaches. And it's been critical to my maintaining the confidence in who I am, even if it feels like other people don't get me.

Your circle might be two people or five people; just make sure they're the *right* people. If you're working to bring a few new friends into your inner circle, make sure you identify the qualities that you really need in a friend. And make sure you're open-minded and open-hearted about who you're open to including. I've found that true friends don't always look like the circles you ran with in high school, or the kinds of people you were raised around. And to find them, there might be some old, superficial filters of judgment that you need to get rid of.

My beautiful group of close friends and I aren't the show dogs impeccably groomed from birth to win. We're much more like strays. Strays who might not know where we were made, but know what we're made of. Strays who've dated our fair share of hound dogs, had surprise puppies, dealt with plenty of fleas, and licked our wounds together. Strays who have overcome the need to hear "who's a good girl?," who don't judge you if you've been to the pound, and yep, we even sometimes pee a little when we get too excited. Strays who howl in laughter together and share dog years of life's wisdom together. Strays born without fancy backgrounds, but with a gigantic fight inside of us. And with only one requirement to join our pack: a huge heart to love. We are strays and underdogs who chose to enter the dog shows anyway, and came out of nowhere to win some of the biggest Best in Show victories, simply because we decided to believe that we could.

# Six:
## *Believe* in the Power of Authenticity

> Be who you are and say what you feel,
> because those who mind don't matter and
> those who matter don't mind.
> — BERNARD M. BARUCH

"Hello Jamie, my name is Sarah Beth, and I'm calling from Texas to order more of your stuff today. I don't know what you're putting in this stuff, but the other day my husband said I look nice. I was like, 'What?' And he said I was *radiating.* Now, you have to understand something: he didn't even notice the time I dyed my hair this purplish-red color by mistake. So for him to say *this . . .* I'm calling to get some more." Callers like Sarah Beth, a shopper I was meeting for the first time live on TV, gave real-time customer feedback.

The QVC experience ended up being filled with important lessons I applied to all areas of our digital, social media, and business growth, and even more so to my personal growth.

A few years into our QVC launch we were still small, relative to the many huge brands at the time, but we were rapidly growing. Our products were selling well on QVC and the repeat purchase rate was high. This means the customers who bought them for the first time liked them, and when they ran out, they came back for more. In business, getting that repeat customer had always been my goal, and the ultimate indicator of success that I cared about. A company can sell something once, that's just a sale. But when customers love something so much they buy it a second time, that's a brand. It's not just building sales; it's developing trust and brand equity. If a customer trusts that your product works and does what you say it does, that's when you can truly build something real.

As our sales and repeat purchases continued to grow, I was getting booked to go on air so often that it took over my life. QVC is on television live, 24/7, every day of the year except for Christmas. There's no script and no teleprompter; it truly is you and a host together, staring into cameras in the studio, while being broadcast nationwide, plus streaming live online. Every minute of airtime counts big-time. For QVC, their airtime is their real estate. When you walk into a Target or Walmart, you can shop thousands of products all right there on the floor. But when it comes to TV shopping, only one product can air at a time. That means all the companies and brands and products are competing with one another to get QVC airtime. So even though IT Cosmetics is a makeup company, we are competing with the best companies across all categories, like Apple, or Dyson, or Vitamix. The airtime, in big part, goes to whoever is hitting the highest sales dollars per minute.

Every time I was live on air, I could see the clock below the cameras telling me how many minutes I had left. And while I was live, I heard the producer in my earpiece telling me if the sales were going well, literally by the second. It was the most stressful thing ever, but of course I had to make it look like I was having fun on air. And here's the thing: You actually *do* need to have fun, because if you try too hard to sell, it will backfire. Viewers are smart, and they won't buy from a salesperson who's trying to hawk product at them. But if you're true to yourself, and you show your authentic love for the product, they can feel that.

Now, just being authentic doesn't automatically mean your product will sell. As I mentioned, at QVC you feel this unremitting pressure that you're only as good as your last show. And even if the last show went well, they still might cut your airtime, *while you're live on air,* if a product isn't selling well. This happened to me many times. I would be presenting a product we had spent hundreds of thousands of dollars making and getting to the QVC warehouse, and if it wasn't doing well, all of a sudden I'd see my countdown clock get cut. Imagine standing there, talking live to 100 million homes about this brand-new product, knowing how much money is on the line for your business and that you have only eight minutes to talk about it. And then you see the clock jump from six minutes down to two minutes instantaneously. You have to keep smiling and championing your product without reacting, but there's a lot going on in your head. You just lost four minutes of your presentation because the product wasn't selling well enough in those first two minutes. Those four minutes represent tens of thousands of dollars in sales you just lost. And to top it off, because it didn't do well, you likely won't get another opportunity to present it on air, which means QVC will likely ship back all of the extra inventory of that product you had already paid to manufacture, and you won't get paid for anything that didn't sell. This might seem brutal, but it's just business like it is in physical retail stores. If your product isn't selling well there, it gets exited and you lose your shelf space. Business is just business and these retailers have to stay in business too, so it makes sense. The big difference, though, is that with QVC it happens almost immediately, and you don't get a ton of days in-store, like in a Target or Walmart, to prove your product will sell. You often get just one shot. And if your track record is stellar, you might get another.

It got to the point where I lived my life on call 24/7. Literally.

The truth is it was really hard. Not having a regular sleep schedule is hard on your health and your body. Add that to the unrelenting pressure to hit sales numbers. The better you do, the higher they move your sales goals and the more airings they give you. Yet somehow you still always believe you're only as good as your last show. And the more time I spent at QVC, the more I saw brand after brand last just one show. So I realized it was an incredible honor to keep getting the invite back because we kept hitting numbers.

QVC gave my company exposure when we couldn't afford advertising, and I owe so much of our success to this day to them. Seeing us on QVC drove people to the stores to ask about our brand, and that demand for our product on the customer level helped us *finally* get those *yeses* from the retailers who had told me *no* for years. The extremely high quality regulations and protocols that QVC demands of its products were expensive and inconvenient to go through as a small company, but they're also what saved us from running into consumer complaint or quality issues that a lot of new and growing companies face. When I look back on this journey, QVC saying *yes* was the biggest launchpad our company could have possibly asked for, and even with all of the struggles, I would do it all over again in a heartbeat.

In addition to catapulting our sales and brand awareness, one of the most beautiful parts of the QVC experience was sharing it with some incredible people who surrounded me (mean girls aside). Helen, one of our models, always had the quickest wit and funniest stories of anyone in our group. Helen was single and in her seventies, and during the long hours on set, she would share her dating stories, and some of them had us all almost peeing our pants in laughter. She was on many of the dating websites, and most of the men she went out with lasted just one date before she'd learn quickly why they were single. One time, she found out that one of the guys who said he was in his early seventies like her had lied about his age. He was in fact in his late eighties. "What? Men lie about their age in their eighties?" I asked. "Men are *still* lying in their eighties?" another model asked. And it got worse. He was married and had lied about that too. On a date with another guy, this time one who really was in his seventies, midway through the date he leaned over and licked Helen's cheek. Yep, with the entire length of his tongue he licked up the entire length of her cheek. Needless to say, that was his last date with Helen. Anyhow, Helen became known as the "man magnet," and when we were doing live shows in the middle of the night and getting to the point where we were delirious, I would actually reference how she was actively dating during our on-air presentations! (With Helen's permission, of course.) And Helen resonated with the viewers, who would call in and mention that she was their favorite model or that they wanted to have an active dating life like hers.

Helen was so sarcastic and so funny that she and Paulo would talk smack to each other in the greenroom like brother and sister. "Jamie, how do you put up with him?" she'd say if he was standing next to me. "Jamie, how did we sell out of that product with *Helen* modeling it? I don't understand," he would say to make her laugh. We spent so much time together, more time than with our own family members. We learned that Helen had a small, old-model TV in her apartment. Her face was now on countless big-screen TVs all across the country. So one year during the holiday season, Paulo and I surprised her by having a large HD TV delivered to her apartment. That way she could record the shows that she modeled in and see her own beautiful face on a big screen.

One of my favorite parts of the QVC environment is that unlike brick-and-mortar stores, where you see a lot of brands' products but rarely meet the company founders, at QVC it's almost always the company or brand founders who are presenting on air. And a lot of the hour-long shows on QVC will showcase products from several different brands. So you end up meeting many fascinating and inspiring entrepreneurs and company founders, because you're all hanging out in the green-room together before your shows.

One of my fondest memories is seeing Paulo and two other brand founders walking down the hall with lobster butter all over their faces, dripping down their chins onto their clothes. One of the food brands had just gotten off the air. After food brands present, they often let anyone who's around eat all of the cooked food they used in their presentations. Some of the food is more coveted than others. See, for me, I would get excited when companies like Cheryl's Cookies were on air. Their free-for-all cookie-fest after their airings got filed under "calories don't count when it's free." But the lobster vendors were Paulo's favorite. When I saw him and the other founders in all their shiny, butter-soaked, lobster-savage glory, I burst into uncontrollable laughter.

"They told us anything not eaten off this display cart in the next few minutes was going to be thrown out," Paulo said with his mouth full as they stood in the studio hallway, ripping lobster tails off the shells, clutching multiple tails in each hand, dunking them in butter, and shoving them in their mouths as if it were one of those hot-dog-eating contests. Often all the founders were exhausted, and in the greenroom during the middle-of-the-night shows, we would end up laughing together over the silliest things, cutting the tension and bonding in the trenches. We ended up forming real friendships.

We all have moments as entrepreneurs when a competitor is doing better than us, and that creates a temptation to consider changing what we're doing, whether it's how we're selling our product, how we're describing our mission, or even what product we're selling altogether. I've seen this play out, over and over, as one of the biggest mistakes any entrepreneur can make. Every time I saw a brand or brand founder change something that wasn't aligned with their authentic WHY or their own authenticity, it failed in the long run. After seeing this happen around me so often, I became passionate about it. Anytime anyone on my team would worry about what another brand was doing, or what was trending at that moment in the marketplace, I began constantly telling my team this: *The biggest risk to our business isn't what the competition is doing. It's the risk of getting distracted and influenced by it and diluting our own secret sauce.* I said this so many times that my team started finishing the sentence for me after a while. Just like in friendships and relationships, the same is true in business. And in business, your authentic relationship is with your customer. Realizing the power of authenticity takes so much pressure and stress off. Because there is only one you. And being anyone other than yourself simply won't work. Realizing this sets you free.

To this day, whenever I flip the channel to QVC, I know many of the presenters I see on any given day. I learned early on that the people who do the very best on the air are the same way off the air. Some of the most successful brand founders have a specific personality, vibe, and point of view on air, and they're the same exact way when they come offstage. On the other hand, the people who go on air with a schtick, or an act, or are hard-core salesy never do well in the long run. There's a revolving door of them. Viewers, and people in general, can connect with you only when you're being authentic. And you can't fake authenticity. Mally Roncal, the founder of Mally Beauty, is a QVC icon. She was Beyoncé's makeup artist, and she's all about peace, love, and really great makeup. On TV she has level-one-million energy. She's flamboyant, fiercely confident, fun, and full of laughter. You wonder how someone can have that much life in her all the time, but in the QVC offices you can hear Mally's laugh down the hall, and she's the exact same way at three in the morning walking into the parking lot. I've had four-hour, one-on-one lunches with her, and we're still laughing at the end. I could call her up and talk for four more hours right now and still have more to share, because she's that charismatic and full of love. That's why she's such a massive success. She is who she is, on and off the air.

Another incredible example of this is the late, legendary Joan Rivers, who was one of the original queens of QVC. She went on air with wild, over-the-top, kind, but often shocking gusto, but that's how she was in real life too. I'll never forget one day inside the crowded QVC greenroom when it was such a slow sales day that you could cut the tension with a knife. I was sitting there preparing, surrounded by a lot of other silent and very stressed-out brand founders, when all of a sudden the large metal entrance doors flew open and Joan walked right in with her arms flung open and loudly proclaimed with her fully infectious irreverence, "Let's wake up America and sell some sh%$ today, people!" You just couldn't help but smile and love her. And she loved her customers. And was always herself, and always succeeded. Selling is a short-lived outcome. Longevity comes from making sure your product does what it says, building trust, being yourself, and truly connecting. Whether you want real lasting customers, or real lasting relationships, or to build an online following or community that lasts, you have to show up with authenticity.

Authenticity doesn't automatically guarantee success . . . but inauthenticity guarantees failure. While growing my company, I've watched thousands of other companies succeed and fail. Authenticity is something you can't fake. And knowing that's where your true power lies is one of the greatest life and business lessons I've learned.

*Two models who've been with us since the beginning and now, ten years later, are part of almost all of our QVC shows: Alisha and Helen (aka Man Magnet).*

*Me, Paulo, and Jacquie watching my niece's graduation from the QVC greenroom. One of countless family events we missed in order to grow the business.*

*Our team celebrating our wins in the QVC Customer Choice Beauty Awards. These awards always mean so much because the winners are chosen 100 percent by customer vote.*

# Seven:
## *Believe* You Can Go from Underestimated to Unstoppable

Do you believe that little girls can fly?
— *NADIA,* THE STORY OF NADIA COMANECI

"We would like to offer you $1.2 billion dollars to buy your company." I still can't process that I heard these words. But they were real. This girl, who started with a dream in her living room, was being told that what she'd created was valuable. Really valuable. Even though it had been dismissed by so many experts, for so many years. Hearing these words made me believe that unrelenting passion and resilience really do pay off. But there was a lot more yellow brick road to go before I got to Oz. The road was winding, interrupted by stop signs, detours, and a lot of lessons in persistence and perseverance.

In 2013, we were doing over two hundred live shows for QVC a year. There are only 365 days in a year and we were doing over two hundred live shows. We had relocated from California to Jersey City, New Jersey, so we could begin building a team while still being close enough to QVC in Pennsylvania. And when we weren't at QVC, we were either back at our office or traveling to retailer meetings nationwide. I started doing in-store appearances at ULTA Beauty stores across the country. Hundreds of customers would travel to the events to meet me and our IT Cosmetics team. We were also getting ready to launch internationally in Southeast Asia and Australia.

We had built an incredible team led by our very first employee, Jacquie, that supported all the QVC shows, from prepping the props, to setting up the shows and casting the models, to producing the show documents and planning the shows, to being there live with me and Paulo for every show.

Building a great team of employees, and then learning how to let go and delegate, was what kept us alive. We were finally able to hire people who were experts in areas where we had just been winging it, such as human resources, digital, global education, and sales. And at the year-four mark I got an assistant named Zega, who quickly dove all-in.

But our business was growing so fast, it was hard to deal with the mounting demands. I didn't want to create a culture of burnout, so I was hiring as quickly as I could. Meanwhile, all of us kept taking on more and more hats and were maxing out.

Paulo still led operations, finance, IT, digital, and legal and oversaw all of the warehousing functions, shipping and customs, and forecasting (so thankful I married the supersmart guy in class, lol). I was still leading more than half of the company's departments as well, in addition to ideation of all products, overseeing development of our education and sales strategy and initiatives, writing product and marketing copy, campaign approvals, product formulation and testing approvals, presenting at retailer meetings and conferences, speaking at customer events, interviewing and hiring employees, doing all company press and media interviews, and presenting on QVC, all while still managing the day-to-day of the business and making sure we hit sales projections.

But if you've ever started a business, you'll know all too well what I'm about to say. While being able to hire people is a gift and a huge milestone as an entrepreneur, managing the people you hire is an entirely different full-time job! We were burned out but kept running as fast as we could. Many days I felt like a hamster on a wheel. But a hamster on a wheel that was now powering an entire company, so she had to run faster, with the huge weight of that company on her shoulders. A hamster convinced that she was running for her life, and like she never knew when the wheel of success would collapse. I had heard *no* so many times, and I'd had no money for so long, that when we finally had *yeses* and the company's bank account was growing, I was never able to fully believe it was happening. Every single day, I felt like it could all come crashing down at any moment. Sometimes it's called imposter syndrome, when you can't believe the success that is happening to you is real or deserved. I didn't come from this type of financial success and hadn't seen anything like what I was experiencing. How could a girl like me have this happening? I knew I was working my butt off. But it felt like at any second it might all disappear.

As the years passed, the burnout got worse. I gained a lot of weight, and Paulo did as well. I started getting hives caused by stress, raised welts that appeared on various parts of my face and body and itched like crazy.

This had begun to happen regularly. One time in an important board meeting, both of my elbows looked like I had giant red baseballs on them. Many times on air at QVC, I would have to change to a different dress to cover them depending on where they appeared that day. I always carried three things with me wherever I went: coffee, cortisone cream, and Benadryl. And, despite the hundred-hour workweeks and nonstop stress, Paulo and I were also trying to start a family. Not sure what we were thinking, but it was our dream to both adopt and have a baby the traditional way. Paulo and I hid this personal part of our life from just about everyone. We suffered a few miscarriages. I started the process of fertility treatments, egg retrieval surgical procedures, and trying to figure out why I wasn't having successful pregnancies.

When your body isn't doing what you feel like it's supposed to, it's really hard not to feel like a failure. It was a period filled with heartache and the feeling of constant disappointment. Woven into the stress was the worry of how we could have a baby and continue to work from the moment we woke up until we fell asleep. Paulo and I didn't have date nights, and when we tried, it felt like another meeting to schedule. We ordered in every meal and I drank coffee all day. Every once in a while I'd have on reality TV in the background, one of my favorite guilty pleasures . . . can I get an amen for *The Real Housewives* and *The Bachelor*?! We didn't move from our laptops. At the end of a twenty-hour workday I would feel exhausted, like I'd run a marathon, and then I'd look at my Fitbit and see that I'd only gone two hundred steps.

I had to be poised and articulate whenever I appeared on QVC, but one time the exhaustion really got to me. I was trying to say that our products had no shimmer or glitter. This was an important point, because customers who didn't like the shimmer and glitter in other products could rely on ours to be free of that. But, live, the first time I said "shimmer and glitter," it came out "glimmer and shitter." Oops. I saw the host cover her mouth off camera. Not a good blooper on a channel where cursing is completely unacceptable. But once I'd made the mistake, it was hard to fix. That night, every time I said "shimmer and glitter" it came out "glimmer and shitter." The models off camera were dying laughing. I was trying so hard not to say it, but it kept happening. Seriously, try it right now. Say "shimmer and glitter" five times fast. It's really, really hard not to say "shitter."

Zega was with me for almost every single QVC show. When they were scheduled in the middle of the night, she would often drive me home, or straight to the office, afterward. During the two-hour ride to Jersey City, I tried to sleep in the passenger seat so that I could catch some rest before we arrived at the office, where there was a shower and I kept changes of clothes, a toothbrush, and toiletries. Often, I didn't have a window long enough to shower and arrived just in time for morning meetings. I couldn't have done the round-the-clock schedule without her.

These overnight drives from QVC shows straight to the office for morning meetings became so routine that one year, as a Christmas present, Paulo surprised me by turning the passenger seat of my car into an electric recline flat seat. I remember Paulo's face when he proudly said, "It's like the ones in that TV show *Pimp My Ride*. Now maybe you can sleep a little cozier during your commute." I've always wanted Paulo to get a tattoo, but he never has because he's so conservative, so I think getting me a Christmas gift that resembled *Pimp My Ride* made him feel cool and edgy.

We missed weddings, holidays, and birthdays. I once took part of my family to Turks and Caicos on a vacation, but I stayed in the hotel room on my laptop the whole time. There was no stopping.

It was unclear how this would work with a baby. Would the baby grow up the same way I did, with parents always at work?

During IT Cosmetics' stretch of hyper-growth, running the company felt like the only thing I was doing really well. Paulo and I were working so much that we didn't feel human. We felt more like robots. Our business was thriving, but our health wasn't, our marriage was almost nonexistent, we barely saw our friends and family, and literally every other part of our life suffered.

At one point, Paulo and I realized that for years, we had spent almost every single wedding anniversary, birthday, and national holiday in the QVC greenroom. The only exception was Christmas Day, the one day they didn't have live shows, but we often still were at QVC for Christmas because we had or hoped to get booked for shows on the days surrounding it. We were so driven that when we knew a huge snowstorm was coming, we would drive over to QVC and stay in a hotel room even if we didn't have any shows booked. We would let them know we were there and ready to go on air, just in case any other vendors' flights were canceled due to weather and they had extra time slots to fill. We got to the point where we could afford to take a calculated business risk and do the buyer's job for them, in hopes it would pay off. By now, we had a good idea of the kinds of products and kits that were selling well. Since products often take four to six months to make, we started strategically ordering excess and taking the gamble that we might get more airings than they had promised us. And if another brand wasn't hitting sales targets, or a show fell through at the last minute, when QVC asked if we had additional inventory to fill in unexpectedly, we did, and we were ready. The hustle was real, and we hustled to drive the hustle harder.

In our early years, just as our brand was really starting to resonate with customers, I received an email that a woman at L'Oréal wanted to meet with us. Her name was Carol Hamilton, and she oversaw all of L'Oréal's luxury brands for the United States. I knew right away that this meeting was happening because of a seed I had planted (well, more like a seed the fearless squirrel had planted) many years earlier. A seed I never knew had sprouted. I'd once heard Carol give a talk at an industry event where she shared her top ten favorite products of all time with the crowd. There weren't any IT Cosmetics products on her list, so the fearless squirrel in me decided to send her a handwritten note to be delivered to her offices, explaining that if she tried our products, they would surely make her list. Along with the note, I sent a gift basket of IT cosmetics. Much to my surprise, it turned out that not only had she received the note, I would later learn that she had kept it. As if she had a gut feeling about it. When she sent the email asking to meet with us, I told Paulo, "I think L'Oréal is going to want to buy our company!" We invited her to our office and the meeting went extremely well. She asked a lot of questions and told us that she believed in what we were doing, how we were talking to a group of women who were typically ignored by most others in the beauty industry. (*Um, I think almost all women are being ignored by most in the beauty industry,* I thought to myself.) She said what we were doing was brilliant and that she believed it was so needed. And also thought that we would be huge. I thought to myself, *Yes, she gets it!*

I assumed this meant she wanted to buy

our company. But I was about to learn it wasn't that simple. That year, Carol shared with the heads of L'Oréal in Paris that she thought our brand was doing something really special and they should take notice. But we were way too small for them to assess whether we had potential to be a large global brand, or if our brand would only resonate in the United States. So for the time being, they weren't interested in buying our brand. Learning that felt like rejection, but by this point, I was a pro at being rejected. And it was just amazing to me that Carol Hamilton recognized what we were doing — because at the time, even though we were doing really well, we were still a relatively unknown company.

And, of course, the other part of this equation was whether we would consider selling if the opportunity emerged. We were running on empty, so it was hard to take the time to think it through. Would we keep our company and pass it down for generations? Would we go public? One thing we knew for sure — we were addicted to work. We couldn't keep running the company as we were and have any kind of a life.

As the years passed, the burnout got worse and worse. I still wasn't pregnant, and we were still working 24/7. We looked for ways to shift the workload. We brought on an additional minority investor, Guthy-Renker, a direct-to-consumer marketing company known to be the very best in the infomercial space. I'd always dreamed of partnering with them because not only are they the best at what they do, but an infomercial would allow us to get our message out to women everywhere without me physically being awake and live on TV to do it.

We filmed an infomercial that quickly started to air at all hours. Many viewers who saw it were interested in the products but wanted to try them out before they felt comfortable ordering. That drove even more people to physical stores to test-drive the products. Our retail partnerships were thriving. And our global expansion was well underway. We learned superfast how hard it is to expand to other countries, though. Each has its own product regulatory compliance and human resource laws. There weren't enough hours in the day, and we didn't have the expertise internally to figure it out on our own, all while managing everything else.

We expanded our team further, thinking that might relieve the pressure, but the business continued to get more complex, so our jobs didn't get easier. And Paulo and I never learned how to set boundaries. We were both just all-in. When my phone rang and I saw it was him, I realized I was thinking of it as a work call, not a personal call. Late at night when one of us would say, "Okay, no more work talk," the other — or even the person who'd said it first — would still bring up something about work. We realized that something needed to change, because this just wasn't sustainable if we wanted to stay alive. Literally.

It had been a few years since our initial meeting with Carol and L'Oréal. I had kept them up-to-date on every successful milestone we hit along the way, just as I had once sent news of our successes to retailers during the years they kept saying *no.* And just like "Marie" had once sent updates to beauty editors, before we were getting press. And Carol continued to share all of our brand's growth with the big bosses in Paris. Then, one afternoon in the spring of 2015, we got the phone call that I had been waiting for. Carol called to say that L'Oréal was interested in having a larger, more formal meeting.

We weren't 100 percent sure we wanted to partner with them, or even to sell a piece of or all of our company, but we needed to do something. Paulo and I couldn't go on like this! We spent weeks preparing for that meeting. The materials we prepared were worlds away from the presentation books I'd brought to Sephora years earlier. By this point we had brought on a private equity investor, TSG Consumer Partners. And unlike the other potential investor who said no because of my weight, TSG couldn't care less about that and was supportive of the authentic me, and our authentic mission as a company. Our investors and lawyers, along with Paulo and our head of finance, helped us to assemble full financials, presentation books, and videos on the brand. We had dozens of people in our creative department dedicated to graphic design, so we now had beautiful product graphics and branding assets. It's true that these presentation books still had those same acetate covers, but otherwise, looking back at the ones I put together in the beginning would be like looking back at art you did in kindergarten.

It all felt surreal. Somehow this girl who started with an idea in her living room was about to present her company as a potential acquisition to the largest and most glamorous beauty company in the world, L'Oréal. You know, the kind of thing that when you see it in a movie, you think it only happens in movies. But this time, it was happening in real life!

Their offices were a fairy-tale world of men in custom suits and women in couture, many of whom had flown to this meeting from the Paris headquarters. I didn't sweat my outfit. By this time, I knew that I might not fit in, but that was why I was there. Freedom! I didn't do exactly what they were doing — I complemented it. So I didn't feel pressure to conform. I had learned this lesson: Not fitting in can be a superpower. It probably would have been a huge turnoff to them in the earlier years, but my confidence in my vision had grown into confidence in what I stood for. I was there to talk to women differently.

You have to be odd to be number one.
— DR. SEUSS

The meeting went very well, and they asked really smart but really tough questions. L'Oréal had over 86,000 employees and owned dozens of other brands, all of them beautiful, none of them similar to us and what we were doing. They were perfectly capable of launching a new brand without buying an existing one, so we had to show the power of our brand and customer connection. Ultimately, they understood that you can't fake authenticity. That day I told them, "I believe we will be the number one brand in the country one day." I knew Carol saw the conviction in my eyes that told her I truly believed it. And I could see by the spark in hers that she did too.

L'Oréal had teams of experts on the ground in over one hundred countries, was already set up to distribute our products and our message of empowering women to women all around the world, so if we partnered with them, instead of us struggling to launch one country at a time out of our own office, they could impact so many more women with our message so much more quickly. I daydreamed about partnering with them and using their leverage to help get us even more shelf space in stores so we could expand our shade and product assortment further, then partnering with their army of chemists to help us expand the product with an even higher level of expertise.

After the meeting ended, a few weeks passed as I waited for my phone to ring, and then it did, and it was Carol. I got butterflies instantly. She said that everyone had enjoyed meeting us and was impressed with what we were doing, "but it's going to be a *NO.*"

WHAT? Nooooooooo! She went on to tell me that we hadn't yet proven that we would be successful on a global scale. L'Oréal would need to see more of that before partnering with us. I was sure Carol believed that they were making a mistake. She was too professional to say so, but I could feel it. As we talked on the phone, I paced back and forth in my office. I was disappointed, but not crying as I had when Allen Burke gave me the *no* on behalf of QVC. I was full of conviction when I said, "Carol, one day it will be a *yes.* I believe that. And one day I will share this story to inspire other people."

She professionally and unemotionally simply responded, "Best of luck to you, Jamie. Congrats on all you're doing."

I thanked her and told her again, "One day it will be a *yes.*"

She gave me a courtesy chuckle and we hung up the phone.

There I sat, deep in the pit of burnout, with another *no.* Okay, I'll admit it. I cried for a day. But this time it was more exhaustion than rejection. Then I got back up, and with God, grace, and grit, I kept hustling.

> The genius thing that we did was, we
> didn't give up.
>
> — JAY-Z

Without truly knowing why I was doing it, I now owned twenty of the same black shirt and twenty pairs of the same black pants, and that's what I wore each day. It was an instinctive survival tactic to conserve energy. To make even one less decision a day felt important. (To this day, I still do this when I know I need to focus all my energy on one thing, like writing this book. Yep, I am sitting here writing in those same black pants and shirt.) I wore my hair in a bun every single day, and for every single QVC show. Every time the image consultants at QVC suggested that I wear my hair down, I explained that I was better able to show the products on my face when it was back, which was true. But the dominant reason was that I was barely surviving the burnout and needed to save every ounce of energy I could.

I took all the energy I conserved in some areas and poured it straight into driving the growth of the business even harder. QVC was shocked that while sometimes other brands would get tired or their on-air presenter would complain they needed sleep (and they definitely did; we all did), Paulo and I took a different approach. We pushed our bodies harder than we should have and showed up and asked for more, whether it required an all-nighter or a few. The QVC buyers started calling me the "Energizer Bunny" every time I went on air. But the thing is, in those commercials the bunny never runs out of batteries. In my real life I felt like I had burned through my batteries, worn out the backup generator, and was on my own version of life support powered by resilience and persistence. Some days, I would be joined by three different sets of our employees rotating through their full eight-hour shifts before I would leave the building.

I drove myself so hard, I started noticing I was progressively starting to forget things. Some days I couldn't remember simple things that had happened, like what Paulo and I had for dinner the night before or even for breakfast that morning. Even to this day, there are a lot of moments during this season in my life that others remember vividly, and I simply can't recall. When I realized this was happening, it scared the heck out of me. But I kept driving myself harder and harder anyway. Yet while that was the story off air, on air you'd never have known it. Even though I was beyond exhausted, we were crushing it, and often doubling our sales goals for our QVC shows. And in some of the group beauty shows that had multiple brands sharing the same hour, the screens in the greenroom showed us everyone's sales performance, and there were many shows where we hit sales totals that were double everyone else's.

Now that we had shown L'Oréal financial projections in the meetings, we had this entirely new level of pressure — we had to hit them if we ever wanted to partner with them in the future! So now the pressure to hit sales goals on every QVC show felt even greater than before. As we grew and grew, I also became superstitious, like a baseball player on a winning streak. I don't even believe in superstition or luck, but I figured just in case, I would cover my bases. I didn't go as all-out as a baseball player who doesn't shave his beard or change his underwear while he's winning. But kind of. I wore the exact same pair of shoes for every single QVC show. And the exact same earrings. By now it had been hundreds and hundreds of shows. The original pair of shoes, these gold strappy heels with a small strip of embellished stones down the front strap, were being held together by a safety pin, so I was forced to get a second, only-lucky-ones-I-would-wear pair. I scoured the internet to find the same exact pair but couldn't. So I found these rose-gold sparkly heels that almost seamlessly blended into the color of my legs and wore them for Every. Single. Show. Thereafter. Yep, still have them to this day!

When you pull up to QVC headquarters, along the entrance road there is this giant neon letter *Q* sign that fades in and out of rainbow colors. It takes about one to two minutes for it to slowly transform from red, to blue, to green, to purple. Well, I adopted another superstition and decided that I would wait until the *Q* turned green, for luck/growth/money, before I would drive through the entrance. Some days I would have to sit there the full two minutes waiting for it to reach green while cars behind me started to honk. I didn't care and would turn my flashers on so they would know to go around me. I wouldn't go unless I saw that green. In hindsight, I just didn't know how to process the success and the pressure that came with it, and the superstitions were a coping mechanism. At the time, wearing the same shoes and earrings, and waiting for the *Q* to turn green, among other things, just made sense.

■ ■ ■ ■

We continued to grow and grow, and the beauty industry was starting to take notice. And then, in February 2016, after year upon year of courtship and firing on all cylinders, the phone rang. It was Carol Hamilton. L'Oréal was interested in meeting again.

Dreaming, after all, is a form of planning.
— GLORIA STEINEM

This time, we went through an even more formal evaluation with L'Oréal. Our bankers and lawyers started talking directly with theirs. We weren't going to mess around. And we also didn't want to spend all our time and energy to end up at a *no* again if we could help it. There was a far more detailed examination of every aspect of our business. I had told Carol that one day it would be a *YES,* and now it just felt like it was finally happening.

We kept these meetings secret because we didn't want rumors to spread in the industry. We also didn't want employees to get excited, only to be disappointed shortly afterward if the partnership didn't happen. Plus, we knew that no matter what, we had to keep hitting our sales projections. We couldn't risk our team getting distracted. The downside to this secrecy was that it meant we couldn't involve our team to help with all of the meeting preparation and workload. Most of this fell to Paulo and one other employee who knew, the woman who helped head our finance department, since the financials and operations were a big part of L'Oréal's due diligence.

We were right in the middle of filming a second infomercial at the time. We spent weeks on set all day long, and then we were up all night long working on the meetings and negotiations. I wanted this to happen ASAP, but L'Oréal wasn't in a rush, because for them there was no need to be. I think they knew that at that point they were the only ones interested in buying our company. There was no competitive tension. Until there was . . .

Precision beats power, and
timing beats speed.
— UFC FIGHTER CONOR MCGREGOR

Our phone rang again. Our private equity partner had received an offer out of the blue from another company to buy us. In a moment that felt like the stars were all aligning, we now had what's called in business deals *competitive tension.* L'Oréal now had competition in the process. Game on!

Then, at the very same time, another company that was known to be up for sale in the beauty industry sold, and the day it did, some of the companies that missed out on buying it became interested in buying us. YESSS!!! It's human nature — when other people want something, it makes us want it more. And that's what happened.

L'Oréal finally made an offer to acquire IT Cosmetics. My jaw hit the floor. It was for SO much more money than what we would have said *yes* to a few years earlier. But here's the thing: the offer they made was lower than the other offers that were now coming in. Even though I knew in my heart that L'Oréal would be the best partner for us, and I was anxious for them to get our message of empowerment into the lives of billions of people globally, I also knew that this was our one shot to do a deal. And I knew that we had built something more valuable than their first offer reflected. So we said *NO* to L'Oréal! I can only imagine what they must have thought when, after years of us jumping every time they said how high, we were now the ones saying *no*! I knew how to hear the word *no,* but I was brand-new at saying it.

I believed in us, and I believed in my power. I was scared, but we held firm to our *no* to L'Oréal. By then, they knew from their own investment bankers how many companies were interested in us. Then L'Oréal came back with a way better offer. And we said *yes*.

> Even miracles take a little time.
> — FAIRY GODMOTHER, *CINDERELLA*

From that point forward, it all moved very quickly. There were moments when doubt crept back in and I still didn't believe it was actually going to happen. But it kept moving forward. We got into the details of things like employment contracts. I did everything in my power to make sure L'Oréal knew how valuable each person on our team was, how brilliant and talented they were. A big part of our success was the people who were scrappy and egoless right alongside me. I spent hours explaining in detail what many of our key talent did and asking L'Oréal to promise me that they would protect and value them.

Initially, L'Oréal wanted to change my title from CEO. At that time at L'Oréal, the heads of zones/countries held CEO titles.

The guy who was head of another one of their recently acquired US prestige makeup brands also held a CEO title, and of course the head of L'Oréal was the CEO. But there was debate over whether I should keep my CEO title. I had earned every ounce of that title for the company I'd built from scratch. I wasn't open to dropping it. I couldn't fathom that.

I'll never forget when Carol Hamilton got wind of the debate over my title. She immediately began the fight for me to keep it, because it meant more to her than I could understand at the time. Carol was a true advocate. She wanted all women to rise and used her power to lift them up, to lift *me* up. I will never forget this, and I will always be grateful for and inspired by it. I would later learn I became the first woman in L'Oréal's hundred-plus-year history to hold a CEO title. But here's the thing: I believed in my heart that, given her instincts and business acumen, Carol should have been the first. Yet she wasn't. And she used all of her might to lift up another woman, me, to that spot.

One of my greatest passions has always been championing other women. And that day, Carol sparked a new level of passion for this in me. Whenever possible I believe in bringing another woman as your plus-one. And if you don't get a plus-one, ask for one. Bring another woman to the table. Pull up an extra seat for her. Bring her to the room where it happens, whether it's a boardroom, a PTA meeting, or a special event. So many women don't get to have these experiences, and sometimes they have to see what's possible in order to dream bigger, and to believe it is possible for themselves. Proximity can be power. We each have this power in some way and we can freely give it.

Okay, back to the L'Oréal negotiation. I agreed to stay on and run the brand for three years after they acquired it. Paulo did as well. We agreed to a very short window to close the deal, and because L'Oréal is a public company, everything had to be kept extremely confidential while it was all happening. This meant that during this short window filled with a million action items and balls in the air, our team still couldn't know. Paulo worked around the clock to make it happen, and we barely slept for a few weeks (thank goodness QVC had prepared us for this type of exhaustion, lol). The deal wasn't done yet, and we still had to pass what's called *diligence checks.* These are where teams of lawyers and bankers and experts scrutinize every record, every number, every formula ownership agreement, every contract, all of your intellectual property ownership, and get to know literally everything about your company. It felt almost like we were standing naked in front of them, and they were looking for any flaw in our business they could find.

The night before the deal was set to happen, we had a problem. I couldn't find the document that proved we owned the formula for one of our key products. I filmed an infomercial all day, and then stayed up all night on legal calls and calls with the manufacturer, trying to track down proof of ownership. Our lawyers were freaking out that if we didn't have something in writing, it could halt the deal. (Note to all entrepreneurs: get all of your IP and formula ownership in writing and in a safe, organized place early on, when you are small. And before manufacturers might want to keep it from you. If you ever think you might want to sell your company one day, learn everything you'll need to have to do it, and then do that stuff from the beginning!) The manufacturer was being difficult and wasn't sending us written confirmation, even though they knew that we did in fact own the formula. Our investors and lawyers were starting to worry that the issue could kill the deal, because this particular product was such a significant amount of our business. Before I hung up the phone that night, I told my lawyers and our investors that I was going to pray the rest of the night and it was going to be okay. They were skeptical. I tried so hard to believe myself. And I prayed so hard that night. And I cried so hard. It had just been so many years, and so much pressure, and it all was boiling up.

In the morning, the confirmation in writing that we owned the formula came through. On the phone my investors and lawyers said, "I want to pray to whoever you were praying to." They were shocked that the email had arrived.

We were about to officially sell our business to L'Oréal. And no one knew. And I felt like I was living inside a dream.

> When you want something, all the universe conspires in helping you to achieve it.
> — PAULO COELHO

The deal was signed, and the day arrived, July 22, 2016, when we could finally tell our team. I had just learned the night before that L'Oréal was going to announce the all-cash purchase price of $1.2 billion in the public press release. It would be the largest US acquisition in their history. To this day, I still can't even process that. All I knew was that it was finally happening. We sent out a notice of a company-wide all-employee meeting to happen that day and timed it with L'Oréal to happen at the exact moment the press release went out. Just a few short minutes before the release was made public, we had scheduled phone calls with all of our retail partners, to hear firsthand from me, Paulo, and Carol that L'Oréal would be acquiring IT Cosmetics.

While virtually no one inside the company knew what was happening yet, one moment almost gave it away. Carol was flying to New York from Paris, and, because of flight schedules, when she landed at JFK Airport that morning, she had to take a helicopter to reach our offices in Jersey City in time for the planned announcement and press release. That morning, I looked out my office window and saw the helicopter land on a helipad about fifty yards away. It didn't seem real. Moments after it landed, Carol Hamilton hopped out in this gorgeous pink-and-white couture dress and designer heels, with white sunglasses on. She lowered her sunglasses to look around, then raised them back up and started walking toward our building. I was so worried employees would see this movie-like scene with a helicopter and Carol out their windows and know that something was going on, or worse, start posting pics on social media of the super-cool scene.

While Carol made her way to our office, we gathered our senior executive team into a room, had everyone place their phones inside a box as an extra precaution, and shared the news with them first. The room was filled with shock and tears and excitement.

Then, along with Carol and the other heads of L'Oréal in the US, we made the calls to retailers, then gathered all our employees company-wide in the largest boardroom we had. The press release went out. It was real. It was happening.

As my heart pounded out of my chest, I stood in front of the incredible people who felt like family, who had built this company and vision with so much love. I said, "We have some exciting news to share with you . . ." and we told our entire company that we would now be part of the larger L'Oréal family, and we would now be on a path to expand our mission globally. Everyone cheered. L'Oréal was known for having great employee benefits, and I remember some of our employees burst into tears, grateful that even better benefits could really help their families. Paulo and I spoke, the heads of L'Oréal spoke, and together we all celebrated.

I didn't yet know how it was all going to work out, or that both the size of our company and our revenue/total sales would close to double in the next two years. (Yep, we doubled the size of the business in the two years after the sale!) I didn't yet know what challenges and highs and lows were to come. But what I did know in that moment was that life as I knew it would never be the same.

As the celebration continued, everyone was buzzing like crazy. It almost seemed to be happening in slow motion. French champagne was popped, and Carol gave me an Hermès bracelet and Paulo an Hermès tie on behalf of L'Oréal. It was my first-ever piece of jewelry from the fancy store Hermès. I had learned by then that it was pronounced "ehr-mez" and not "her-mees" like I had once thought. Since it was my first piece, I didn't know how to open the bracelet clasp to put it on. It was a little embarrassing. Or at least it was embarrassing for Carol, based on the look on her face.

I think she assumed I was much more sophisticated when it comes to fashion. She quickly covered for me, the way a mom covers for her kid naively flashing her underpants in a restaurant. She showed me how to twist the *H,* then helped me put it on my wrist. I battled the feeling of being an imposter, which at that moment came in the form of feeling like someone who doesn't deserve to have this happening to her. Like someone who isn't cool enough or fancy enough. I kept smiling anyway and pushed all of that self-doubt out of my head as best I could, and tried to enjoy this crazy, surreal moment.

I felt like Cinderella. And wondered if all the pumpkins in my life would now turn into stagecoaches, and if all of my shoes would now turn into pretty glass slippers, especially the ones I'd been wearing to QVC for more than six years straight. I wondered if all the people who didn't believe in me, the way Cinderella's evil stepsisters never believed in her, would now be kinder.

At this moment, my family and friends still didn't know what was going on as, legally, we had to keep the deal private until it was official. And now it was. The news quickly hit the homepage of the *Wall Street Journal* that day, then spread like wildfire from there, so they were surely about to find out. My friends and family had barely seen me since we launched the company, and I had a feeling their reaction was going to be, "Does this mean when we go on vacation you'll stop working and come out of your room?" As I tried to be present and celebrate with everyone, so many thoughts kept swirling in my head. *Will my parents be proud? Will Paulo and I be able to curb our workaholic tendencies? I hope the investor who told me women wouldn't buy makeup from someone who looked like me hears the news.* And, a thought I put aside for later: *Maybe my kids will see me after all.*

In the boardroom, everyone's spirits were flying, as if they were playing a role in a real-life fairy tale unfolding before their eyes. Paulo kissed me on the lips, in front of all our employees (which I never let him do), and everyone cheered. And amid all the cheering, while our smiles told everyone "we did it!," Paulo and I looked at each other and shared a deep knowing of all we had been through to get to that very moment. We had been through the trenches together, the sobbing on the floor while down to our last few dollars together. The years and years of hundred-hour weeks together, hearing *no* more times than we could count together. The hundreds and hundreds of QVC shows together, dividing and conquering the unremitting workload — together. I don't know a smarter, harder-working man than Paulo. And we both knew in that moment that we couldn't have done it without each other. It felt like we were walking off the battlefield, with the warriors who had been fighting alongside us, and together, we were victorious. It felt as if we were holding up the victory flag together and we had defied the odds.

As my eyes welled up with tears, I glanced over and locked eyes with Jacquie, who had spent the past several years building this company with us. Jacquie, who was standing there that day cheering the loudest in the room for me and Paulo because, no matter what, she always stood by my side cheering me on. As Jacquie and I made eye contact with each other, we both knew that her life would now take a very different turn. That this was the first day of the rest of her life too, and in a very different and major way. To explain what I mean, with her permission I want to share a bit of her story that she's never shared with anyone before. And a bit about the wild story of our friendship. You might discover parts of your own story in hers. And it might just change your life, the way it did mine.

Before I do, remember the power of believing in your power. That, along with working hard and never giving up, made all the difference in transforming an idea that began in my living room into a billion-dollar company. And in turning a journey filled with underestimation into a dream that was unstoppable.

# EIGHT:
## *BELIEVE* IN SERENDIPITY

Her victory is your victory. Celebrate
with her. Your victory is her victory.
Point to her.
— ABBY WAMBACH

When Jacquie and I locked eyes in that
room with everyone cheering, nobody knew
the depths of what we'd been through
together, and how something that often
tears women apart — dating the same
sketchy guy — was in our case what actually united us and kicked off what would
become a roller coaster of life decisions
together.

This is the story of Jacquie. You know, IT
Cosmetics employee #1 Jacquie. My brides-
maid Jacquie. One of my best friends of over
twenty years Jacquie. The Jacquie who left a
stable job to come to work for me in my living room. The Jacquie I cried tears of joy
with after selling out for the first time on

QVC, the Jacquie I've sobbed tears of pain with when haters have torn me to shreds or said hurtful things about me online. The Jacquie who is my ride-or-die friend. What I've learned is that in a single instant, a person can enter your life in the most unexpected of ways and change it forever.

You know how Oprah says the universe is always talking to you? First it speaks in whispers. And if you don't listen, it will thump you upside your head. And if you still ignore the warning signs, then it will come in the form of a whole wall of bricks crashing down on you. Well, Jacquie and I met right smack-dab in front of a wall of bricks about to come crashing down.

The day I met Jacquie, I was hanging out with my college boyfriend Dirk, in my college apartment, and there was a knock on my door. I opened it, and there was a beautiful girl with gorgeous long, wavy brown hair and these soulful eyes that looked as though they had both light and pain in them at the same time.

"Dirk, what are you doing?" she demanded as tears began to fill her eyes. Dirk was my boyfriend of just a few months. Ours had been a whirlwind romance, and we already hung out almost every day. He had once mentioned to me that he had a roommate who was a bit crazy, but that was all he told me. We were both students at Washington State University, and with our busy class schedules he ended up hanging out at my place a lot, but I hadn't yet been to his, which was eight miles away. So I hadn't yet met the "roommate," but here she was.

My first reaction to seeing a girl crying at my door is to say, "Oh my gosh, are you okay? Come in!" And that's what I did.

"Dirk, what are you doing?" she said again. This next part just sucks.

Dirk said, right in front of her, "Jacquie, I'm with Jamie and you need to understand that." They then got into a back-and-forth argument, and it became clear that she thought he was cheating on her — with me.

"You're lying, why are you lying?" she pleaded.

"I'm not lying," he insisted.

"I can't believe you're doing this to me — are you kidding me?"

"You're crazy."

It was like a scene from a soap opera. I glanced over and saw that my roommate, who was from Japan and was attending a semester of college at WSU to perfect her English, was definitely understanding every-

223

thing that was happening. She was relaying this dramatic love-triangle confrontation to a friend on the phone, giving a play-by-play in Japanese. Her narration went from dramatic emphasis at full volume to bursts of laughter. I couldn't understand the words my roommate was saying, or what parts she was finding funny, but in hindsight, I think she was ahead of me in that moment and already felt like Dirk was the one lying. And perhaps she knew this was the moment he'd been busted. But at the time, it wasn't so funny. Dirk ended up repeating the story he had already told me about his life — that Jacquie was his roommate who wanted a different type of relationship than he did — and asking her to leave. She did. And she left him too. She moved out of their apartment and into her closest friend's apartment.

As fate would have it, her closest friend's apartment happened to be in the same large house as mine. It was one of those older homes that was divided into several units. Now Jacquie the crazy ex-roommate or sane ex-girlfriend, depending on who you believed, was living in the same house as me. In the days and weeks to come, when Dirk came over to my place, she was in an apartment upstairs.

On a phone call to his sister that he intended for me to overhear, Dirk described the scene with the ex-roommate in my apartment as if to prove to me that what he was telling me was true. I didn't have any obvious reason to doubt his story. Except for the fact that I felt, deep down inside, like something was off. That's the universe whispering to us, right? If you've ever dated a sketchy, dishonest person, you know what I'm talking about. Something just didn't feel right to me. But I still wasn't ready to listen to that feeling.

As time passed, Jacquie ended up putting a letter under my door that told me their whole history and her story. She and I ended up running into each other at the gym, and while working out, we started talking. I knew in my heart she was telling me the truth, and I finally got Dirk to admit it. They had been dating for a few years and were living together. That was all I needed to hear. I broke up with Dirk the Jerk. And Jacquie and I ended up becoming good friends. And then great friends. And then . . .

She got back together with him. They dated for a few more years. She even ended up molding her post-graduation plans around him, following him to Seattle so they could move in together. Believe it or not, she and I stayed great friends throughout all of this. And the cool part was, she was never weird toward me even though I had previously dated her boyfriend. And I never judged her for going back to him. (Although, as a friend, I of course didn't think it was a good idea.) But we were both in our early twenties and hadn't yet learned that ALWAYS true lesson in life, in the words of the late Dr. Maya Angelou: "When people show you who they are, believe them the first time."

A few years later, they had bought a home together and were engaged. Dirk had gradually started mistreating Jacquie more and more. He would put her down in front of other people, especially when it came to her body and appearance. Jacquie told me that when she'd go to eat something, he would say things like "Are you sure you want to eat that?" In group settings he would announce, "Jacquie is on a diet," which she wasn't, simply because he thought she should be. Not that this matters, but Jacquie was a size 6. And then, as if he hadn't hurt Jacquie enough already, Dirk the Jerk ended up cheating again. And again. And finally, after staying with him hoping he would change *FOR OVER TEN YEARS,* Jacquie had had enough. She got up, packed her bags, and left him. This time for good.

As I got to know Jacquie more and more over the years and learned where she'd come from, I discovered that she's one of the strongest women I know. She's a warrior. And has the scars to prove it.

Jacquie was raised in Montana by a mother who was physically and emotionally abusive. They moved around from one trailer park to another, and her mom was on welfare through Jacquie's entire childhood. Jacquie never knew who her father was. As a little girl, when Jacquie would shovel snow for the neighbors or earn extra money however she could, hoping to buy food and clothes, her mom would often take the money away from her and spend it drinking at bars. Jacquie learned how to survive and fend for herself far too young. And she had to hide her school achievements from her mom, because her mom would get jealous and not want Jacquie to excel, and often forced her to quit anything she was doing well at. Some of Jacquie's hardest times growing up involved her mom's boyfriends. If one of them broke up with her mom, she would become physically and emotionally abusive and take it out on Jacquie. As the abuse continued, Jacquie hit her breaking point and at age fifteen ran away.

She didn't know where she was going, but it was as if God was guiding her steps.

The police officer who arrested Jacquie for running away became an angel in her life. He and his wife ended up adopting Jacquie. And they are the ones she calls "Mom" and "Dad" to this day.

Jacquie went off to college by pure grace, filled with the grit and determination to create a better life. After college she did well in every job she had. At one point, a few years after she left Dirk the Jerk, she was working as a disc jockey and traveled the world getting booked to deejay parties. There was even a huge building in China with a mural of her on the side of it for a tour she did there. (Hence the full forearm "DJ Jacquie Jack" tattoo that made hundreds of QVC appearances successfully demonstrating our concealer.) She and I always stayed close friends, even while living in different parts of the country and the world.

In 2009, while we were running IT Cosmetics out of our apartment living room in Studio City, California, Jacquie and I met for coffee one day and I shared with her how passionate I was to change the conversation about beauty. To change the way women look in the mirror so that instead of seeing what's wrong, they see what's right (which is everything). I explained to her how sick and tired I was of seeing all those images we're told are "beautiful" that just make us all feel bad. And she could totally relate and was as passionate about it as I was. She told me that if we could pay her at least enough money for her to eat and cover her bills, she would quit her way-more-secure and better-paying job with benefits to come help us make this dream happen. She was six months pregnant at the time. In the beginning, we couldn't even afford to offer her benefits. But she truly believed in the mission and wanted to help do whatever she could to be part of it.

Jacquie was soon to become a mom and was unsure what lay ahead with her boy-friend at the time, who was also her son's father. I knew that nothing would mean more to her than being able to give her child a better life, filled with more opportunities than she was given. Her faith in the potential for IT Cosmetics to give her a bright future filled me with both incredible gratitude and also an incredible sense of pressure and responsibility. I didn't want to let her down. If you're an entrepreneur, you know how hard it is the moment you realize you have employees depending on you to pay their bills and counting on you for their families' security and future. And Jacquie was so much more than an employee to me; she was like family.

She officially joined our company on full payroll with the goal of a long-term career. Every day she came to work in our living room, and, like me and Paulo, she wore every hat. Like us, she tackled tasks she had no idea how to do and did her best to figure them out. When we launched on QVC, she worked every single show with us. And in our early years at QVC, when it was our primary revenue stream and when we didn't know how long the success would last, Jacquie, like us, often spent more nights in that greenroom than she did at home. She was living with her boyfriend and their son and she was the primary breadwinner of the household.

For the first seven years of her son's life, Jacquie worked the same hundred-hour weeks that we did. And, sure, she believed in our mission, but I know in my heart that her bigger WHY was her son. And his future. I saw her cry her eyes out more times than I can count driving to and from QVC, because she was missing him so much. I hid my worry that her sacrifice wouldn't be worth it. I felt guilty that the needs of our business, and my inability to afford to hire additional help, were robbing her of spending that precious time with her son. I knew this was, of course, her choice, but I also knew it hinged on her deep belief in me. When we moved our business across the country from California to New Jersey, Jacquie moved along with her son and boyfriend. She was truly, truly all-in. It used to keep me up at night sometimes, and we were barely sleeping as it was. What if our QVC success came crashing down? We had no idea if our business was going to make it or not. And on many occasions, it looked as if it wasn't going to survive. She was trading her life for an uncertain future. What if I was never able to give her the security she wanted? But Jacquie was ride-or-die. I truly don't know many people who could have or would have worked as hard as she did for so many of those years.

People say never work with friends or family, because it will ruin your relationship. Unfortunately, in my ten-year journey of building my company there have been a few times when I've definitely learned that the hard way. It can be complicated to navigate the boundaries and not take things personally. What might be a healthy dynamic for friends doesn't always translate into a healthy work environment, especially when one person becomes the boss. It's too easy for the lines to get blurred and the relationship to suffer or be ruined altogether. I found this in almost every case, except with Jacquie. We've somehow managed to always keep our work and personal relationships separate. On days when I've totally disappointed her or upset her at work, or vice versa, we've managed to shut that part off when we'd go to grab a coffee or a meal together. I think it's because we've always truly wanted what's best for the other, without an agenda.

I used to pray that one day I could repay Jacquie for all her years of sacrifice and commitment. I used to pray that she wasn't missing so much time away from her son and her boyfriend, all for nothing. And here's the thing: Jacquie never asked for anything from us in return. She didn't have some grandiose expectation that someday there would be some big payoff, and she never asked about that. After brutal days on QVC when we missed a sales goal or lost a product, we would soothe ourselves together by reading customer letters and stories of how our message and products inspired women to feel good about themselves again.

Jacquie truly loved our customers and believed it was an honor to be part of growing this company.

She also truly loved breaking up tense moments with humor. Have you ever seen a stage mom on TV or even in real life? You know, the kind that dance in an over-the-top way right behind the judges while their kid is performing onstage, hoping to remind their child to smile big and mirror their choreography? Many times I'd be live during an intense show on QVC while completely stressed out knowing we were missing goal, and Jacquie would pop up behind the camera in the studio and start tap-dancing with jazz hands and full commitment, while I was right in the middle of the on-air presentation. I would try to stay focused on selling the product, and often could barely hold back from cracking up on live TV the way the comedians do on *Saturday Night Live* when they try to stay in character but find the jokes too funny to keep their composure. Jacquie would make full-out stage-mom facial expressions behind the camera, pointing both of her fingers to the dimples in her cheeks, reminding me to smile and appreciate the moment more. To this day, if she and I can't solve a problem or are stressed out, she'll often break out these old stage-mom dance moves and they still make us crack up every time!

There were also some really, really hard days when we couldn't be that thoughtful, and chose to drown our sorrows in red wine instead. It was a good day when we could afford to graduate from boxed wine to bottles. Sometimes it's the small victories!

Once the company grew, we could finally afford to start paying Jacquie a much better salary. Paulo and I prioritized paying her better before we even began paying ourselves at all. Jacquie was the one who thought of the CC cream concept. CC cream is a moisturizer that is infused with color-correcting and coverage pigments, so instead of wearing a traditional heavy makeup to get coverage on your skin, using CC is like wearing a simple moisturizer and getting treatment plus full coverage. When other brands were working on a product called BB cream, which stands for Beauty Balm, the idea of a CC cream, which stands for Color Correcting, was just sprouting in the best skin care labs in Korea. Jacquie was ahead of other brands in researching this and developing ours to cover and perform even better than what existed. To date, this is still our best-selling product of all time.

And because of her beautiful, brilliant, creative thought process, we were way ahead of the competition when we launched our CC cream.

Breast cancer runs in Jacquie's family. Contributing to this cause is something that we're both passionate about. It was Jacquie's idea early on to partner with Look Good Feel Better™ and begin donating our products to women facing the effects of cancer. We started doing this even before we started paying ourselves. We've donated over $40 million in product to the cause. Today, Jacquie runs two departments at IT Cosmetics and is an on-air presenter at QVC for our products.

Again, with Jacquie's permission, I'm going to share something with you that not even my or her closest family knows, and I am not sure I can get through this next part of the story without crying as I write.

Paulo and I put aside a piece of ownership in the company for Jacquie — she had earned it. And the day we sold to L'Oréal was the day that Jacquie's life changed forever, as did her son's future. It was the day when God showed up in such big ways, showing her why all the closed doors and open doors in her life made sense. Why the wrong people came into her life and led her to the right ones. Why her intuition told her to keep going when the hours seemed too long. Why she felt like it was the right thing to do as a mom when people around her wondered why and at times shamed her for working so hard. God showed up for Jacquie, for that beautiful baby girl, who never knew her father and was born to a mother who didn't know how to show her love. That beautiful little girl forced from trailer park to trailer park, who on many days grew up feeling hungry and forgotten. But God never forgot about her. He made her born to fly; she just had to learn it for herself, and she did. Jacquie has always been the incredibly loving mother to her son that she never had, but now, on top of that, she is able to provide all of the opportunities she never had to her son.

When we announced the sale of IT Cosmetics to L'Oréal, on that day, in so many ways, I was happier for Jacquie than I was for myself. That day, together, we sobbed. We did it. We had a dream, and we worked our butts off, and we showed up for each other, and she believed in me, and I believed in her, and we did it! Our friendship began in the middle of a mess, and together we

*Jacquie and I leaning on each other, like always. I chose this photo because we had no idea it was being taken. Wow, am I grateful she knocked on my door that day. Thanks to Dirk the Jerk for introducing me to my incredible friend and sister of now over twenty years.*

learned such a powerful, serendipitous message. First through a dishonest guy, then through each other. Dr. Maya Angelou's words bear repeating: "When people show you who they are, believe them the first time." When you do that, it helps you weed out the people who are going to keep you from your dreams, and helps you open up space to welcome in new people who are truly destined to join you on the ride of your life!

# NINE:
## *BELIEVE* LIFE ISN'T MEANT TO DO ALONE

You are a mighty person in the making,
a masterpiece in progress, a miracle
in motion.

— TIM STOREY

Every time in life when I've tried with all my might to force something to happen and it doesn't, whether it's a big dream I'm trying to make come true, or when I'm literally trying to force a door open, over and over, and it just won't budge — every time life doesn't go my way, something better and even more miraculous always seems to happen. It's as if God is saying, "I love you way too much to give you what you're asking for. Just trust me."

My birth mom got pregnant unintentionally during a onetime encounter. Meanwhile, Paulo and I spent close to a decade trying to get pregnant. Between fertility procedures, countless needles and hormone injections, and more negative drugstore pregnancy tests than I can count, I had spent so much of the last decade in tears, feeling like I was failing and like my body was letting me down. Both Paulo and I did test after test, working with doctors to try to uncover the problem, and their consensus was that the issue was the shape of my uterus. Its heartlike shape meant I had a higher risk of miscarriage. It was possible that I could carry a healthy baby to full term, but risky. We kept trying, and I kept either failing to get pregnant or miscarrying. All of this was happening in private, in parallel to the explosive growth of IT Cosmetics and the demands of our nonstop work schedule.

After we sold the business, I was about to turn forty and I knew we wanted to really prioritize growing our family, however that ended up happening. When we were dating, I used to tell Paulo that one day I wanted seven kids, and to have at least four of them be adopted. And that was before I found out that I was actually adopted myself. We started seriously looking into both adoption and surrogacy and decided to go full speed ahead with both. At the time, I felt like surrogacy was the scariest option. I'd heard crazy stories on the news and in movies of a surrogate running away with the baby or coming after the parents for custody. The thought that someone else would be literally carrying our child in her body was overwhelming. But I decided to be open to all options and to keep faith in the journey we were on. We began talking to an adoption facilitator, and at the same time we agreed to work with a separate surrogacy agency.

The surrogacy agency was moving at a much quicker pace than the adoption agency. After all the legal paperwork was completed, we were ready to be set up on a "match call." This is a video call led by the agency to introduce intended parents to a potential surrogate.

If you're not familiar with this process, there are so many layers to it that I never could have imagined. What I mean by this is that you have to actually talk through all the hard stuff ahead of time. Including life-and-death decisions that you might not have to think about if you got pregnant the old-fashioned way. The agency presented a number of questions for us to discuss. For example, we had to answer how we felt about excruciatingly painful possibilities pertaining to the pregnancy and baby, and how we would want them handled. If this is a tough subject for you, you might want to skip the rest of this paragraph. There were heart-wrenching questions like: *If your embryo splits into twins or triplets, and doctors determine that you have to do a reduction (terminate one of the embryos to have any chance at all for the others to live), what would you do?* Questions like: *What if the surrogate gets pregnant and the pregnancy becomes a threat to the surrogate's life — would you be okay terminating the pregnancy?* And here's the REALLY HARD thing: you have to hope you align morally with the surrogate, because, for instance, even though it's not her baby, your surrogate might be so strongly against pregnancy termination that she would rather risk losing her own life than terminate a life-threatening pregnancy. These questions are not about what's right or wrong; they're about making sure you are able to articulate what's right for you and where you stand on all of these extremely difficult topics, and then making sure you are paired with a surrogate who shares the same beliefs. So this moral alignment of all of these situations that you hope and pray never happen has to be discussed up front. It's so overwhelming to have to think about what you would actually do in those types of situations, let alone decide and then verbally commit to what you would do in them. I completely understand why it's so important, it's just also so hard.

Once Paulo and I had those difficult conversations with the surrogacy agency, the next big hurdle turned out to be my own fear of the whole process. I was potentially about to partner with someone I couldn't un-partner with. Someone who might carry my baby. That would mean handing over all of the trust of my heart to someone I didn't even know.

My fear grew as we approached our first match call. I was worried that the surrogate might know who I was. At that point, I was still doing more than two hundred live TV shows a year on QVC and we also had an infomercial airing all the time, and millions of loyal customers across the country. On any given day, a few people would come up to me on the street or at the mall and say, "You're Jamie — I watch you on QVC" or "You're that makeup girl on TV" or "I love your products" or, occasionally, "I ordered your product and the shipping was late and it ended up not arriving on time from the store, and then when it finally arrived, the box was dented, and I wasn't happy about this at all, so I posted a bad review online for you, but you need to know about this problem; also let me show you the product I have in my purse because I don't think it was filled up all the way, or at least not filled up as much as it could have been, when I opened it brand-new — look, I have it right here." (Thank goodness the last example doesn't happen too often, but when it does, I just figure it comes with the territory of being an entrepreneur.) So when it came to the match call, not only was I worried that the potential surrogate might recognize me, I was also worried that if she knew our names, she might google us and then want to be matched with us for the wrong reasons. Since L'Oréal had released the terms of our deal, there were now countless articles all over the internet about the $1.2 billion purchase price. Plus, I was scared about those disturbing stories you hear in the news. The surrogacy agency promised us that no names would be shared at this stage and that I could even do the match call in disguise if I wanted to. So I did.

I bought glasses and a light blond wig. No joke. The glasses came from the drugstore and were the lowest strength I could find, since I don't normally wear them. They were only slightly blurry. I put them on along with the wig, and Paulo put on a baseball cap, and we prayed. I was *so* nervous for the approaching call. I had to channel that famous quote from rapper 50 Cent, the one that says, "Either pray or worry, but don't do both." Such good words. So true. If you pray, but still worry, it's like you're not trusting your prayer and not trusting God. So I prayed, remembering those words, and stopped worrying.

Our laptop was open and ready for the video match call. My wig and glasses were on. I was going by my middle name, Marie, and Paulo was "Paul."

"Marie is hot," Paulo said, trying to break the nerves with his humor, one of the things I adore about him.

The screen was ringing. It was time.

"Hello," we said with huge smiles. On the screen was the most kindhearted woman and her husband. Her eyes were bright and warm, and she just seemed so genuinely good. She and her husband already had five kids of their own, and she shared that for her entire life, she felt called to do something like this for another family that was having a tough time getting pregnant. She also said she loved being pregnant. The facilitator took us through all of the difficult questions, and we all seemed to be aligned. I had an overwhelming sense of peace that grew stronger than any of my fears. After the call, we were given the weekend to decide if we felt like it was a match . . . or if we wanted to continue to interview other potential matches. The potential surrogate and her family had the same choice. Paulo and I felt such peace, and we both knew right away. Minutes after the call ended, we called the agency and said we felt that she would be a great match and that we wanted to move forward if she felt the same way.

Minutes after that, she called the agency to say that she too wanted to be matched with us! When we heard that, tears streamed down both my and Paulo's faces. We didn't really know what we were getting ourselves into, and there was still a part of us that was totally scared, but we were going to do it anyway.

We started the official surrogacy journey, and of course we all shared our real names. We went through the embryo transfer process, where we were all together in the doctor's office as they transferred embryos made of my eggs and Paulo's sperm through a tiny tube and into her uterus. Together, Paulo, our surrogate, and I all held hands, prayed, and cried. We met her kids and her husband, because they were all part of this journey too.

We transferred two embryos at the same time. Paulo and I had hoped for twins, and our surrogate had always wanted to carry twins as well. Once the embryos are transferred, you wait about ten days to see if any of them took, and if in fact you have a positive pregnancy test. Our surrogate was so anxious to know that she bought a drugstore test a few days before the official appointment to do the test, and it was positive! She texted me the picture of the positive pregnancy test. And while I didn't want to get my hopes up too quickly, since it wasn't the official appointment, I couldn't help it. I was freaking out, and Paulo and I cried, and I immediately started writing out a list of potential names for twins!

A few weeks into the pregnancy, at one of the ultrasounds, we saw only one gestational sac on the monitor. The nurse checked again and again, looking for the second. The doctor came in and did the same. There was only one baby.

I instantly comforted our surrogate, who was really sad. I knew that one of the embryos not making it likely meant that that embryo wasn't viable and wouldn't have made it no matter what. But I realized she felt this great responsibility for her own body to deliver and that she was both sad for the loss and also disappointed, as if she had failed in some way. I tried to reassure her the best I could. And while I was sad too, I felt this overwhelming gratitude to have such an amazing human being as a partner with us on this journey. I felt like it was a miracle that another person could be so selfless as to feel it was her calling to carry a baby for someone else. To me, just the simple idea of her being willing to and wanting to do this qualifies her as a real-life angel. To this day, when I think about her heart, I cry. Because it makes me believe in the heart of humanity. It reminds me that there are so many good, kind people in this world who truly want to be good and kind to others. On that day, I told her she was a real-life angel on Earth, and that God was in control of all of this. We held hands, and there was this unspoken knowing, that we were all meant to be on this journey together.

As the months went on, our baby was growing and growing, and we learned we were going to have a baby girl. And then one July afternoon, three weeks before her due date, she decided she was going to show up early! We flew to our surrogate's hometown, filled with abundant anticipation. We all checked into the hospital together, and Paulo and I got to be in the room with her the whole time during labor and delivery. Our surrogate felt strongly that right when she delivered, she wanted the baby to be placed onto me so I could do skin-to-skin with her in the first moments she spent in this world.

Labor continued, and our surrogate told me and the doctors that with one of her children, she knew she was about to deliver but because she wasn't fully dilated the doctors didn't believe her, and the baby came out fast. She warned us and the doctors of this and said to make sure to trust her when she said the baby was coming.

As the hours passed, the nurses frequently came into the room to check how dilated her cervix was. They would say things like, "You're at a six still, you have a ways to go," but our surrogate started to feel like she was getting close. She pushed the button for the nurses to come and said, "I'm close now, check again," and they did. They reassured her that she wasn't fully dilated yet and left the room. Then I heard words come out of our surrogate's mouth that I had never heard her say before. All of a sudden she yelled, "Get the f(*&^%$ doctor! The baby is coming!" and her husband went running out into the hall to yell for a doctor. She was right; they should have listened to her.

My heart was racing. There were still no doctors or nurses in our room, and I glanced down and saw that my daughter's head was all the way out. I rushed over, not having any idea what the heck I was doing, but I was ready to catch her. I reached to cradle her head just as a group of nurses (still no doctor) swarmed in front of me and pulled the baby all the way out. Our baby girl was born. She had broken her collarbone on the way out, but she was healthy and beautiful. The doctor rushed in shortly after, Paulo cut the umbilical cord, and I sobbed uncontrollably. It was the most beautiful thing I'd ever experienced in my life. Our beautiful baby girl. Born in a community of love from the womb of a human being volunteering her own body to give life to another family. We named our daughter Wonder. With the way our journey had led us to the miracle of finally welcoming a baby into this world, the name Wonder felt so fitting. She let out her first cries and they placed her onto my chest, inside my robe, skin to skin. I couldn't believe God had blessed us with such a miracle. We were parents. I was a mommy.

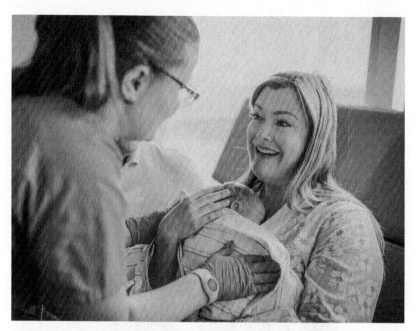

*Wonder being placed in my arms for the first time, then inside my robe for skin-to-skin.*

When I saw you I fell in love, and you
smiled because you knew.
— ARRIGO BOITO

I've always been the kind of person who does things on my own. Who trusts myself more than I trust anyone else. Who worries that other people will end up letting me down, so it's better to just do it myself. Doing things independently felt like a way of showing my strength. I aspired to be strong enough to not need anyone else for anything. Like that was a badge of honor. And that often meant not only doing things alone

*Paulo and I, overwhelmed with gratitude and awe for our real-life miracle.*

but being lonely. I'd never fully understood or embraced the power of community. Until that day. Another woman, and her family, went on a journey with me and mine, and gave us a gift that we couldn't give ourselves. She did something for us that despite all of my might, I couldn't do on my own. I needed her. And because she truly felt that her calling was to do this for someone else, she needed me too. Our surrogate, and my daughter, changed my heart, and my life that day.

Failing over and over to get pregnant felt like a closed door and like rejection from my own body. Wow, I am so thankful for my closed doors! Sometimes it takes years before I'm able to see that what ended up happening and the lessons I learned from it are so much more meaningful than what I was trying to accomplish. The hard part is having faith that a better outcome awaits us. Of course, we can't know this for sure. And in the moment, these closed doors and rejections and things that feel like failures are difficult to bear.

On that day, I learned another powerful lesson: life isn't meant to do alone.

My daughter, Wonder, is a healthy and happy and blessed little girl, who is silly and strong and loves dancing with her Elmo doll. Paulo does all the *Sesame Street* dances, and even though he can't keep a beat, he fully commits and makes me and Wonder laugh, although we're laughing for different reasons. Our surrogate and her family have become our dear friends. None of the things I was worried about ever happened. And instead, my life was infused with a love and joy I couldn't have imagined.

I'd always been the lone wolf, who carved my own path, who was determined to succeed in my life and career despite what anyone else told me, despite those who doubted me, despite those who failed me, despite where I came from. I'd always felt like men held women back and we could do everything on our own, but realized I had gotten one big thing wrong. We can't do it all alone. Or at least, we can't truly live our best lives all alone. I never could have had the kind of success I had with IT Cosmetics without Paulo, and Jacquie, and our amazing team. And I never could have had my daughter without another incredible woman and her family.

I learned that when we want to do things all on our own, it can come from a deep-seated fear that we're not worthy of other people showing up for us. But that's simply not true. You are worth showing up for, and so am I. And we can't ever live our best lives, or reach the fullest, highest expression of ourselves, all alone. And to have true human connection, we need to take the risk of being our authentic, vulnerable selves. We need to take the risk of asking for help. We need to take the risk of sharing our stories with those who have earned our trust. We need to risk counting on other people, even if some of them might let us down, because to live our best life, we need to share it. We need to risk having the wrong people reject or hurt us, in order to find the right people who love us. We need to risk truly loving other people in the hope that they will love us back. We need to risk speaking our truth, and brave being hurt, in order to be fully alive. We need human connection to feel true love. We need community. We need each other.

And, when it comes to needing each other, I was about to ask my own birth mom to show up for me in a way she hadn't yet. When I held my daughter for the first time, it was truly one of the most miraculous moments in my entire life, and it led to the realization that it still hurt my heart that my own mom had never held me the day I was born. While I understood why she didn't, I still didn't feel peaceful about it. I still felt pain over knowing this. It almost felt like since she'd never held me, her own baby, I wasn't validated, or acknowledged, or real. And at the age of forty-two, I decided to do something that felt both risky and overwhelmingly scary. I decided to share how I felt with Rosemary and then ask her for what I needed. Here's the thing: In my heart I just felt like I needed her to hold me, the way a mother holds her newborn baby. In my head this seemed irrational, and maybe even a bit crazy. But in my heart, it felt like it was the missing ingredient in me breaking through a barrier of disconnection with her.

I invited Rosemary to come down to Southern California to spend the weekend together. This might be one of the most difficult things I've ever done in my life.

We sat down on the couch. As she sipped her water, I wrapped myself in my favorite cozy blanket and sipped on some cinnamon dolce–flavored coffee. The warmth of both helped soothe the butterflies in my stomach. "So there's something really, really important to me that I need to share with you," I said.

"Okay," she replied. I spoke my truth, and I showed up in full vulnerability. I shared how in awe I was when my daughter, Wonder, was being born, as I was experiencing and witnessing the miracle of life while at the same time realizing the overwhelming blessing of God trusting me to be the mother of my beautiful baby girl. I shared with her how holding Wonder on the day she was born was one of the most powerful moments in my life. And I shared with Rosemary that I felt this void over my being born and never being held by her.

And then I took a deep breath, and with my heart pounding, I asked her, "Will you hold me? Your baby. Like a baby?" Her eyes started to well up with tears, so I quickly made a joke and said, "Do you think I would crush you?"

She laughed and said, "Of course not," as she started to cry. Rosemary is tiny. She's a few inches shorter than me and very thin. I estimate I'm about fifty pounds heavier than she is. And in that moment, I didn't care. I swept aside all of those distracting thoughts about size or if she was going to think I was heavy. I couldn't let my insecurities cost me this moment in my life that mattered so much more. I made sure, asking again, "Would it be okay if I sat on your lap and you held me like a baby?" Would she do it now, forty-two years later, since she never did it the day I was born? I knew I was risking rejection again.

She looked at me and said with overwhelming emotion, "Okay." I could tell she was praying. She once told me that when she's scared, she imagines Jesus sitting in the chair next to her, and it helps her to be confident in any situation and to know she's not in it alone. I felt like she was imagining Jesus sitting across from her in this moment. She sat closer to me on the couch. And I climbed on top of her, then sat sideways with my full body across her lap. I wrapped my arms around her neck, and she wrapped her arms around me and we both started crying. Then, my sixty-one-year-old birth mom held her forty-two-year-old baby for the first time ever. She got to hold her daughter for the first time, and in the same moment, I got to be held for the first time by my mom. As we both cried, I said to her, "Promise me you won't ever let me go again." She started sobbing. So did I. I continued, "I feel like you gave me up, but then when I finally found you, you disappeared, and it felt like you gave me up again. Promise me you'll never let me go again."

Still crying, she said with the purest conviction, "Jamie, I promise. I'll never let you go again." And I believed her. We hugged. And we cried. And we healed.

Believe in the power of asking for what you need, whether it's from someone else or yourself, in order to heal. For me, I had to shift my perspective on how I saw needing something from someone else. I used to think it was a weakness, but now I know it's a strength — even if it means being vulnerable or risking embarrassment or rejection.

It might mean asking for an apology. Or giving one. It might mean asking for someone to change a behavior. It might mean looking in the mirror and asking yourself to love your body, and then committing to do the hard work of understanding and overcoming why you don't. It might be asking and expressing your need to your partner for more affection. It might mean finally telling someone the truth about how their words hurt you. It most likely will mean having a tough conversation. But I've learned that revealing how you truly feel, even when it's hard, can be key to connection, freedom, and healing.

■ ■ ■ ■

# PART TWO: RISK

■ ■ ■ ■

# Part Two:
## Risk

# TEN:
## *BELIEVE* IN BEING BRAVE OVER BEING LIKED

I am not throwing away my shot.
I am not throwing away my shot.
— *HAMILTON,* THE MUSICAL

My printed-out papers quivered in my hands, and I hoped everyone thought a fan must be blowing somewhere offstage. Standing on the podium, staring at an audience filled with what the world taught me power looks like, I knew I needed to pull my hair back, stare my fear straight in the eye, and know that my faith was bigger than it.

I was being honored with the Cosmetic Executive Women Achiever Award. It's one of the highest honors you can receive in the beauty industry, almost like getting an Academy Award in the beauty world. And it's usually an honor bestowed on someone after they spend their entire career in the industry. I was only eight years in. The awards event itself is a really big deal. It happens once a year and is attended by every major beauty brand's founder, CEO, and senior executive. Basically, on that one day, in that one room, the decision-makers responsible for almost all of the major beauty brands you see globally gather to celebrate. To top it all off, I had also just been asked to join the board of CEW. By the woman who heads it all. She had personally recommended me to her fellow board members, they had voted, and they had agreed, and I was invited to join this very prestigious, very exclusive board. *WHAT???!!!* In the beauty world this is like being asked to join the most exclusive sorority. But the thing is, I've never been part of a sorority. Initially it felt too exclusive to me. I've always believed in the words of poet Cleo Wade: "If the cool kids club doesn't include everyone, it's actually not cool at all." I mean, I had always attended the CEW events and will forever be thankful that it was at their product demonstration event that I was able to sneak away from my booth and meet the QVC buyer in person. Their events had given a budding entrepreneur like me proximity to others in the industry. Plus, I knew they did a lot of great work to support great causes. And even though I always saw their board as very high society–

like, that might have been my own un-
founded bias. Maybe this group was inclusive, and I was worried for no reason. I
wasn't sure yet. But what I was sure about
was that this was definitely a world I hadn't
come from and had never been exposed to
or part of, and it felt like a gift to have a
chance to see inside it. So I stayed open-
minded and I joined. Now all of a sudden
receiving this award added even more pressure, because I was a board member too!

It wasn't just all of the retailers and beauty
stores that had said *no* for years. Up until
this point, I had rarely felt embraced by the
beauty industry itself as a legit player. During all the years I attended all the big
organizations' awards shows where they
would give an award to the newcomer that
showed the most promise, we never won. I
was never the hottest new brand founder
thrust onto the stages of event panels
highlighting the future of the industry.
Many of those brands ended up being
short-lived, but still. It had seemed that
inside this fancy industry, we were almost
always underestimated or just completely
counted out. My best friend Natasha always
helped me get through this, whether by
reminding me to be the squirrel or through
famous words she'd share, like "God says,

'You weren't rejected, I hid your value from them because they were not assigned to your destiny.' " So learning all of a sudden that I was going to receive this incredible honor, in addition to being welcomed onto this elite and prestigious board, was the first time I felt acknowledged, seen, included, and celebrated. It was like going from zero to hero in the blink of an eye (with eight years of hundred-hour weeks pouring my heart and soul into building a company determined to change women's lives, and the beauty industry as a whole, in between).

In the weeks leading up to the awards event, I had learned I would have ten minutes or so to give my acceptance speech. My first instinct was to prepare some remarks filled with gratitude for all the people who had supported me in this journey, which is what I do almost every time I'm blessed to win an award. Something in my gut felt like a traditional thank-you speech wasn't special enough for an event this big. But I wrote one anyway.

Then, as the event loomed, it hit me like a ton of bricks. What was I thinking? How could I just write a regular thank-you speech for this event? Maybe this award I was receiving and the stage I was about to stand on weren't about me. As soon as I had that thought, it took hold and I couldn't let it go. I knew in my gut it wasn't about me. I realized that in that one room on that one day when I spoke, almost all of the key people who control the images of beauty that billions of women see globally would be sitting right there in front of me, listening. Holy s(*&!). Why would I waste that opportunity simply talking about myself, or saying thank-yous that, while sincere, were also wrapped in the desire to make everyone like me? What if the reason I'd been given this opportunity and this moment was so I could take a shot at making an even bigger difference in the beauty industry? An impact beyond what I was doing with my own company. What if I explained to them that my success was proof that if they changed their ways, and changed the unrealistic, highly altered images they blanket the world with, they could have even greater success?

Was I crazy?

Do you remember that commercial Steve Jobs did for Apple? In it, he reads a powerful excerpt from a letter written by Jack Kerouac that ends with him saying, "The people who are crazy enough to think they can change the world, are the ones who do."

If you haven't seen it, google it. The morning of my speech I watched that commercial over and over. And I prayed. And I cried. I got still and tuned in to my intuition, and I just knew.

I knew if I took this moment that was supposed to be celebratory, and instead used it to fight for something I was passionate about, it might not go well. But I had lived enough life to believe in the truth of one of my favorite quotes from "The Man in the Arena" by Theodore Roosevelt (explored so powerfully in Brené Brown's best-selling book *Daring Greatly*):

> It is not the critic who counts; not the man who points out how the strong man stumbles, or where the doer of deeds could have done them better. The credit belongs to the man who is actually in the arena, whose face is marred by dust and sweat and blood . . . who at the best knows in the end the triumph of high achievement, and who at the worst, if he fails, at least fails while daring greatly.

If I used my one shot in that one room, in that one moment, it would take all of my bravery. I could fall flat on my face and maybe even lose some of my friends in the beauty industry. But I also knew, in my soul, that it was my time to walk into the arena and to dare greatly. I would rather be brave and stand up for what I believe than be popular.

The day of the awards ceremony arrived. I felt like a gladiator about to risk it all. Except in my battle instead of armor I wore a sparkly awards-show dress, and my arena was a fancy New York City ballroom. I sat on the stage, heart pounding in my chest, while I received the most beautiful and elegant introduction. I stared into a packed audience of impeccably dressed executives. People in the beauty industry definitely know how to dress. They probably had no idea that my favorite version of couture was my sweatpants, no makeup, and a hair scrunchie. (Pair that look with some junk food and a glass of red wine, or sometimes even a coffee cup of red wine . . . but that's another story.) On this day, I looked the part that was expected of me, and they had every reason to believe I was about to give a people-pleasing speech, as was expected of me. After all, ever since the acquisition by L'Oréal I'd been treated like the beauty industry's golden girl.

Instead, I stepped up to the podium, and

I shared the words on my heart. I didn't know that some of what would happen afterward would be disruptive in the best way, and some of it devastating in the worst.

Excerpt from my acceptance speech from the 2017 Cosmetic Executive Women Achiever Awards:

What will you do, with the power that is YOU?

Thank you so much to CEW for this recognition. IT Cosmetics was actually discovered by QVC at the CEW Awards in 2010 and it was life-changing for me and for the brand and I will forever be grateful. That then led to our amazing partnership with ULTA Beauty, and TSG, and Sephora and then L'Oréal, so I am forever grateful to CEW. I want to say thank you to Paulo and to my entire team at IT Cosmetics, thank you for being brave, for taking huge risks, for daring greatly to do things differently with me! Thank you for changing lives with me every day and for forging ahead with me on this mission to change the conversation about beauty!

In the early years of running IT Cosmetics, I heard *NO* more times than I can count. *No* from every retailer, *no* from just about everyone. I was still running the brand out of my living room a few years in, and I really didn't know how we were going to stay alive. And then a defining moment happened. I met with a potential investor who was a pretty big deal in private equity, and after doing their due diligence they decided to pass on investing in IT Cosmetics. And I'll never forget when I asked why — he said to me, "I'm just not sure women will buy makeup from someone who looks like you. You know, with your body and weight." I remember looking at him straight in the eyes in shock, and then feeling something deep down inside myself that said, "No. He is wrong." And then I set out to prove it . . . not only for myself but also for women everywhere.

When we launched on QVC in September of 2010, we had ten minutes on QVC and I decided to remove my makeup to show my bright red rosacea to show live how our product works, and cast real women as models. If I looked around the beauty industry at the time, no one had ever done this, and every indicator told me this would not work. We went live with ten minutes . . . and when the "sold out" sign went up . . . I cried. I cried not only because my company was going to stay alive but I cried because I realized that when it comes to the images of beauty that we see as women, it was a moment in time that showed me this iconic statement to be true: The power of the people is greater than the people in power!

(Side note . . . this is the moment in the speech when I saw a lot of smiles in the room drop into stoic stares. The room was about 50/50 men and women, but all of their faces seemed to drop equally. Continue speech . . .)

It was proof of an ah-ha moment for me . . . because I always wondered — is it that women will only buy cosmetics from flawless airbrushed ads with supermodels or celebrities . . . or — is it that no beauty company has been willing to risk doing it differently?

So I decided to grow IT Cosmetics and ignore everything being done around me in beauty at the time. We used real women and real before and after shots. Many retailers and beauty experts told us that by doing this we didn't look luxury enough. Today almost all of those same retailers now use real women in images. And I am proud of that. When you turn on QVC or any TV shopping channel today, now seven years later, you see almost all makeup brands showing real women as models, and when I see that I smile . . . I am really proud of that. Today we are blessed to be a top-performing brand in every retailer we're in. And I share that because for the longest time I believe that in the beauty industry we have all bought into the notion that you have to show images of unattainable aspiration to sell products . . . and me standing here right now, and the success of IT Cosmetics, is proof that this isn't true. When we sold IT to L'Oréal recently in the largest acquisition in L'Oréal history, I actually got an email from that investor who passed on investing because of my weight. By the way, had he invested, it would have been the most successful investment in his company's history. His email said, "Congratulations on your deal with L'Oréal. I was wrong." And that he regrets his decision. It felt good for a moment. But what I realized was that he had bought into that same definition of beauty that we've been seeing our whole lives.

And in the beauty industry — I'm proud

of L'Oréal and the brands helping to break the mold including casting transgendered models, it's about time! — but I feel like as an industry we're just starting to scratch the surface of what needs to change. If we as beauty companies want every woman to buy our products, why do we show her photoshopped images that don't look like her? And more than that, what impact do these images of beauty have on the world? And right here, right now — we are the ones who have all of the power to change this.

Look around . . . sitting in this room right now are the people who singlehandedly decide the images billions of women see around the world.

In this room right now are the executives from all of the top beauty brands, and the next generation of decision-makers for those brands. All of the most influential beauty brands in the world are right here in this room.

In this room right now, you control the images women see globally — the images put out as what is aspirational. What starts as a marketing idea and campaign in your offices, many just a few blocks from here, reaches billions of women on a global scale.

I want you to think to yourself and answer these questions honestly. When you look at the images of models and of beauty that your brand uses . . . have they ever made you feel insecure? Or less than? Do the images you use and put out to the world empower you? Or do they make you feel disempowered?

Oprah once asked the question — "What will you do with the energy that is you?" It's a question that has impacted my life in a great way, and today I want to build on that question. Because each one of you in this room has a lot of power. You have a lot of power to make your mark on the beauty industry and in the world. It's easy to get caught up in the day-to-day of our jobs, competing for bigger numbers, getting a high when we achieve them, but today I want to ask you to take a huge step back and think about what really matters. And what difference are YOU going to make on the lives of women and girls globally — in your career. How did the images you see of beauty impact you as a little girl? How did they impact you as a young woman? And how do they impact the woman you are today? Each of you sitting in this room right now has the power to make the decisions to change this for other girls and for other women. You truly have all of the power. You, in this one room right now, are the decision-makers for all of the top beauty companies in the world and you control all of the images that billions of women and girls see globally . . . you have all of the power to change how these images shape their lives. Today I leave each of you with one question . . . What will you do . . . with the power . . . that is YOU?!

Thank you.

As I stepped away from the podium, I could feel the impact of what I'd done in the deepest part of my gut. I had broken the unspoken rules of engagement, and I called out the entire beauty industry, to their faces, and challenged them to change.

What will you do with the power that is you? It's a question we have the gift of being able to ask ourselves each and every morning when we wake up and open our eyes. Will we use our energy and power to be liked, or to be brave? To take risks, or to play it safe? To challenge the status quo, or to numb out in the comforts of our surroundings?

On this day, standing in front of the decision-makers for the largest, most powerful beauty companies in the world, I chose being brave over being liked. A choice that's almost always the right one, and in this case, I would soon face the unexpected consequences of making that choice.

# ELEVEN:
## *BELIEVE* HATERS ARE JUST
## CONFUSED SUPPORTERS

Hate. It has caused a lot of problems in
the world, but has not solved one yet.
— DR. MAYA ANGELOU

"Your face is wider than an elephant's ass."
"How far along are you?" "You should
consider getting a chin reduction." "I've
noticed you've gained some weight back.
What was the diet you tried that didn't work
for you?" "I'm not trying to hurt your feelings, but you should look into hiring a styl-
ist." "Don't take this the wrong way,
but . . ." These (and many other) criticisms
are all real things people actually posted on
my social media pages. And, get this, all of
these are from people who have *chosen* to
follow me on my page! Some might think
they're coming from a good place. I mean,
clearly not the elephant's ass one. But even
with that person, who really knows?

Have you ever had haters? Or trolls online

that say mean things about you? Or even people you know who say mean things about you? If you have, you know how much this can hurt. And you're not alone.

Three years before I met Paulo, when I was twenty-two years old, I had just won the Miss Washington USA competition and at the time reality TV was making its debut. There had been a show on MTV called *The Real World* where strangers lived together with cameras capturing it all, but other than that, reality TV wasn't mainstream yet. As the year 2000 approached, two competition reality TV shows were about to premiere — *Survivor* and *Big Brother*. In *Big Brother*'s first season, ten contestants would be locked in a single house to live together and compete to make it to the finale.

I was nearing the end of my senior year of college, and some friends and I, on a whim, thought it would be fun to apply to be on the show. We each sent in a tape. (Yep, a VHS tape. Remember those?) I got a call saying that out of thousands of submissions, I'd qualified for the callback rounds in Los Angeles. I flew to LA having literally no idea what I was getting myself into, and feeling excited and invincible, nonetheless. (Ahhh, our early twenties.) Then I made it to the round of the final seventy-some applicants.

At that point I was subjected to background checks, psychological interviews, blood work, and lots and lots of on-camera interviews, and then it happened! I got the news that they'd chosen me to be on the show! Holy s(*&!

I tried to explain to my family what I was about to do. Remember, this was the very beginning of reality TV becoming a popular genre. No one really understood that the editing could create storylines all on its own. And blogs and social media were just starting to go mainstream, so that massive arena filled with unsolicited opinions, haters, and anonymous critics was all brand-new.

Dozens of cameras filled every room of the *Big Brother* house so the outside world could watch how nine strangers and I lived together. The footage captured was edited (highly) and aired six nights a week on prime-time network television. In addition, there was a live camera feed 24/7 where people in the outside world could watch (spy) right into the house. Yet we had no access to phones or television and had no idea what was going on in the outside world for three months. Each week, all of the contestants would vote to kick someone off.

The two who received the most votes would be put on the "chopping block." Then the vote was open to the American public. They called in or went online to vote on who they wanted kicked off. The final three contestants to make it to the end of the show won prize money.

Being on the show, at that point in my life, especially as an introvert, was the craziest thing I had ever done. Imagine being locked inside this house full of cameras and microphones with nine strangers and having to wear a microphone 24/7. Everything I did and said and didn't do and didn't say was recorded. The infrared cameras even recorded everything that happened in the dark and filmed us while we slept. All of the mirrors were two-way, so there were either cameras behind them or camera operators standing with cameras behind them, filming every move we made. Imagine the things you do all day long — waking up, getting dressed, washing up, your habits and quirks and everything in between — all being filmed!

I would look into the mirror of the medicine cabinet while brushing my teeth and know someone was standing there filming me. Every once in a while, I could even detect a slight movement behind the mirror. It was so bizarre and the weirdest, most invasive feeling, especially because you couldn't see the face of the person filming you. Oh, and I am going to get TMI with you for a second. Because here's the thing: The *Big Brother* house had only one toilet. It was inside a very small toilet-only room. This was the only place in the house that wasn't on camera (yep, even the shower had a camera), but even the toilet room had a hanging microphone inside. Imagine yourself sitting on a toilet, and there's this long cord hanging from the ceiling with a microphone that falls just above your head and slightly in front of your face. While the microphone was there presumably to make sure no one slipped into the toilet room to have a private conversation, it recorded everything. That's right, everything. This is going to sound so ridiculous, and super embarrassing, but there was a moment when I was sitting there on the toilet, a couple of months into being locked in the house, terrified to fart. Now, I know everyone farts. But not into a microphone! Seriously, just for a moment, try to imagine yourself farting into a microphone. With strangers listening! (I later learned there was an entire control room with dozens of people listening!) For weeks, anytime I had to, I held it in! It feels so embarrassing to write this, but at this point we're friends, so I'm gonna get real with you. Day after day, I did whatever I could to go to the bathroom making as little noise as possible. Plus, I was Miss Washington USA at the time, and for some reason I thought I was supposed to be extra classy, whatever that means.

Let's all be honest for a second. How many times in a public restroom do you wait until everyone leaves to finally go to the bathroom? Or you flush the toilet extra times to mask any noise. Or you cough loudly. Or roll the toilet paper holder to mask noise. What's wrong with us? Seriously! It's so time to end this and be free!

Anyway, one day I was inside that small bathroom, sitting on the toilet, and I just decided life is too short. And let's just say I let it rip! Yep, fully rip! I felt both embarrassed and empowered all at the same time! FREEDOM! And I fully committed! It was fully committed freedom! I'm not throwing away my shot at freedom! *You only live once* freedom! My dad who used to say "pull my finger" freedom! Swing-'em, Fearless, Ballsy Squirrel Freedom!

Okay, I think by now you probably get the point that literally every single move we made for three solid months was captured.

At the same time, all that footage of us was edited into a show with story lines that we weren't privy to, and broadcast on national network TV six nights a week. My year, Season One of *Big Brother,* seventy episodes aired on prime-time TV. Do you ever watch reality TV shows, say *The Bachelor,* or *Bad Girls Club,* or any of those, and wonder why everyone is crying or why their emotions are heightened? Well, here's the deal. When you're locked away from the outside world, it's like you're living in this bubble. And as the weeks and months go by, everything inside that bubble becomes super intense and your emotions become super heightened, which of course makes for great TV! As the days and weeks passed in the *Big Brother* house, every moment felt so intense that I could never let my guard down. Not even while sleeping.

Because *Big Brother* was a competition, and because a lot of money was on the line (the winner got $500,000, second place got $100,000, and third place got $50,000), the competition became fierce. Every week we would vote another person off, and the public really got involved. Since this was all happening in real time, and we were locked inside the house without any awareness of what was happening on the outside, the only way fans could communicate with us was by hiring small airplanes to fly banners over the house we were living and filming in. You know those planes that fly those long ribbon banners that normally have advertisements or say things like "will you marry me"? Those. Fans got so into this show that they would pool their money and fly messages over our house, trying to pit contestants against each other. It was crazy. Especially because it was the only info we had from the outside world. Every time it happened, all of us would run out to the small backyard to look up.

When a plane flew over saying something like "Jamie, watch out for So and So, they voted to kick you off," I never knew if it was true. Some days I would get kind messages from fans like "Go Jamie Go, We Love You!" but then many days there would be planes that flew over with comments like "Jamie sucks and she's two-faced" or other hurtful messages about me or the other contestants. I started getting a sick, physical reaction every time I heard the engine of one of those small planes approaching overhead. As I share this story, it sounds so crazy and a bit silly to me. But at the time, I couldn't bear the thought that people were actually paying money to hurt me. The other contestants would get equally upset. It felt like anonymous bullies were using airplanes to spread banners of hate across the sky for all to see. To this day, anytime I hear a small plane overhead, I have a yucky feeling in my gut from these memories. Crazy, right?

In other ways the show was a ton of fun, and I'm grateful for getting to see inside a reality show experience like that, especially in the pioneering days of the genre. Plus, as an introvert, I was so far outside my comfort zone that I lost many of my inhibitions (I let them rip, literally!), and that was such a good thing for me. I have no regrets about doing the show — YOLO, right? I lasted all three months, was the last woman in the house, and got kicked off the day before the show ended. Fourth place, and no money. And I thought that was the end of a thrilling, once-in-a-lifetime experience. But, boy, was I wrong. I was about to find out that the hater airplanes were just a warm-up act for what was to come.

The day after the show ended, I went out for a meal with my friends and family. To my complete shock, I couldn't walk down the street without being stopped every few seconds by someone who recognized me from the show. Many of the people were kind and just wanted a photo; others would tell me how they loved or hated something I did or said, and then let me know their opinion about it. They'd tell me they loved the comedy skits I did with another contestant called Chicken George, or they'd ask, "Were you and Josh secretly in love?" or "Do you really sleep in your makeup?" (The answer to that one is no; the editors just rarely showed me without makeup because the show wanted me to come across as a beauty queen.) I didn't know how to handle any of this attention.

In my first twenty-four hours after leaving the *Big Brother* house, I learned that people had created hundreds of websites in response to the show, including opinionated sites supporting or hating on each contestant. I had fan sites and I had hate sites evaluating everything about me. *WHAT???* I didn't know what to do or how to process this.

By the way, because I was one of the few contestants who wore makeup in the house, and I put it on in front of the mirror, fans and critics took note. One of the questions I got most frequently was "What lip gloss do you wear?" Women would come up to me and say stuff like, "I have to get that lip gloss for my daughter for her wedding." On the other hand, some of the most hateful websites were focused on criticizing my makeup. One hater created a mean online game where you could smear lip gloss all over my face. Others posted photos of me with makeup covering every square inch of my face like an abstract painting. It was funny, not funny, then funny again. Here's what I mean. At the time I had no idea that I would create a makeup company one day, let alone a makeup company that would become one of the largest in the country. How crazy is that? So thanks, haters, for planting that seed and helping manifest my future! Hah! God is so good! But I digress. Back to the effects of all this love and hate.

My first response to the hate sites was to curl up in my blanket at home, with a pint of ice cream and bags of candy, crying in pain. Emotional eating made it slightly better — or made me slightly more numb. But that was the other thing — there were also countless websites judging my weight and body. Fun times. I don't mean to give less attention to the many amazing, beautiful, and kind fan sites. But here's how our brains work. We can be getting all the positivity in the world, and yet our brain's default is to magnify it when one person says something negative. At the time, I didn't know how to take control over my attention and mindset. All I knew was that it felt like I was facing hatred and rejection. I internalized the criticism and many days felt alone and unlovable.

On the flip side were the superfans. Many were kind, and would send gifts in the mail like dolls with my face on them, tons of T-shirts with special messages, paintings, and jewelry. There were even letters from prison inmates.

Then I learned one of the big downsides of having overnight fame, which is that it comes not just with fans and haters but also with people who aren't well.

Prior to the show, I was just a regular person. I had graduated from college and was working super, super hard at an internet startup in Seattle, and made just enough to pay my bills and make my student loan payments. When I went on the show, we didn't get paid. We only made a $50 stipend per day, though we still had to pay all our bills somehow. When you become famous overnight, without a career that pays, you end up famous, but without any money. This means that when crazy people stalk you, you don't have any money for security or to protect yourself.

Stalkers aren't fans. They are people who are mentally disturbed, and who often become obsessed with another person. Because the live feed of the show was being streamed over the internet, there were people watching from their homes. And not all of them were well. One scary stalker decided to show up at the FedEx store where I stopped to print a few things just outside the town where I grew up. He lived many states away and had been following me. He said hello in person in FedEx that day. I later learned he had built some sort of mannequin robot that he believed was me, and he was also under the misconception that I was living with him. I had to get the police involved.

As the months and years passed, and the fifteen minutes of fame from the show was over, the fans and haters from the show also faded away. At the time I didn't have real tools to know how to process it all, but I grew thicker skin.

There are all types of haters out there. The kind that know you and the kind that don't. The kind that truly want to hurt you, and the kind that are just so hurt themselves they don't even realize what they say is hurting you. The kind that are brave enough to show their face are in the few-and-far-between group. And then there's the majority, who do it anonymously or disguised as someone else, or by spreading gossip so that it ends up getting out there and somehow causing collective hate. With the rise of social media and all forms of technology, kids aren't just being bullied in small groups at school anymore where they know with certainty who the bully is; they're being bullied online in public forums, often anonymously, and the painful content often stays online permanently. Recent studies show loneliness, depression, and suicide are on the rise, and many studies link this to the rise of cyberbullying, social media, and the rapidly evolving role of technology in our lives. Haters and critics are taking up growing space in all of our worlds, and now this negativity is often reaching us daily in a device we not only can't seem to look away from but in many cases are full-out addicted to. A lot of the new research being done on all of the feel-good chemicals released in our bodies from receiving likes and followers is scary, especially given that it's addictive to everyone, including young people during the years when their brains are still developing. With that said, all signs point to technology only increasing its role in our lives. So figuring out how to get a handle on processing hate and criticism in a healthy way is an absolute necessity for ourselves, our families, and the younger generation who will be raised in this new reality.

It's easy to say just stop caring. Just don't worry about what other people think. Because what I know for sure is that the famous words are true: hurt people hurt people. So just don't pay any attention to haters, right? But here's the thing that makes that so difficult. At our core, we all yearn for human connection and belonging. And when you completely stop caring what other people think, that also comes at the price of disconnection from humanity. And that's not great either. So what's the solution?

This has been a long battle for me, because I've learned that anytime you put yourself out there, anytime you take a risk, anytime you speak your truth, anytime you step out and do something brave or great or public, it always comes with critics. And pretty much the only way to not get any haters or critics is to not do or say anything with your life.

Albert Einstein once said, "Great spirits have always encountered violent opposition from mediocre minds." Now, if I were to say this quote, I would replace the word *mediocre* with *unevolved.* But either way, the price we all pay for doing anything great at all is that not everyone is going to like it, or like you. And when that happens, it hurts.

Pastor Joel Osteen famously said it this way: that all of our difficulties in life aren't just *setbacks,* they're actually *setups* from God, to help make us strong enough to carry the weight of both the highs and lows of our future calling. While I didn't know it at the time, this experience of having fans and haters was preparing me for what was to come.

My next introduction to the court of public opinion came when I decided to enter the world of journalism. When I was twenty-five, I went to graduate school to get my master's in business from Columbia University in New York City.

When I got into Columbia, an Ivy League business school, I knew how to work my butt off and make things happen. I deserved to be there. But neither of my parents who raised me had gone to college, and I wasn't raised going to fancy private schools. I was so insecure and worried that I wouldn't fit in in an Ivy League environment I had only seen portrayed in movies.

But I believe in the popular idea that growth happens on the other side of our comfort zone. In my first year of business school, I quickly realized I was learning even more from the stories shared by other students, professors, and alumni than I was from the actual case studies or coursework. I deeply valued the proximity to all of these amazing people. There were days I would just look around the classroom and think about how much money we were each spending to be there. While it was worth it, I wondered how we could all get even more out of the experience. That's when I had the idea to do in-depth interviews for the school newspaper with super-interesting students, professors, and alumni. I published them under the headline "Uncovered," and told the story behind the story, in their own words, of all of these fascinating people. When I did interviews, I felt a sense of intuitive flow and fell in love with sharing other people's stories.

That's when I began to tune in to that state of flow and follow its direction, letting it, instead of other people's opinions, guide my decisions. Getting an MBA is a two-year program. In between those years, most students do a summer internship in finance or consulting or investment banking that pays very well, sometimes $10,000 a month for three months. And those high-paying internships are also seen as the first step toward a student receiving a fancy, high-paying full-time job offer at graduation. And here's the thing: a university's ranking often comes down to all of these numbers, like how much their graduates get paid in their first job after graduation and what the average salary is for the graduating class. There's a lot of pressure on MBA students, including from themselves and from classmates, to get a high-paying "successful" job. It's seen as a badge of honor and acceptance. You also feel the pressure of stewardship. There's this unspoken feeling that your peers and the alumni are counting on you to maintain the school's high status through your own accomplishments.

I could have gotten a high-paying consulting or finance job for my internship. But I knew in my heart I would be miserable doing it. So what did I do? I took a massive risk. I found an UNPAID journalism internship at a local TV station in the middle of a small farm town called Yakima in Washington State. Yep, unpaid. Zero dollars. I flew out there, borrowed my stepaunt's station wagon because I couldn't afford to buy or rent a car, and worked my butt off. For free.

I learned how to write story copy. I learned how to shoot video, how to record myself and others' audio and voice-overs, and how to edit all of it.

I learned how to one-man-band report. One-man-band is where you're all alone as a reporter. You load up the news car with gear, drive to the scene of a story, set up the camera, mic the people you're interviewing, and film them. You then mic yourself and set up your camera to film your own part of the story. Then you drive back to the TV station, log all of your footage, write your story, get it approved by your producer or news director, and then edit the story and turn it in to air on TV that night. Some days you might also introduce your story live on the air.

I spent my summer learning everything I could about this process. I covered boring stories and exciting stories and very sad stories. I ate a lot of Kraft Macaroni & Cheese. Often, I had to pull off to the side of the road when the door panel to my borrowed station wagon fell off mid-drive. I bonded with all the other reporters, who taught me the ropes. And I had one of the best summers of my life. When I left Yakima, I didn't have a dollar to my name, but I did have a full heart, an audition tape, and the dream that one day I could get paid for listening to, connecting with, and sharing other people's stories.

In my final year at Columbia Business School, I was chosen by my peers as class speaker at graduation. This was such a shock to me, mainly because I was about to *totally hurt* the curve of Columbia Business School. The year I graduated, 2004, the average salary plus bonus of a Columbia MBA student after graduation was over $100,000. Want to know what mine was? Approximately $23,500. About half what I was earning just out of high school at the health club I'd quit to go to college nine years earlier. With no idea how I was going to pay my bills or my student loans, I accepted a job as a morning TV news anchor/reporter at KNDU TV in Tri-Cities, Washington.

You should have seen the look on many of my classmates' faces when I shared what job I was taking after graduation. It was usually a confused yet inquisitive look mixed with disappointment, embarrassment, and a dash of pity. Many of my classmates, filled with the best of intentions, worried that I was making a mistake and not living up to my potential because I wasn't going after a higher-paying job on Wall Street, which in their eyes was a bigger achievement than following my gut to the middle of nowhere and making no money. But I was strong enough then not to make major life decisions based on other people's expectations. I knew they meant well and wanted the best for me, but I had to turn down the volume and listen to that still, small voice deep down inside. In my class speech at graduation, I talked about all the things I imagined for the future of our class. I even mentioned how excited I was to one day surely see some of us on the front page/homepage of the *New York Times* or *Wall Street Journal.* (I had no idea that would actually be me one day.) I left Columbia Business School with what I believe might have been the lowest starting salary certainly that year, if not of all time. But I followed what I believed was my calling. The university itself supported me and cheered me on. Which is why today I am one of its greatest cheerleaders. Being underestimated by others never matters if you are following your truth. And sometimes people only see where you are, they can't see where you're going. I was probably the lowest-paid person out of my Columbia Business School class. Fifteen years later, I received the university's highest honor, the medal of excellence. Just a few people receive it each year. I was also asked to join the board of overseers. When you follow your calling on your life, all things are possible!

I soon found that taking a job in TV threw me right back into that world of haters. "Are you pregnant?" "You're gaining a lot of weight." "It looks like the buttons on your suit are popping off!" "Your voice is super annoying and is ruining my breakfast when I watch you. I have to change the channel." "They have surgeries now that can reduce your chin size. I really like watching you, but you should really look into this." Welcome to TV!

When you're doing something that is public, or something that actually makes a difference, or anything that has you stepping outside your comfort zone on the path to something great, everyone seems to have an opinion on it. And I've learned that the more brave or successful you are, the more other people seem to think you're not human like them and that you don't have feelings. I hear this from actors and other friends who have public or prominent jobs. People write or say things about them as if they assume they won't feel it or actually get hurt by it. But we are all human. As I grew in my TV career, I learned that my experience doing *Big Brother* had set me up to be able to handle the good and the bad on my next step in life as a journalist. I was so much more resilient than I'd been years before. Every time I got a hate-filled email or read a negative post online, it might hurt my feelings for a bit, but I got better and better at letting it roll right off me like water off a duck's back. And I started intentionally paying more attention to the kind emails, and to the letters, messages, and notes of viewers who shared how their days were brighter because of our morning show, or how they felt less lonely, or how they loved getting their news from us. What we focus on we magnify, and we have to choose our focus wisely.

When it comes to internet trolls and haters, there can be so much negativity that it's hard to see through to the positive. Motivational speaker and former NFL wide receiver Trent Shelton has one of the most insightful ways of reframing haters in a positive light. He describes haters as people who actually admire what you do, they just have a different way of showing it. He says, "Haters are just confused supporters." And he has some very valid points. He says haters often follow you on social media; that's love. They sometimes even create fake accounts to follow you. That's love too. So, basically, what he's saying is that haters, deep down inside, are actually loving us too. Beautifully said, Trent.

That made sense when I looked back on the mean girls who worried about our growing success and when I thought about the large company that stole one of our products. They wanted what we had. They admired us!

Next time you encounter haters or face opposition, start by asking yourself if there's any truth to their words or actions, and what might be the intention behind them. If there's no good intention to be found, then most likely the criticism is meant to be destructive instead of constructive and they're simply taking out their own pain on you. In this case, these famous words apply: "Don't take criticism from someone you wouldn't take advice from." It's important to look past their words, focus on what matters, and stand in your truth. And always remember, these setbacks might hurt our feelings, but they also might be setups to make us strong enough to carry the weight of future successes.

■ ■ ■

With years of both public praise and scrutiny under my belt, I thought I could handle whatever my Cosmetic Executive Women awards speech was about to bounce back at me, but the attacks that followed it were different and painful in a completely unexpected way.

# TWELVE:
## *BELIEVE* IN KNOWING YOUR VALUES AND LIVING THEM!

Take away what you're known for,
and whatever's left is who you are.

— BOB GOFF

"What will you do with the power that is you?" I stood up in front of the entire beauty industry, in the same room as the giant companies' executives, collectively responsible for deciding the images of "beauty" that billions of women see globally, and I challenged them to change. I knew in my heart it was the right thing to do. My entire career so far had prepared me for that moment. I believed that perhaps part of the reason I was blessed with the great success of my company was so that, at minimum, the other companies, which often seemed to be driven only by their bottom line, would listen to me. Or at least copy what I was doing, to try to make even more money. (And unlike knocking off our products, this was actually a way in which I wanted to be copied!) Which, big picture, would still get me closer to my goal of shifting culture and changing the conversation about beauty.

After I finished my speech, the majority of the room applauded passionately, and about a third of the room stared at me with cold eyes and pursed lips and gave a light courtesy clap. I felt the conflicting energy take over the room. As the event wrapped up, some of the industry legends who are normally very warm toward me snubbed me as they walked by. I knew that might happen. But my goal wasn't to offend them or belittle their accomplishments, it was to shed light on what I truly felt needed to change. And in the room there were not only the people who control the giant department store and luxury brands but also the heads of the multibillion-dollar brands that you see for sale in the drugstores and big-box stores, so I knew I was bound to offend somebody.

Before I could worry too much, I was quickly swarmed by woman after woman, many of them in tears. Several of the women who came up to me shared their own struggles with feeling beautiful, and their own internal conflict of loving their work in the beauty industry but not loving the part about it that made them feel like they weren't enough. Many women shared how they related to my story about the investor who said he didn't believe women would buy makeup from someone who looked like me, with my body and weight. The event was also attended by beauty editors and members of the press. Several of them approached me afterward with great enthusiasm for my boldness in taking on an industry of giants. So as I left the event that day, I knew I had ruffled some feathers, but overall, I felt brave. Standing up in front of them all and challenging them to change how they see their own responsibility to the world had been the right decision. I might have tarnished my crown as an up-and-coming "industry darling" that day, but I took a stand for real women everywhere, and for what I believed in. And I will always believe in those famous words, that "the power of the people is greater than the people in power."

That said, I was not remotely prepared for what was about to happen next.

First, I received a scolding phone call from an industry legend who was sitting in the audience that day. One I had always admired from afar. She was fuming. The decision-makers for probably 90 percent of the global beauty market had been in the room, and she said that I should be embarrassed by what I had done, and that I had surely offended many of the other industry icons in the audience as well. She also shared that she had always been fond of me and even had championed me inside the industry. I explained to her that I had hoped she would have known in her heart that what I was taking a stand for was true, and that as an industry legend she would be proud of me for taking a risk with an authentic intention to move the industry forward. I told her that I truly believe the famous words about how the people who are crazy enough to believe they can change the world are the ones who do.

She snapped back at me, "Are you kidding me? YOU WILL NEVER CHANGE THE BEAUTY INDUSTRY."

Even though the call wasn't on speaker, she spoke so loudly that Zega, who was sitting in the room with me, heard what she said. Her jaw dropped to the floor.

My reply was calm and collected. I simply said, "Actually, I already have."

The call didn't end well. She told me she was going to put in a call to the head of

L'Oréal about this, as what I had done was not acceptable. It felt almost as if she was going to call my parents and get me in trouble! She said to me, "You'd better hope there isn't a backlash." I wasn't sure exactly what she was talking about. Was that a threat, or did she think others in the industry might be offended and blackball me from their events?

I just said, "I am really sorry if you're upset over this, but I truly believe in my heart that I did the right thing."

We agreed to disagree, and the call ended. Not amicably. Not really with closure. It just ended.

I thought that was it. I'd burned whatever bridges I was going to burn, but I'd stood up for what I believed in. Little did I know that was only the beginning. First, the good. Several top magazines and websites quickly published incredibly positive stories about how I was a trailblazer and had challenged the entire industry to change. They shared all of the ways I had already changed the industry as a brand and on air by using real women as models and showing women of diverse ages, sizes, skin tones, and skin challenges. Several articles also came out sharing the story of how I'd been turned down by an investor because of my weight. My speech went viral, and our company's Facebook post of it got over a million views. Now women everywhere, not just those shopping for makeup, had a chance to hear my message.

THEN I learned the hard way why so many people are scared to ever speak out like this. Because the beauty legend who was so upset with me on the call was right about one thing. When you take a stand, you risk backlash. And backlash can really suck. Especially when it falsely attacks the core of who you are.

As quickly as I was praised and placed on this pedestal by article after article in the press, touted as the brave and rebellious girl fighting to change the entire beauty industry and pushing for inclusivity of women everywhere — I was suddenly attacked online for *not being inclusive enough.* And when I say attacked, I mean, it was brutal.

These attacks weren't coming from the mainstream press, but rather from people online. Anonymous comments started popping up saying I was a hypocrite because I didn't show models of *all* ages, or sizes, or skin tones, or skin problems, or gender identities. Then the attacks snow-balled. My social media, my company's social media, and my email inbox started exploding with hate-filled messages, threats to my safety, including death threats, and photos of me where people drew hurtful things on my face, including one with devil horns.

I thought I'd built resilience and had thick enough skin not to let this hurt me. But this was a different kind of criticism. I'd spent most of my professional life fighting for inclusivity, and to be attacked in this way hurt my soul. It took every ounce of my being not to lose my faith in other people. It hurt so, so bad. I felt like I was the one taking a stand to fight for what was right, only to be attacked for not doing every possible part of it well enough.

I could have played the role that everyone wanted me to play. I could have made a beautiful speech that made everyone in the room happy that day. I'd already sold my company. I had nothing to gain from the attention. There was no upside for me here other than really trying to effect change and shift culture.

As for the parts I didn't do well enough, I own them fully. There is a difference between passionate constructive criticism and personal attacks. One helps us learn and grow; the other does the opposite. Even though the attacks, especially in the hurtful form many of them took, were hard to bear, I decided that I needed to be strong enough to listen to them, in case they were in some way a gift. A gift to know more, to learn more, and to do better. When we feel attacked, it's so easy to defend and deny. But we can't ever grow that way. I spent countless hours, days, and weeks racking my brain to see if there was any truth to these attacks and how I could have done better.

I had tried to capture all forms of diversity with the models we used, but I missed the mark at including models who were differently abled, which wasn't intentional, but was a clear oversight. I used models who ranged in age from teenagers to their seventies, but perhaps could have made even more effort to find models in their eighties and above. At the time of the speech we had been working hard on expanding the assortment of our concealer to forty-eight shades, and launching a campaign around it where we used forty-eight of our actual employees to model each shade, but maybe I could have fought even harder, sooner, for more retail shelf space so we could expand the shade assortment even earlier. I failed to do all of those things. And probably many others.

I tried with all my might to be everything

to everyone, but I know that's simply impossible to do. I also know I am far from perfect and I can always do better, and I'm always open to listening and trying. As painful as these criticisms were, I took them in, I listened, and I really did some deep reflection. And they lit an even stronger fire under me to challenge myself and our incredible team to do better and do more. And we did.

This learning was a gift that then led to change. And it came from the messages I received, read, and heard, along with the conversations I had and the work I put into understanding anything I might have been missing. This is the positive side of backlash.

Unfortunately, for every extremely insightful message, there were dozens of very ruthless attacks, death threats, and accusations that weren't constructive and were clearly aimed to cause hurt and fear. And here's the one thing about that that made me extra sad: When you attack people who are the ones brave enough to stand up, all you do is discourage other people from standing up. This is something that often has a deep impact on women. We're conditioned that unless we do things 100 percent perfectly, we shouldn't try. A recent study shows that on average, men apply for a job when they meet only 60 percent of the qualifications, but women wait to apply until they meet 100 percent of the qualifications. It's just one of many powerful examples of this mental model. Women are often taught we need to be perfect to take a chance, and we avoid taking risks due to fear of failure. This same mindset shows up in all areas of life, including underestimating our worth in negotiating salary and raises. Lack of confidence and being unwilling to put ourselves out there and ask for what we want hold us back in both our personal and professional lives. I had mustered every ounce of bravery I had not to throw away my shot, and to do what I could do, the best that I could, with the best of my understanding at the time, where I was, to effect change. I showed up imperfectly, but at least I showed up and tried.

While this was all happening, I got quite a few calls from friends who worked in the press. Trying to make me feel better, they explained that because my speech went viral and made so many headlines, it was a prime target for trolls who, by attacking it, would ride the coattails of its popularity. They explained that people will do anything for clicks and views because it's often how they make money. But no matter what they said, or how well-intentioned it was, it didn't make me feel much better.

I then decided to google all the people I admire most. The people who I see as the ultimate contributors to humanity, the ultimate in success, achievement, and service. I suspected, and wanted to confirm, that anytime you do anything of significance, it comes with opposition. From people who don't agree with you, don't like what you're doing and therefore don't like you, or just flat-out hate for no discernible reason. So I googled them all — my greatest mentors and the most incredibly successful human beings on the planet. Sure enough, they all had tons of haters. Websites devoted to attacking them. Tons of lies or hurtful, hateful things written about them. Some of these are people who strike me as bringing such value to the world that I don't see how anyone could possibly hate on them, yet they do. While doing this didn't make me feel any better, it did help me feel less alone.

For a while, I worried for my safety while walking into the office, flashing back to my TV news days of covering crime, and my *Big Brother* stalker days, remembering just how many unwell people might have seen some of the attacks and want to join in. But the worst part, really, was the all-consuming anguish I was in. When our character is being challenged, and especially when it doesn't feel true, it can be torturous.

When someone attacks who you are, it's so important to truly know yourself, and take hold of that knowing. When it feels like the world is coming against you, the only thing that can keep it from taking you down is knowing your truth. And my truth is that I always stand up for the right thing. I might do it messily and imperfectly, but I always do it.

I see the differences all around me and find them beautiful. Size, age, skin color, gender, who you love, how you vote, how you pray. These differences are beauty in all forms, and my heart connects to your heart; I believe we're all connected. And I know who I am.

Good timber does not grow with ease:
The stronger the wind, the stronger
the trees.
— DOUGLAS MALLOCH

I believe so strongly that, especially as women, we have a responsibility to be mindful not to attack other women just because they aren't doing it all perfectly, or just because they've made mistakes in the past, or just because they don't do things the way we would do them, whether it's how they parent, how they lead, or how messily they show up in the world when they're often just doing the best they can. As women we also need to overcome the fear of facing opposition. While criticism often hurts, in my case the constructive feedback was a gift. It truly helped me see blind spots I'd missed and helped me challenge myself to grow and do better. Today I have nothing but gratitude for the people who spent their precious time giving me their thoughtful feedback. We all should be able to speak our minds, loud and proud, and should always speak out against anything unjust, of course, and we also have a great responsibility to change the environment around us that robs women of the confidence to step into the game imperfectly. As women, so many of us end up sitting on the sidelines of life, and the sidelines of our dreams, because we feel unready, or unqualified, or not enough. So many women are still so critical of ourselves and other women. And this just holds us *all* back. We need women to take chances, launch businesses, challenge industries, speak out against injustices, and shine their own lights brightly, without being afraid to fail or worrying about getting shamed for it. We need to have grace for each other. We need to lift each other up. And celebrate each other.

> The warrior knows that her heartbreak is her map.
> — GLENNON DOYLE

I don't regret choosing to be brave over being liked that day. I showed up and entered the arena. I didn't throw away my shot when I had one shot to take. I used the heartbreak from a lifetime of seeing unattainable images of beauty as my map on my quest to take on something far bigger than myself. And when I realized I could do even better in my own company as well, I used the heartache that came from hard criticism as my map to live my values and challenge myself to learn, grow, stretch, and lead better. When it comes to knowing and living your values, it's always the best decision for your soul to do the right and brave thing, even when it is the hard thing.

I can't completely change inclusivity in the beauty industry all on my own, but I sure as heck have tried my butt off. And maybe, by challenging the entire beauty industry publicly, I moved it one step forward that day. Maybe I moved it five steps forward that day. Today, some of the biggest brands in the world feature models of all ages, sizes, skin tones, skin challenges, and genders. Maybe they're changing because they want to do the right thing. Or maybe they saw our success. Whatever the reason, I hope what I did that day played some small part in it.

I also learned that I failed to check all the boxes perfectly. But I entered the arena and I charged onto the field. I didn't sit on the sidelines; I played my heart out. And my hope is that the decision-makers of the beauty industry will catch the pass that I aimed to throw with all the precision I could find in my soul right into the end zone, to win the game for us all! Because I do believe that together, we've got this.

■ ■ ■ ■

# PART THREE:
# EMPOWER

■ ■ ■ ■

# THIRTEEN:
# DON'T *BELIEVE* IN BALANCE.
# IT'S A LIE!

The price of anything is the amount of life
you exchange for it.
— PARAPHRASED FROM
HENRY DAVID THOREAU

Have you ever anticipated an exciting event,
meeting, vacation, family gathering, holiday
party, or school reunion, and instead of feeling excitement and joy, felt nothing other
than stress . . . not stress about the actual
event, but genuine, persistent stress about
whether the clothes you planned to wear, or
bought to wear, would fit? Then when you
tried them on, you got so upset you didn't
even want to go? If so, I've been right there
with you. Far too often. Including the day
before I went to the Oscars "Night Before
the Night Before" party. I pulled the dress I
planned to wear out of my closet. It was
made of a beautiful sheer stretchy organza
fabric with sparkly hand-sewn beads, and

I'd bought it when it was just a tiny bit too tight *knowing* it would fit by the night of the party, and, guess what? Yep, it was still too tight. I turned to the side of the closet where I had moved the bigger sizes, the ones I hoped I'd never wear again but couldn't quite commit to getting rid of just in case. Do you have a section in your closet like that? I also had a section of still-too-small items, some with tags still on them, that I somehow decided made sense to buy because I was *definitely* going to fit in them eventually.

On this night, the party was such a huge deal that the disappointment of my dress not fitting didn't stop me from going, and it's a good thing, because at that party someone said something to me that just blew my mind and shifted my perspective forever. It came out of nowhere. Okay, let me set the scene. Because of the company I built, I now get invited to some pretty cool parties a few times a year. And the Oscars Night Before party and the Night Before the Night Before party and dinner are a couple of them. Each year I've attended, I've spent countless hours fretting over what to wear, what will fit, and then, of course, what look to aim for with my hair and makeup. It's one of only a few times a year when I hire a hairstylist and makeup artists (aka a glam squad) to come to my home and help me get ready. After the sale to L'Oréal, I was catapulted into a world where for the first time I experienced the kind of glam squads that celebrities use. That's when I learned that for those hair and makeup looks you see on celebrities at parties and events, they typically spend thousands of dollars and many hours getting ready. From hair extensions (in case you didn't know this, there's almost no one on the red carpet without extra hair added on any given day), to body makeup to cover veins and enhance muscle tone, to enough face makeup and contouring to make any feature appear a completely different shape, to fake eyelashes, to a fresh manicure, and, depending on the dress, often double Spanx (yep, one pair on top of another!). And these are just the basics. It's a lot. A lot of time and a lot of energy. All for a photo op on the red carpet that will usually get edited to perfection by someone before it ever surfaces anywhere. And all for a single event that day. Seeing inside this part of the beauty industry was quite the contrast to my daily life at IT Cosmetics. I loved experiencing the masterful hair and makeup artistry and each artist's talent firsthand.

And every time I am fortunate enough to have this experience, I'm also mindful of just how much time it takes to maintain this lifestyle for the people who are able to and choose it.

After all the hours spent getting ready, I pulled up to the pre-Oscars party and first posed for those all-important red-carpet photos. Once that was done, I made my way inside, where everyone had a drink and was working the room, from A-list celebrities to a whole lot of entertainment industry execs who all seemed to thrive in this environment. Lots of schmoozing, lots of agendas, and for many people, it seems, lots of fun!

Because I come alive and get fired up on television when I am talking about something I truly care about, especially when I am talking with other women or listening to another woman's story, people assume I'm an extrovert. But, as I mentioned, I'm actually a true introvert off camera. Especially at parties and social events. If you've ever walked into a party and felt so painfully shy or awkward you want to go hide in the bathroom, or you literally do hide in the bathroom, I'm right there with you. So I try hard to challenge myself to be social, but it really is hard for me in these types of settings. I find "small talk" depleting and challenging. If I have a choice, I'll always try to bring one of my extroverted friends with me to these events as my plus-one so that they can carry the conversations with new people, and I can just listen. Even with the public nature of my job and the company I've built, socializing at parties with people I don't know is just still so, so hard for me.

For whatever reason, even though I'm an introvert, I almost never get starstruck. Aside from Oprah Winfrey and Victoria Osteen, I don't think I've ever been nervous or starstruck around anyone. Maybe it's because I've met so many celebrities as part of my job, and I know they are exactly like you and me. They have the same insecurities, the same fears, the same highs and lows, and the same need for love and belonging and community. So as I walk into a celeb-packed event, instead of worrying about who's who, or who I would love to meet because they're famous, I always trust that I will meet exactly who I'm supposed to meet. It's a kind of blind faith about events like this, which I learned from my friend Natasha, that gives me peace. And it takes any pressure off feeling like I have to force being social. Sometimes I end up meeting the most interesting people this way

— by not trying to. And other times I end up listening to someone that I later learn really needed to be heard and reminded that they matter.

On this night, like at all events, Paulo immediately began devouring as many of the passed hors d'oeuvres as he could get his hands on. No matter what healthy eating plan he's on, hors d'oeuvres are his kryptonite. At this point in time, Paulo had been vegan for a long while and had been loving it. His cholesterol went way down, and I didn't think anything could break him. That is, until we were at the pre-Oscars party. One glimpse of those shiny silver trays and all rules went out the window. From across the room I saw his hand reach over and grab two chicken satay skewers with peanut sauce. I debated whether I was going to tell him that I saw him do this later. But before I could really consider the thought, there he was, devouring Wagyu sliders. Then mini pork buns. I admired how joyful and free the look on his face was, and wished I felt that carefree when I saw the tempting hors d'oeuvres being passed. And I couldn't help but laugh, the way I did the time he was devouring those lobster tails in the QVC greenroom. Although back then he wasn't a proud vegan or surrounded by A-list celebs who he was supposed to be *sharing* the hors d'oeuvres with. On this night, Paulo had transformed into a no-holds-barred *non-*vegan!

In moments like these, when I'm part of something that feels straight out of a movie (no pun intended in this case), I always try to feel the moment. To look around, take it all in, and truly feel it. And feel gratitude for it. As I was panning the room, noticing all the A-list celebs, I saw Meg Whitman from across the room. What I didn't know was that in a few short moments, she would say something so simple that would forever change my perspective. And to this day, she probably has no idea she did. Meg Whitman, in case you're unfamiliar with her, is an icon for many in business. She's been the CEO of companies including eBay and Hewlett-Packard, she's on several boards, and according to *Forbes,* at the time I'm writing this book she's the second-richest woman in America. She's also married with two children and has her MBA from Harvard. She's commonly referred to as a BFD (Grandma, that means big . . . um . . . deal). And seeing all those A-list celebs sashay up to meet her was pretty cool.

Meanwhile, I was deep in a conversation about women and confidence with Carol

Hamilton from L'Oréal, who is as passionate about this topic as I am. We were talking about how a recent study had shown that less than 50 percent of women are confident in themselves, and how traditionally the beauty industry speaks to only those confident women and ignores the rest. Then someone introduced Meg Whitman to Carol. When Meg shifted her gaze to me, I reached out to shake her hand (normally I am a hugger, but this time a handshake felt like the right thing) and said hello. I'd barely gotten my name out when Carol, who always champions other women, started to sing my praises to Meg, sharing the changes I'd made already and continued to push for in the beauty industry, in particular how I'd been helping inspire confidence in women. I saw a sparkle appear in Meg's eyes and she reached out and gave me a fist bump! OMG! As far as I'm concerned, getting a fist bump from Meg Whitman is cooler than anything that could have possibly happened with any big celeb in that room. Getting a fist bump from Meg felt like an acknowledgment from one badass woman to another. It felt like this woman, who broke through one glass ceiling after another, who was truly the only woman in many of the boardrooms, who was and is a trailblazer for countless women, actually saw me. And said "well done" to me. All in the form of a single fist bump. P.S. After the fist bump, she didn't do the explosion sound or open her hand into an explosive firework motion, but listen, I got a fist bump from Meg Whitman! I'll take it.

Post–fist bump, I all of a sudden retreated into my introvert mode, standing in the middle of a party with no idea how to keep the conversation going. Introverts, if you're out there, I know you feel my pain right now! So, I decided to ask a question that I actually really wanted to solve for myself and for all women. I knew Meg was usually asked business questions, but that wasn't what was on my heart to ask. I took a deep breath and used the Mel Robbins 5-Second Rule, a tool that's helpful when you might chicken out of doing something. I counted backwards: *five, four, three, two, one,* and then blurted out my question without allowing the time to second-guess myself. I blurted out, "Meg, I have a question and I might never get this shot again, so I'm gonna ask it. I've been blown away lately by how many women, almost everyone, no matter how successful they are, all have one thing in common — they've spent energy worrying about and being insecure about their body, weight, or appearance. In fact, almost all of the incredibly successful executives I know, and other hugely successful women — lawyers, CEOs — they all admit that they often measure their self-worth on any given day by what dress size they fit into. Meg, have you ever felt this way, or do you ever worry about these things?"

There was a brief pause. (Note — in that pause I worried about everything from *Does Meg think I am crazy?* to *Did she just lose her respect for me as a businesswoman?* to *Does she want to take her fist bump back?* to *Maybe, like almost every woman I know, Meg is insecure about her body/weight too and is angry that I asked her and she doesn't want to admit to me, a total stranger, that she does spend time worrying about it* to . . . well, you get the picture.) The brief pause felt like an hour, and I couldn't wait for the answer. Did this business mogul spend time worrying about her body and weight too? It seemed as if the whole room went silent for a moment. Then Meg looked at me and very directly said, "No."

I said, "Really?"

And then she proceeded to say something that was so simple, yet so profound. Something that has been one of the biggest lightbulb moments for me. She said, "Something has to give. And something had to give. With everything in my life I had to decide what had to give. I have kids. And a career. I couldn't keep my house the way Martha Stewart would. Things have to give. And that wasn't something I worried about."

Whether out of necessity or choice, she had figured out that she couldn't give her energy and time to worrying about things like her weight of the moment or what her house looked like and still accomplish what she needed to in her career and parenting and other aspects of life. Now, I should say Meg seems to be in great physical shape and, who knows, her house is probably in great shape too, but the point is that she said she couldn't give either her focus. Because the things we focus on come at the price of other things that we then can't give our time/energy/focus to. She made that choice knowingly. But so many of us — often unknowingly — feel like we have to do it all and end up feeling like we're failing at everything. Or we choose to spend time worrying about our body/weight/appearance, or what someone else is going to think about us, or if someone else likes us, or those internet haters/trolls who say hurtful things, or all of the other things that don't serve us, every single day.

BUT something has to give! So that means if we're worrying about weight/body or other people's opinions or any of these other issues, it's coming at the price of something else we could be spending our energy on. Big picture, we know which things really don't matter in life. Let's take body image — we often obsess over it, spending money on diets, going down social media rabbit holes reading about diet trends and success stories, searching for clothes to make us look thinner. What price have we paid for the energy we've given this? Think about the things we focus on that take our time, energy, and hard-earned money that don't serve our souls or our dreams or our health and well-being or others. As Meg so brilliantly pointed out, something's gotta give. She chose not to worry about body image or appearance/weight or how her house looked. And instead she used that energy to raise her family and also become one of the most successful businesswomen of all time.

Then this question hit me, thereby prolonging the huge ah-ha moment. How much time do women actually waste on things that don't help us and each other move forward? Think about quantifying and adding up all the precious hours and hard-earned money spent toward things that don't really matter, like what we're going to wear based on what dress size we fit into, or how we're not (fill in the blank) enough. I feel sick thinking of the hours I've wasted on what size I am and how to change it. All those hours, and the opportunity cost of them, for me, for virtually all of us. All of that time could be going toward things like education, or a career, or a cause we're passionate about, things that actually serve us or others. As women, so many of us are taught to not leave the house without looking nice. So many of us are raised, whether it's by well-intentioned people who love us or by society in general, to be perfectionists and people-pleasers. And to be nice. And not take up space. And cross our legs. And as we get older, we learn we need to shrink to be pretty. Literally to get thin and take up less space on this earth (I've fallen victim to this for years), even when for many of us it comes at the price of our health and physical energy and time. Then we learn to wear high-heeled shoes (me too) for our legs to look longer and thinner. Those ridiculous shoes keep us from being as physically able as we could be. Think about it. We now take up less space and we slow down. Then we get long, often fake, fingernails. But those make our hands less physically able. These acrylic nails (for years of my life I always got the French manicure style — you know, with the white tips!) also take our time and money. I mean, these things are great if they truly bring you joy, or help you express your individuality. For me, they usually only felt like obligations to meet some expectation I'd given myself.

I realized that those years of wearing the same black pants and shirts and my hair in a bun were a survival tactic because something had to give, and I couldn't give time to hair and wardrobe choices and still have energy to ideate and create and drive the business. I've never loved spending hours getting ready, which is why I created and launched products that could save time and were super quick and easy to apply. I also truly believe my rosacea is beautiful, with or without makeup, and that every person is beautiful with or without makeup. To me, makeup is an optional expression of individuality, almost the way clothes are. Some days you feel like wearing sweats or wearing no makeup. Sometimes you feel like dressing up or spending extra time perfecting an eyebrow arch. I had learned through the years of working with Look Good Feel Better™ (the charity we've supported since

Day One that helps women face the physical effects of cancer) that the simple act of applying makeup can boost your confidence, not just because of how you look but also because the time spent doing it is an acknowledgment that you're worthy of that self-care. I thought I was in a good place when it came to deciding what I wanted to trade my time for and what felt worth it. Some days I got way more joy out of wearing sweats versus making sure my accessories matched my outfit. But I realized in that moment with Meg Whitman that when it came to body and weight, I wasn't there yet. It had consumed my thoughts and time and energy in a joy-depleting way for as far back as I could remember.

"Something had to give." I stood there talking to Meg Whitman, contemplating all the hours of my life I'd given up, even that very day, to look the way I did and fit into the dress the way I did. Those were hours that could have been spent in so many better ways. And listen, there's nothing wrong with spending time getting ready, or spending time any which way you want to spend it. Whatever you decide is right for you. Some people love the artistic expression of hours of glam. For them it's a good use of time because it fills their soul. But in that moment, I realized I needed to do some major soul searching about what was right for me. Because whether we like it or not, we can't do it all. It's impossible. If we try to do it all, something's gotta give. If we're trying to balance it all perfectly, likely everything will lose, and we'll be feeling like a failure all the time.

When I look back on my journey of starting my company in my living room, then working nonstop for over a decade to grow it, a lot of things had to give for me to successfully grow my business at that rate. And when I think about it, truly, I've never successfully achieved balance. I was a great CEO, but I wasn't present for my friends and family the way I wanted to be, I wasn't a present and connected partner to Paulo, I wasn't a great owner of a body or steward of health, I lived out of a suitcase, and my house was often a mess. And even though on the outside everything looked like a success, I felt like I was falling apart on the inside. Because I thought that there was this thing called balance and I wasn't achieving it.

But I don't think achieving balance is possible. I believe balance, as it pertains to juggling all the important aspects of our lives equally, is a lie. And when we believe that lie is a truth, we end up feeling like a failure all the time. And feeling that way takes even more energy, which means even more has to give. If we're feeling like we're failing all the time, it means we're feeling that way in the presence of our kids, on date night with our partner, and in the time we carve out for self-care. So it means we're actually robbing ourselves of being fully present in all of those moments. This is a lesson I wish I had learned so much sooner in life. But it's one I know now.

We have the power to decide where our focus and energy go. And we need to choose it carefully, because something else will give when we make this choice. Once you choose what matters most to you in life and where you want to focus your time and energy, then you have the opportunity to do your best at being present in the moment. When you're at work, be all-in and fully at work. When you're with your kids or family or friends, put your phone away, don't allow yourself to think about work, and be fully present and all-in with your family. When you're carving out time for true self-care, be fully present and fill yourself up unapologetically. Realize you will never be able to do all of these things in balance. If you believe the lie that you will, it can rob you of ever being present and truly enjoying all of the most important areas of your life.

I've come to believe that not only is balance a lie, it can be a form of self-sabotage that so many girls and women fall victim to. Instead, believe in the power of choosing your focus and being intentional with your energy. And being present in the moment! Because no matter what, something's got to give.

Meg Whitman likely had no idea of the impact her wisdom and mentorship in that moment had on me. Mentorship, in all its forms, as both a mentor and a mentee, has significantly shaped my life. Whether it's from a chance encounter like I had that day with Meg; an ongoing mentoring relationship with a colleague, friend, or boss; another entrepreneur who I mentor; or a mentor from afar, perhaps someone whose book I once read and still to this day have never met. We can all learn from each other, teach each other, inspire each other, and impact each other's lives. We are all in this together.

# FOURTEEN:
## *BELIEVE* IN GIVING
## WHAT YOU NEED

To let love be the answer no matter the
question . . . .
— CLEO WADE

"I'm good, thanks. How are you doing?" I
waited for a response. There was an odd
pause and the barista looked caught off
guard, as if the question took him by surprise. I felt the habitual pull of my cell
phone and was about to look back down,
when he smiled and said, "Actually, it's my
birthday so it's a great morning."

"Well, happy birthday," I said.

"Thanks, you're the first person I've told."

I love moments like this, when two people
connect, and they hear and see each other. I
realized that morning, in the long line for
coffee, that I felt a bit disconnected from
the feeling of being alive. I mean, how often
do we go through the coffee line on auto-
pilot, not even making eye contact with

anyone else, not because we don't want to but because we're numb or busy or distracted? And I've learned this powerful lesson in life: If you want something, or need something, give it. And you will surely get it. I've gone through periods of time in my life when I wondered why I wasn't feeling life's moments more, or wasn't feeling more joy, and learning this lesson — to give what you need — has been a tool to help change that for me. Sometimes the simplest lessons can transform our lives the most.

This has become a guiding principle in my life and has proven true time and time again. If you're saying, "What the heck are you talking about? How can I give something I don't have?," let me explain. I promise you this will make sense, and when it does, and if you start to practice it, like me, you might find it game-changing.

My dear friend, best-selling author, and one of the most impactful human beings I know, Brendon Burchard, says, "At the end of our lives we all ask ourselves three questions: Did I live? Did I love? Did I matter?" I believe we can achieve all three of these things each day, simply by giving appreciation to another person. Imagine if every time we thought something authentically positive about another person, we made the effort to tell them. The key is it has to be 100 percent true. I've found that doing this changes so many people's lives, including our own. If you like a stranger's hair in the coffee line one morning, tell her. If the checker at the grocery store takes great care to say hello to each customer, tell him you see him and how great he is at brightening everyone's day. Send a text message to someone you authentically appreciate, telling them why. When a coworker shares a smart idea, celebrate them. If you notice someone who's all alone at an event or gathering, go up and say hello and tell them that you see them. (Even if you're an introvert!) I incorporate this practice into my life and it brings me such joy. And purpose.

I've always felt that, especially as women, we are born confident — and then we learn not to be. Words have so much power. And sometimes we all need to be reminded of our power. Sometimes we all need someone to believe in us, so that we more easily believe in ourselves. That doesn't make us weak; that makes us human. We're made to be in community. We need to uplift each other, as fellow human beings, in this shared experience. We are each a steward of the power we have to lift each other up. And it's free to use! Living by this practice has truly been life-changing for me, on more days than I can count. And this lesson was brought to life so beautifully and powerfully on one of those days, when I had the chance to meet former first lady Michelle Obama at a launch event in Los Angeles for her book *Becoming.*

The day of the event, my eyes were swollen and puffy from crying all morning, and I was just trying to hold it all together. My mom, Nina, had been in and out of the hospital all year, and that week she was back in the emergency room. She has an autoimmune disease called scleroderma that causes the tissues in your body to harden, and the more the disease progresses, the more painful it gets. The morning of the event, I was having flashbacks to riding in the back of an ambulance with her on the way to the emergency room, always overwhelmed by the fear that she might not make it back home. For a few years up to this point, I'd been in that new season many of us go through when our parents get older, or face health challenges, and we have a kind of emotional role reversal where we instinctively worry about and feel we have to start taking care of them. What made it even more difficult this day was that I was in Los

Angeles and my mom was across the country in New Jersey. I wasn't there with her, or even in proximity to her, and felt helpless. I almost didn't go to the event that day, but the gift of being able to meet Michelle, a woman whose strength of character and generous heart had always inspired me, just like my mom's had, felt like a bright light during a difficult moment.

While there were tens of thousands of people packed into the stadium to hear her speak, the tickets I had came with the opportunity for me and my friends and Paulo to go to a meet and greet before the onstage event, while the audience was finding their seats. I was directed to a special line when I arrived, and there were about one hundred other people in this line, all waiting to meet Michelle. Secret Service agents engulfed the space, and as we got closer to the front of the line, we were asked to place all our belongings, including our phones, in a special secure area. We were instructed to step up to Michelle when directed, on the step-and-repeat photo wall (a wall with a special backdrop — you know, the kind of wall you see behind all the photos taken of celebs on the red carpet). We were told clearly that we would have just a moment to say hello and then pose for the photo, and under no circumstances were we allowed to hand Michelle anything, like a business card or gift.

As I watched the line move in front of me, I started seeing people walking back from having just met her. Many were crying; others were squealing with delight that they had met someone who meant so much to them. It's important to note, this story isn't about politics or political affiliation. If you happen to have seen that now famous moment that made the news at John McCain's funeral, where former president George W. Bush passed former first lady Michelle Obama some candy, it's one of my favorite TV moments of all time. I believe that we can and should all have true friends in our lives who might not vote the way we do, or look like we do, or love like we do, but who are good human beings like we are and who believe in the power of love and humanity like we do.

As the line moved closer, and I got a glimpse around the corner to the room where she was standing, I wondered how she was feeling. She smiled and shook hands graciously in the few seconds people were allowed to say hi and smile for the photo, before a security team ushered them quickly to move on. It was a well-oiled machine. I wondered what I would say to this incredible, powerful woman whose contribution to the world I truly admired. What could I possibly say in just a few seconds that would matter?

I recalled my own experiences of being in similar situations meeting our amazing customers at IT Cosmetics events and what I've heard from friends with public jobs who have also greeted fans or customers at a step-and-repeat. I imagined how she might be feeling after giving her energy individually to so many people, so I decided I wanted to say something to her that hopefully uplifted her or brightened her day in case she needed it. I also decided to give what I needed. I truly needed to raise my own spirits that day, so, living by this principle, I decided to pray about it. "God, please give me the right words to say. Help me give her something that she actually needs to hear or would enjoy in some way." I wanted what I said not to be for me, but for her. I could never have predicted what was about to happen . . .

I was next in line, and my heart fluttered with anticipation. I had once seen a sitcom episode where the character about to reach the front of the line kept letting people go ahead of them so that they got the continuing thrill of being next in line! I literally felt like doing this, though I'm sure the Secret Service wouldn't have been so keen on the idea. When Michelle's team gestured over to me that it was my time to step out of the "next in line" position and walk toward her, I still had no idea what I was going to say, but I had faith the right words would come out. My eyes met Michelle's, and I felt her strong, kind presence instantly. And just as I opened my mouth, she spoke first. And in that moment, she said something that astonished me.

"You have such a light inside of you," Michelle Obama said to *me* as I walked up to her on the step-and-repeat. I felt as if time stopped. I remember saying the words "thank you," while being overwhelmed with surprise. And I have no idea what I said after that. She smiled at me with fully present and kind eyes, and her team immediately made it clear that we needed to stop talking and smile for the photo. We did, and then I thanked her again.

My entire intention had been to somehow say something that was of value to *her,* just in case she needed it, and what happened is she did that for *me.* She called something out in me that made me feel so special. That reminded me of who I am, and what's inside of me, on a day when I was tempted to forget. She said exactly what I needed to hear in that moment, and especially during such a difficult day. When we do this for someone else, we have no idea of the impact it just might have on them, and on the people around them. I called my mom from the event that day. "Mom, I met Michelle." My mom cleared her throat; I could tell she was mustering up extra strength to be able to project volume into her voice so I could hear her.

"Oh, Jay . . . that's wonderful. How was she?" she asked.

"Mommy, she was amazing. And beautiful. Just like you."

Earlier I talked about the power of turning down the volume and taking your microphone back from the people you don't want speaking into your life. When you give what you need, it's a way of using your own microphone to uplift others. It's also incredibly powerful when we turn *up* the volume on the right people and right words, whether it's in the form of helpful advice, valuable ideas, or inspiring and uplifting moments. After that day, I did something I make a practice of whenever someone says something that uplifts me or inspires me. I intentionally decided to let Michelle's words take root by remembering them often and almost ingraining them in my mind. On days I need to lift myself up, I recall those words and hit the repeat button on them. This practice, of turning up the volume on the positive things that empower us, is like creating a playlist of positivity that we can keep in our toolbox for the days we need it.

We all have a light inside of us, not just to light the way for ourselves, but also to illuminate the beauty in others. And some of us dim it, or we haven't sparked our light in a long time, or we start to doubt how strong our light is and how brightly it's capable of shining. Or we forget we have that light at all. I've always believed that when you give an honest compliment to someone else, you change the world for the better in that moment. Because we are all connected to each other. And what we give, we get. When we authentically (it can't be fake or dishonest, it has to be real) uplift another person, we get lifted up ourselves! It's like the golden rule. It's like Newton's third law. Whether or not we see it right away, it's already true.

If you want something, the best way to get it is to give it. Now, in life, this doesn't always happen so instantaneously and obviously as it did with Michelle that day, but it does always happen eventually. I've seen this lesson as a common thread woven through great human beings and great leaders: to live life in a way that sees and serves others. Think about it. Almost everyone who has made a great, positive impact lives this way. The aunt or grandma in the family who everyone is devastated to lose. The teacher or school janitor who gets that big, tearful celebration when they retire — you know the kind, where even past students show up because they lived a life where they truly saw, cared for, and served others. From Oprah showing up day in, day out for her talk show decades after she never needed to work another day in her life to the bus driver who forgoes retirement because they cherish giving a smile and hello to every passenger each morning knowing it might be the only one they get that day. When you truly see and hear another human being, it's often the greatest possible gift you can give them. And yourself.

The same is true in business. As a boss or leader, one of your jobs is to make sure your team feels seen. And heard. And safe. And like they matter. And you have to really mean it. In addition to higher morale and lower turnover on your team, the added benefit is that since you get what you give, you are then even more strongly and authentically seen and heard and valued as a leader. It's one of the ingredients that was key to us having extremely low turnover at IT Cosmetics. And for something that seems so simple, it's amazing how rare it is, especially inside leadership structures in companies.

Giving what you need is such a simple but powerful practice. When you're intentional about it, I've found it to be even more powerful. For me, it's been transformative to look up from my super-addictive cell phone screen and take a moment to feel the day, to pay attention to whether I'm truly feeling alive and am truly seeing and connecting with other human beings. When I'm having a hard day, trying to give joy or acknowledgment to someone else is one of my tools to snap out of it. And often I realize I'm not practicing it enough and that's why I'm feeling off.

The best part is, we all have the power to give in this way right now. If you want friendship in your life, be a friend. If you're feeling lonely, give community to someone else. If you feel like your voice isn't being heard, ask someone else to share their story with you and then fully listen. If you're not feeling beautiful, see the beauty in others and tell them about it. If you're feeling unseen, let someone else know that you notice them. If you don't yet have the material possessions you desire or as much wealth as you want, share what you can with someone in need. Believe in the power of everything inside of you right now that you have to give. And if you want or need something, give it. Then watch what happens.

# Fifteen:
## *BELIEVE* IN THE POWER OF LETTING YOUR LIGHT SHINE!

"I love your dress."

> *"I got it on sale."*

"You should be so proud of yourself."

> *"Oh, I had a lot of help."*

"You're beautiful."

> *"No way, I've gained so much weight."*

"Your husband is so thoughtful."

> *"Yeah, but he can't change a lightbulb to save his life."*

"Your hair looks great!"

> *"I totally need a haircut."*

"Your child is so clever."

> *"Oh, but she's a handful, and I'm a hot mess today."*

352

*"Your skin is so beautiful."*

*"Seriously? Do you see this zit?"*

Have you ever responded to a compliment by putting yourself down? So often women bond with each other over perceived problems, not successes. We learn early on to fear that sharing our personal victories puts us at risk of disconnection and alienation.

Women are often raised to play it small and be nice and polite and not offend anyone. So on the one hand, I'm bold and fearless and a rebel and filled with the unremitting grit to build a successful company from the ground up, and I'm happy to share, mentor, inspire, and empower others by talking about how I did it; and on the other hand, I was taught to feel uncomfortable talking about my actual success without it feeling boastful. And I was definitely taught that you never discuss financial success, and that anything to do with wealth should be kept as private and discreet as medical records. I was raised to think that people who broadcast their own success are arrogant, insecure, and pretty much total jerks.

So when I got the phone call from *Forbes* saying they were going to put me on their "America's Richest Self-Made Women" list,

I didn't call back. I had my company's head of public relations let them know that I wasn't interested in commenting on my personal net worth, figuring if I didn't participate, they wouldn't include me. The reporter followed up with an email saying they had gathered enough concrete data to publish their estimate of my net worth anyway, and that it was going to press whether I commented or not. *What the &\*$@?* I thought instantly! As my heart beat faster, I continued to read the email. The reporter's message said that since it was going to print no matter what, it would be ideal for me to confirm the details of my assets. I panicked. Thoughts raced through my head, like *How do they know what my actual net worth is?* and *There were so many bankers and lawyers involved when I sold my company, but who could have shared info like this?* and *There's no way I'm going to comment on such personal info!* and *Oh no, if they publish this, how is it going to impact my life?*

When L'Oréal included the $1.2 billion cash purchase price for IT Cosmetics in their press release and the story hit the news, people instantly came out of the woodwork asking me to pay off their mortgages, threatening to sue me, trying to extort money, asking me to cover their medical bills, and everything in between. But the sale price of a company is one thing; disclosing my personal net worth was entirely different! I told the *Forbes* reporter I absolutely wouldn't comment. This was a hard decision because even as a young entrepreneur, when I made cookies at home and sold them at school for $1 a bag, even then I dreamed of being on the cover of *Forbes.* So for *Forbes* to actually have any clue who I was felt like a dream.

I believe the reason my company is so successful is because of the great products combined with the authentic mission we have to shift culture, and to change the beauty industry on behalf of all women. Sharing that mission in *Forbes* would be an amazing moment and help accelerate it. In addition, I thought sharing some of the details of my own arduous journey as an entrepreneur could give hope to others. So I decided to tell the reporter that I *would* share my story, but I wouldn't ever talk about personal financial numbers. And we never did. She kept her word and didn't bring up the subject when she interviewed me, and her beautifully written story was inspiring and from a place of intention to serve other entrepreneurs.

BUT she told me that she still had to publish a net worth number, and since I didn't provide details, they would publish what they believed it to be based on the publicly available data. Here's the thing: There was no way for *Forbes* to accurately know my net worth. They knew the sale price of our company, but they also knew that by the time we sold, we had private equity partners and investors. There are people who sell their companies for $1 billion and get all $1 billion of it, and others who, after investors are paid, don't end up getting even $1 million. So what *Forbes* does is publish their best guess based on the data they collect and whatever sources and insights they believe to be accurate.

The day the *Forbes* list was released, there it was in print: "Jamie Kern Lima, CEO IT Cosmetics," then it listed their guess of my net worth. My team got the copy fresh off the press, and as they handed it to me in my office, my heart was in my throat and all I could say was, "WTF!" (Note: I built a company by asking God to use me and help me be of service in the most significant way . . . yet now I was blurting out WTF loudly in my office, and not just the three-letter acronym.) Why was this such a big deal to me? Why was I so torn between feeling proud to be on the list on the one hand (was that my ego?) and so embarrassed, mortified, and basically ashamed that I might come across as arrogant or showy on the other? Then I had thoughts like *I wonder if during those days as a waitress at Denny's I could have truly believed I'd one day be on the* Forbes *list?* and for a split second I had a small-minded thought: *I hope all those people who didn't believe in me see this!*

I've always believed in the powerful principle of this Lewis Howes quote: "A true billionaire is someone who positively impacts a billion lives." Beyoncé, Taylor Swift, Meg Whitman, and Oprah were on the list, and I knew I was in the company of women who made huge impacts. One of the best parts about monetary success is being able to use it to help people, the way Paulo and I have been able to do both during the time we owned and since we sold our company. That intention of serving people is what lights my soul on fire and has me jumping out of bed each morning. I don't measure success by the amount of money or job title you have. I truly view it as the measure of your meaningful service. But was that the real reason I didn't want to celebrate my business and monetary success in a public way? Or was it really that, as a woman, it's ingrained in me to dim my own light and call it humbleness?

Confession: in the past three years, since making the list each year, my public bio has read "Jamie's on the *Forbes Most Successful* Self-Made Women List" when the correct name of the list is *"Richest."* I replaced *richest* with *most successful* thinking it was more tasteful and humbler. For every TV appearance I've done, every keynote speech I've delivered, and every award I've received, the bio supplied by my company public relations team swapped out the word *richest.* Then, just this year, I had a HUGE epiphany! A legit "WHAT have I been doing?" moment. I realized that there is huge power in other girls and women seeing me, a self-made woman who started with virtually no money, on the *Forbes* RICHEST Self-Made Women List! Because when we see that something is possible, it's so much easier to imagine it for ourselves. Seeing what Oprah does in her career, for example, has helped me believe for my entire life that I can accomplish my own outrageously huge dreams as well.

To create a true cultural shift, girls and

women need to see self-made women who have achieved great business and financial success. I worked hundred-plus-hour weeks for ten years and powered through on grit and prayer. For over eight years, I spent countless nights sleeping in the QVC green-room doing more than two hundred live TV shows a year. I was pummeled with rejection from all angles for years. It took keeping my faith bigger than my fear and not letting myself translate hearing *no* after *no* into self-doubt, and that helped me eventually turn every single *no* into a *yes.* The power of women seeing other self-made female millionaires and billionaires is huge. Why had I been playing this down and even hiding it? Why had I been dimming my own light? Why hadn't I realized that I could help illuminate the path of possibility for other women?

When I told the reporter at *Forbes* that I wouldn't comment on my net worth, she mentioned that many of the other women on the list don't and won't either. And that it was a stark contrast to the frequent reaction from men who find out they're making the *Forbes* list. When I asked her what she meant, she explained that not only do men typically *want* to be on the list, they often complain that their net worth number should be even *higher* than the *Forbes* number, and very often go to extreme lengths to provide *Forbes* with financial records to prove they deserve, and then try to demand, a higher published net worth and ranking on the list. The difference in typical responses between men and women is crazy, right?! Or not! For so long women have been taught to shrink (literally), and that we need to be both beautiful and nice to conform to society's ideal of success. We're also often taught that we can't be more successful professionally or financially than our partners if they're male, because that dynamic would destroy the relationship. Similarly, men are often taught to measure their success based purely on financial accomplishment. They're also taught that they need to be the breadwinner. Even though in our conscious minds we know these are antiquated, limiting beliefs, our subconscious minds can still mistake these beliefs as truths. Society, and even our well-intentioned families, often broadcast them as true.

Think about it: even in the most viewed and common images on Instagram, a modern platform filled with all generations but primarily millennials or younger, images of what an aspirational woman is are often body- or appearance-based, or they model how to achieve perfection as a mom; meanwhile, men are pictured in front of monetary or professional accomplishments and images of success and money: cool cars, planes, or at work. Even when you see some hugely successful self-made women, especially in entertainment, they often still shrink themselves. I've seen photos of Hollywood power couples where the woman, often far more successful in business than her boyfriend or husband, is posed in a bikini while the guy stands physically above her, fully clothed in front of a plane, with his arms crossed. We should all be free to post whatever we want, wearing whatever we want, expressing our identities however we want — no judgment here — but what's glaringly missing from the overall picture, especially on the most popular social media platforms, is images of women achieving financial, business, and leadership success. When was the last time you scrolled through your social media feed and saw an image of a woman in front of her desk, or heading a boardroom, or in a business suit, that was celebrated by going viral or by getting millions of likes?

We each choose who shows up in our social media feeds, and we choose with free will to follow the people we follow. And when we follow someone online, it also means we're making the choice to fill our own energy with what that person subscribes to, from what they find funny to how they define success and worthiness. And when it comes to who you follow for business inspiration or motivation, consider this: Follow the people online who have actually done the thing that you want to do. Not the people who are just really good at talking about it. Every so often I like to do an inventory of the people I'm following, and just take a moment to pause and ask myself if I like the way it makes me feel after I see their content. Does it inspire me, uplift me, and fill my soul? Or does it tempt me to feel inadequate, empty or unworthy? Edit who you're following often so you curate the kind of energy and impact you bring into your life. This also helps protect your peace, your positivity, and your potential!

To shift culture and stop perpetuating these antiquated norms, it's so important that girls and women see a new picture of success. And that men do too. To me, that's the power of making it onto the *Forbes* Richest Self-Made Women List! Imagine how powerful it will be when all of us, and especially the next generation, are so comfortable with the concept of a successful businesswoman that business tips spread faster than dieting trends. I've come to see that lists like this help us get there.

While I still won't disclose or comment on my actual personal net worth, I now no longer hide that I'm on the *Forbes* Richest Self-Made Women's List. Sharing our victories, our accomplishments, and even our small wins can feel counterintuitive. I totally get it. Because we're taught to be modest and we're taught, especially as girls and then women, that sharing our wins is bragging and unbecoming. We're taught to minimize big wins and small wins. We learn to hide our talents and abilities. Even as early as grade school, I remember not raising my hand when I knew the answer. When I was awarded "Biggest Procrastinator" in high school, I didn't tell anyone that while I was definitely procrastinating at school, I also had three jobs and had saved up enough money to buy a car. And when I made the dance team in college but one of my good friends didn't, I told her the judges had made a huge mistake and I must have just gotten lucky that day.

We bond over gaining weight, falling off diets, how someone mistreated us, or how great a filtered (aka fake) photo looks on social media. And let's be honest here — imagine what happens to the girl who shows up to the group and says things like "I'm always naturally thin no matter what I eat. It's so great." Or "My marriage is doing so great; my husband just did all the household chores today and then wrote me a love note." Or even something less personal, like "The best parking spot opened up right in front of the coffee shop just as I pulled in today and there was extra money in the meter!" Think about how we're socialized to react to that. With thoughts that the person is gloating. We learn quickly that when we share complaints over how we couldn't button our jeans that week or how our house is a mess, other women relate and connect with us right away. Even when you believe you're a champion of women, this is still often how women bond. Over perceived problems and weaknesses, not over victories. This fear, that sharing our victories is like bragging and can disconnect and alienate us from each other, has got to end! Plus, sometimes when I see women doing this, it also can be to send the signal that they're not a competitive threat to each other. It's ridiculous that we ever need to worry about that. WTF (sorry, Grandma, but WTF!)!

Men are socialized to be so different. They learn to reward and celebrate each other for successes, whether it's being happy about gaining muscle at the gym or getting a great parking spot with free money in the meter. How often are men rewarded for putting themselves down?

For the sake of ourselves, our sisters, our mothers, our aunties, our stepmothers, our grandmothers, our great-grandmothers, our daughters, our granddaughters, and for all women, we need to change this. We need to celebrate our own victories with each other, and we need to celebrate *her* victory as if it's our own. Remember the idea of scarcity — that if *she* gets the one seat at the boardroom table it means I didn't get it? We think if she wins, it somehow means I don't. The opposite is actually true. The more she succeeds, the more space and opportunity there is for me to succeed. The more we celebrate our own victories and her victory, the more examples are out there for other girls and women to see! We need to change this, and it needs to start with you and me. Right now. Deal? And listen, it's not going to be easy. But it's gotta happen. To truly create change and shift culture around this, it's so important to believe that *your* victory is *her* victory! *Your* strength is *her* strength! And sometimes someone else has to see *your* win to believe it's possible for herself.

Next time you have a win or something great happens to you, whether it's big or small, share it and celebrate it with others. And if you feel strange doing it, then pick this book back up and reread this chapter! Share and celebrate your win, whether it's big or small. Do it bravely and confidently. Don't be tempted to keep it to yourself just so you don't make other people feel bad, or uncomfortable, or less than. They might react that way, but it's okay. When something feels too arrogant for you to reveal, or you're worried other people will get uncomfortable or not like you if you share your accomplishment, I get it. That's how we were raised to feel. And sometimes when you share something great that's happened to you or that you've accomplished, other people *will* get uncomfortable or insecure or they'll think you're conceited. Most often this happens because we were raised to play it small and be nice, quiet people-pleasers. But if you really think about it, people-pleasing, which on its face is polite and likable, can be seen as a culturally taught form of keeping you small. How can you rise to the top if you're constantly pulling yourself down? That might make *some* people more comfortable, but this isn't about them. So don't rob the people who need to be inspired by your story and hear it or see it to believe it's possible for themselves, just to make someone else more comfortable. One thing that helps me when I start to feel like I am going to play it small is to remind myself it's *not* about me, that any win can be a moment of inspiration and liberation for another woman, and so with that intention I share my victory.

It's not only about helping and inspiring other girls and women, it's also about doing this for yourself. And for the younger self inside of you. As a little girl, maybe you were scared and unsure of who you were and who you were becoming. Now is the time, as a woman, when you can reach back to your younger self and extend your own hand . . . to that little girl who learned to doubt the strength inside of her, who learned to doubt her own beauty, who learned to stay quiet when she knew the answer, who got put down for being herself and started believing the hurtful words. Reach back to that little girl, take her hand, and say, *"Come with me, we're stronger now. You're not alone. You're beautiful. God made you with a light inside of you destined to shine. You're worthy of using your voice, of knowing the answer, of shining your light so brightly that it illuminates the world."* Don't dim your light. Ever! Because when you dim yours, you dim hers! Believe in the power of letting your light shine. *Her* future, and yours, depends on it!

# Sixteen:
## *Believe* in Miracles . . .
## and in Oprah

You've always had the power, my dear,
you just had to learn it for yourself.
— GLINDA THE GOOD WITCH,
*THE WIZARD OF OZ*

For as long as I can remember, I believed I would meet Oprah one day. As a little girl growing up, she was my TV mentor. When I was home alone, which was a lot, Oprah was my sister, my friend, my mentor, my auntie, and my favorite teacher. Through her shows, and through her vulnerability and bravery of sharing her own story of struggles, insecurities, faith, joys, victories, and pain, I learned I wasn't alone in mine. She played this role for so many of my friends as well. When Natasha was growing up, Oprah was one of the few women on TV who looked like her and who wore her hair curly. For Natasha, seeing Oprah every day in her living room helped her believe she could have her own TV show one day and wear her hair curly too. And she did both of those things! And as all of my friends and I have grown up, and for so many women I know, Oprah's role as a teacher and mentor in our lives has never changed. I believe that she is one of the greatest living teachers in the world.

Of course, like just about everyone I knew, I always dreamed of meeting her. But unlike everyone I knew, I truly believed that I would. I never dreamed of her solving my life's problems or paying my bills, even though I could barely afford to pay bills most of my life. I never dreamed of her giving me a car. I just had this feeling like we were connected in some way. And if you're a lifelong viewer like me, you'll remember that moment in a Barbara Walters interview in 1988 when Oprah told her, "I always knew I was destined for greatness." I remember being a little girl, eleven years old, watching this and knowing that deep down inside I felt a very similar way. Oprah got so much flak in the press for saying that, which isn't surprising — people aren't used to women speaking that confidently about themselves. Society reacts anytime a woman shines her light brightly.

■ ■ ■

If you're an Oprah fan, you probably remember the hamburger lawsuit where she got sued by the beef industry for saying she would never eat another hamburger. And listen, no matter how you feel about the topic, to me that's the least relevant part. I remember being nineteen years old at the time and thinking, *WHAT, this is HUGE! SO huge on so many levels.* I mean, for a woman to have so much influence that simply speaking her opinion on national television got her sued? And not only a woman, but a woman of color. For her to have garnered so much influence that they sued her, simply for voicing her opinion? I remember feeling how meaningful that was, and what a victory it was for all of us women! And remember when she got attacked in the press for the segment she started called "Remembering Your Spirit"? The press said that she was getting all religious on people — this was before talking about spirituality and mindfulness were as mainstream as they are now. She's always been ahead of her time and never got distracted by what other talk shows or their hosts were doing, even during periods when those other shows were winning in the ratings. I'm sure this lesson from her planted a seed in me way back then for my approach at IT Cosmetics. I always told our employees to keep their blinders on and ignore what our competitors were doing. And that the greatest risk to our own success at IT Cosmetics would be getting distracted by the competition or letting their success tempt us to dilute our own authentic mission and our own secret sauce. Oprah's example taught me to instill this lesson in my company. And I know to this day that had we ever gotten distracted and focused on what our competitors were doing, we would never have grown to be a billion-dollar brand.

So by this point, you probably get how great her impact had been on my life, even though I hadn't met her. And then, are you ready for this? I had absolutely no idea that completely unexpectedly, out of the blue, on a day I was so burnt out and exhausted and hadn't even showered, I would MEET OPRAH!!! Here's how it happened. And here's what happened after it happened. Which is even more crazy. Or not. I mean, what's crazy anymore at this point?

My fortieth birthday was approaching, and

I was still working a lot. I had heard about an Oprah SuperSoul Sessions event happening in Los Angeles, so I bought tickets for myself and a few friends. I was going to be in LA for work, and the timing worked out just right. I had been to one other Oprah event in the past, at a stadium in Florida during her Live Your Best Life tour. It was packed with thousands of people and was really fun. This event in Los Angeles was at a theater on the UCLA campus, and Oprah was going to have several guest speakers and guests she interviewed onstage. The morning of the event, my excitement almost overwhelmed my exhaustion from working way too much. I put on my favorite green dress and wore flat shoes to the theater, with high heels in my purse to change into later. I had always worn heels on TV and in most business meetings and knew that sometimes the cameras panned to the large audience. I wanted to make sure my heels were on for that part, just in case. I brushed my hair back into a ponytail and put on my favorite ring and bracelet, both of which are engraved with "She believed she could, so she did." I've always believed in having reminders around that inspire you. That morning, Zega mentioned that she had gotten in touch with a friend of hers, also an assistant, who was able to get us better seats than the ones I had purchased and that our tickets were getting swapped, but that was it. I had *no* idea what was about to happen to me.

We arrived at the event and made our way to our seats. They were really great — the fifth row back and in the center, along the left aisle. I was so grateful that Zega had scored us an upgrade. Just as we were getting cozy, a young blond woman came up to Zega to say hello and then introduced herself to me. She said, "Hi, I am Oprah's chief of staff, Amy. These are her seats you're sitting in, and I'll come back at the lunch break to take you to meet her."

"WHAT???" I looked at her, and that was the only word that could come out of my mouth. Was this a dream? I looked over and Zega had tears welling up in her eyes.

Amy said, "You didn't know?"

"Know what?" I said.

She looked at Zega and said, "I'll let you tell her."

Zega explained that she had written a letter to Oprah's chief of staff. And I don't know what magic Zega worked, but somehow Amy had read it and shared it with Oprah. And somehow Oprah had decided to invite me to meet her that day. To this day, Zega won't tell me exactly what she wrote in that letter. But she did say that she shared the story of how on her first week on the job with me, when we got our coffee at a Starbucks drive-through, the paper cups had sleeves on them with quotes from Oprah. I proceeded to tell Zega about the impact Oprah had had on my life as a mentor from afar. Then Zega told me that she wasn't an Oprah fan. *What?* I was shocked. Say it isn't so! I continued to gush about all the ways that Oprah is one of the world's greatest living teachers, and Zega eventually grew an appreciation for her. Anyway, apparently she shared that story in the letter she wrote, and she also shared a bit about my story and the kinds of things I've done for other people, and how meeting Oprah would be the greatest gift Zega could ever give me. Zega had many friends who were assistants, but she didn't know anyone on Oprah's staff. Yet her letter had somehow risen to the surface.

See, here's the thing. At IT Cosmetics alone, we receive a nonstop inflow of thousands upon thousands of letters, stories, emails, and social media direct messages. Even if I had spent twenty-four hours a day seven days a week reading them, I wouldn't have been able to see 1 percent of them.

There were just too many. So now imagine Oprah. She's a million times more well-known than my company is, and she must get a million times more emails and letters and social media messages. On top of that, she gets them from every country in the world. And I knew this wasn't happening because I was a successful CEO; there are millions of those, and many much more successful than me, and most have never had the opportunity to meet Oprah. What are the odds of a single email from my assistant with no contacts there actually even being received, let alone read by her team and *her*? It's like one in a billion. Then when one gets read, what are the odds of it getting passed along to her? One in a million. Then, out of the surely countless ones she actually is aware of, what are the odds of her deciding to respond? I knew, in every ounce of my being, there was a reason bigger than myself that this was happening. And I knew God was in it.

In the audience of the event that day, I was mesmerized by how insightful the speakers were. Gary Zukav gave the most beautiful analogy of how to know when you're going in the right direction in life. He described it as being like a boat in water. We can feel when we're sailing in a way that's against the current, and it means that we're not going in a direction that's aligned with our soul. Like the opposite of flow. He said, "As you follow your inner sense of meaning, you are sailing in the same direction your *mothership* wants to sail." I also got to hear the powerful Angela Manuel Davis speak about the power of the words we tell ourselves about ourselves. And while I was doing everything I could to be present and take in all of these inspiring words from the speakers, I was also *COMPLETELY FREAKING OUT* that I was going to meet Oprah that very day!

Live for the moments you can't put into words.
— ANONYMOUS

A friend of mine had met Oprah once in a meet-and-greet event line, like the one I went to for Michelle Obama. And I guessed that was exactly what I should prepare for. I would likely have just two seconds to say one thing, then smile and take a photo, and step away. As the lunch break approached, the upcoming moment felt way too big for me to handle, to be honest. I kept remembering what Natasha always says: "Don't put anyone on a pedestal except for God." The truth was, in my journey of building IT Cosmetics, I'd met many A-list celebrities and almost never got nervous. I never felt like a fan. I was always open to meeting every person in the same way and with the same heart that I bring to meeting someone in line at Starbucks. We're all human and we all have the same feelings, thoughts, emotions, insecurities, and needs. But THIS WAS OPRAH! She'd been my mentor my whole life, without my ever meeting her. And now I was going to meet her.

And . . . the moment was upon us! The audience was dismissed for lunch, and Oprah's chief of staff, Amy, appeared at our seats to bring us backstage. If ever there was a moment to change into my high heels, this was it. But for some reason I decided to leave my high heels in my purse and stay in my flats to meet her. I can't explain this; it just felt right in my heart. Maybe it was a way of leaving any semblance of a costume behind and baring my authentic self.

On the way backstage, I was taking deep breaths and praying. I couldn't even play it cool at that point. I looked ahead to see the long step-and-repeat line that I was going to join, but it never came. There wasn't one anywhere in sight. Instead, we got to a door and Amy said, "This is her greenroom. She's right inside. Are you ready?" WAIT, WHAT???

"What do you mean?" I asked her. "Like, you mean she's inside and this is her room?"

Amy said, "Yes," with a big smile.

"Dear God, please give me the right words to say so that I can impact Oprah in some way, like she's impacted me my entire life, and that Your perfect will is done, in Jesus's name, Amen," I prayed to myself as my heart beat faster than I could process. I asked Amy if it was okay for my friends to join me, as I knew this could be a once-in-a-lifetime moment for them too, and I wanted them to experience the same gift of this proximity beyond measure. She agreed.

One of my favorite things to do in life, anytime I get the opportunity to be in the room where an important event happens, is to bring at least one other woman with me when I can. I've earned my way, and sometimes was just given extraordinary grace to be invited into so many incredible business meetings, so whenever possible, I ask for a plus-one, specifically so I can bring another woman I mentor or another woman on the way up. I wasn't raised being exposed to incredible opportunities and often just the proximity to them is true power. So, whenever you are blessed, think about asking for a plus-one, and bring someone to the room with you. Whether it's to a business meeting, a really cool event, a gathering of friends, or in this case TO MEET OPRAH!

I'm physically reliving this as I share it with you. My heart is back in my throat. Okay, back to the story. Amy opened the door and I walked in. I felt like I was completely dreaming for the next few minutes. Stepping into the greenroom, I saw Oprah, all alone, sitting on a couch.

"Miss Kern," she proclaimed from across the room, and all I could think was *OMG, she knows my name.* I walked up to her, said hello, and gave her the biggest hug. And then I stood there looking at her and she put her hands on my face. I think she could tell I was practically out of my own body. And I am sure this reaction wasn't anything new to her. She was kind and gracious, and we took some photos together and with my friends. The only thing I remember saying to her that day was, "Let me know if I can ever be of service to you in your life in any way." At that, she looked at me, perhaps with a tiny bit of surprise, and replied, "I will."

We left her greenroom after a few minutes, and I couldn't comprehend what had just happened. I sat in the audience through the rest of the day's event, and can you guess what I did? Yep, I replayed those minutes over and over in my head and started second-guessing everything I did and said. (Isn't our inner critic so much fun?!)

The next day, I woke up both completely elated and then really, really sad. This doesn't make sense, but I was thinking, *What if that was my one and only chance to meet her, and that's all that I said?* I prayed about it, because I didn't want my self-doubt to steal my joy over something that was SO COOL. Then, to my surprise, I got a feeling deep down inside telling me with clarity that it wouldn't be the last time we'd meet.

Knowing that I hadn't shared with her any part of my story, or really anything at all; knowing that I was freaking out so much that I was practically out of my own body when I met her, I decided to take a huge chance.

I took a weekend trip to Sedona, Arizona, a place known for its healing energy vortexes, and my only goal on the trip was to write a thank-you email to Oprah. Thanking her for her time and for meeting me, and also sharing some of my actual story with her. I felt like I might have, at best, one shot to write this. Because even at that point, the odds of her chief of staff seeing it, let alone reading it, let alone sharing it with her, could again be very, very small.

I checked into an outdoor bungalow-style room at this spa, literally with the sole intention to process what had happened and to write that email. When I reached the front of the bungalow, I noticed that a deer was lying right beneath the deck of my room. She was lying with part of her body under the shade of the deck, but with her face and neck basking in the sunlight, staring at me. She stayed there most of the day. While I normally don't believe in this stuff, I started wondering if this deer's presence was a sign of some sort, or whether she was my spirit animal. I googled "deer spiritual meaning" and the first thing that came up was this: "Deer as a totem animal belongs to those who shine the light so others find their way home." Wow. With that, I prayed for the right words, and I wrote this letter. I'm sharing it with you because if I were reading this book I'd be thinking, *What the heck did you write to Oprah?* I'm not sure if the letter had anything to do with what happened afterward, but just in case it did, here is an excerpt from the email I wrote to Oprah that day:

**From:** Jamie Kern Lima
**To:** Oprah's Chief of Staff (to forward to Oprah)
**Subject:** Oprah - From Jamie Kern Lima (IT Cosmetics)

Dear Oprah,

Thank you. I know how precious your time and energy are, thank you for welcoming me into your greenroom to meet for the first time. I also know you're blessed to not have to do anything you don't want to do, and while I am filled with gratitude (what an amazing surprise!), I also believe it's not an accident you chose to say yes to us meeting. With gratitude and boldness, I want to share this with you. (I am singing *I surrender all* in my head as I write this.) My intention is that it fills a new space in your heart that is of great meaning to you, as our journeys parallel in many ways.

The way you explain how you were connected to *The Color Purple* before you got the call from Steven Spielberg is the best way I can explain this overwhelming energy force for good inside of me and the certainty I have about needing to share it with you. Not any of the countless people I meet while running my company. Not with anyone else. Just with you. I've always known this, but I haven't known why. Until I had an ah-ha moment this week at the SuperSoul Sessions event. Oprah, I now believe our motherships sail together (as Gary Z. would say), and here's why.

- We're both female CEOs who have built incredible companies and are responsible for hundreds of employees.
- I learned my parents were together just one time, in Santa Barbara, CA, and then never again. I was given up for adoption the day I was born. It is a miracle you and I are here. One sperm, one egg and BAM we are here!
- I began my career as a TV news anchor but didn't feel like it was where I was supposed to be.
- While growing my company I heard "no" more times than I can count, from Sephora and ULTA and QVC. But I was guided by a force and mis-

sion greater than myself. Today we are a top brand in all three.

- I'm the only person in my family to have this kind of success . . . or to even think the way I do. Neither of us grew up with an example or an expectation to be doing what we are doing.
- In the words of Dr. Maya Angelou we are both Phenomenal Women.
- I wear heels every day at work, but I wore flats to meet you. This only makes sense in my heart.
- How do I navigate how close I let employees get who are running my day-to-day business/life? What mistakes should I avoid making?
- Right now, TV is using me while I am still running my company (QVC to make money, infomercial selling product, etc.) and I'm working to use it instead, through an authentic and vulnerable connection with women. But I don't feel I've even come close to tapping into this overwhelming creative force inside of me, and I have some big ideas on how I can be using my visibility in ways that could truly inspire women to live their most aware, full, inspired, authentic lives.

- You once said you were born destined for greatness and I completely understand what you meant because I feel the exact same way.
- My favorite color is green.

*Pressed down, shaken together, running over . . .* In my most recent work, as founder of the beauty company IT Cosmetics, I believe I've changed the way millions of women look in the mirror, and I've used myself in full vulnerability and my issues (literally wiping off my makeup to bare my bright red rosacea and sparse eyebrows) as a vessel for women to see a different image of beauty. For the past several years, I've gone on QVC hundreds of times each year and my mission has been for every woman, even those with issues like me, to feel she's beautiful and she's worth it. And I take off my makeup to be brave and to tell her it's okay and we're all in this together! Of course our products are amazing, but it's been this authentic mission and message that has resulted in our company's success. On a daily basis I hear from countless customers of all ages on how they feel beautiful for the first time, or for the first time in a long time. I started the company in my living room, and now it's grown to be the 5th largest prestige makeup company in the US and just a few months ago I sold IT Cosmetics to L'Oréal. While L'Oréal has over 86,000 employees, they just made me the first female to ever hold a CEO title in their 107-year history. It is a fairy tale story that is true. And like you, I don't need to work another day in my life. Yet I know my work, and my calling, is just beginning! This overwhelming energy force for good is inside of me and has been *pressed down, shaken together* and is just starting to begin *running over*!

I know the next step in my journey is to connect with millions of women, to create better lives and be who they were destined to be to their fullest expression of themselves, in a way much bigger than what I am doing now. I believe I can be a vessel to make women's lives better and help them live their best life and I am willing to be vulnerable enough to ask the questions for them, and take the risks for them, and face the fears for them, and be used in that way, so that they connect with the best of themselves and change their awareness of what is possible! And I believe every step so far in my journey has led me to this.

Oprah, I am drawn to connect with you, the way you explain you were drawn to *The Color Purple.* I've even prayed to surrender it and for God to take it from me, because it feels too overwhelming.

When your chief of staff Amy walked up to me last Thursday to my surprise and said "You are going to meet Oprah today" it was like someone came to my track I was running on and told me Steven Spielberg is on the phone. And when we met, I really wanted to be protective of your energy and space in your greenroom, so rather than sharing all of this with you then, I prayed in that moment that it would be just the first time of many that I meet with you! I know this is a bold thing to say, but you created the Bold Move app, so you will understand! So when we met, I simply chose to say, "Let me know when you think of how I can be of service to you." Because I believe this will be true. Because I believe that our motherships sail together, so I know I will inevitably fill a space in your heart that is of great value and meaning to you.

I would be truly so grateful to have the opportunity to meet with you again sometime. And I have faith that you will know the answer to the when/why/how it happens.

      With an abundance of gratitude and love and joy and boldness and soul,
                  Your Mothership Sister,
                          Jamie

*With Oprah in her greenroom the day we met.*

That's the email that poured out of me, to her, that day. And I pasted in these two pictures at the end of it. Just before I prayed

*Oprah touching my face, as I prayed for the right words to say.*

and hit send.

A few months later my phone rang. It was Oprah's chief of staff, calling to say that Oprah wanted to invite me to lunch at her home.

"WHAT?" I said.

She said, again, "Oprah would like to invite you to lunch at her home."

This felt *way* too big for me to handle. Like this had to be God and I was being given this gift for some reason. Like maybe it was all orchestrated by God as a setup for something I was supposed to do, or a way I was supposed to be of service to her or to others that was beyond my imagination. I had no idea, but it felt like I was dreaming, and it felt way too big for me to process.

When someone welcomes you to their home, it's always nice to bring a small gift, like a candle or a bottle of wine. But what the heck do you bring Oprah? I'm seriously embarrassed to tell you how many hours I spent both worrying and praying about this question. Then getting mad at myself because, as you know, one of my favorite quotes is from 50 Cent, who said "Either pray or worry, but don't do both." But this time, I ended up doing both until I finally felt peace about the gift I was going to bring her. Well, actually, I settled on two gifts. First, a baby oak tree. I once had a spiritual reading done by a shaman who told me that I have a force inside of me that he described as an oak tree. He said I would never be happy in life unless I was like an oak tree with large branches, sheltering lots of other people. Since that day, oak trees have been special to me. I knew that Oprah also loved oak trees. So I got her a four-foot baby oak tree in a pot. Don't ask how hard that tree was to find. And don't ask about how, when I heard this tree was in Brentwood, California, I assumed it was the Brentwood area of Los Angeles, only to find out the day before the lunch that the tree was actually in the town of Brentwood, which is in Northern California. I ended up having one of my employees, along with an Uber driver, help bring it the six hours from Northern California to LA.

Any guesses what the second gift was? It will probably shock you. Remember the poster of that fearless squirrel that Natasha found? The one that she and I ended up channeling as our fearless alter ego over the years? Well, yep, my second gift to Oprah was a framed photograph of that very squirrel. Giving it to her felt both totally wrong and totally right. Because if anyone has figured out how to triumph over fear and to teach us all how she's done it, it's Oprah. Plus, if this was my one shot at actually getting to know her, I wanted her to see the real, authentic me. It's totally embarrassing to admit how many different frames I bought and tried out to find the perfect one to give her. My kitchen table may or may not have been filled with more than a dozen different green frames of that squirrel the day before our lunch. But no judgment, okay?!

For me, Oprah exemplifies the strength of character that's possible for us to achieve in our own lives. Before I met her, she was already the best teacher I'd ever had. And I'm going to venture to guess that I'm the only student that's ever brought her a picture of a squirrel with big balls as a teacher's gift.

> God can dream a bigger dream for you than you can dream for yourself. And your role on Earth is to attach yourself to that divine force and let yourself be released to it.
> — OPRAH WINFREY

Oprah went from being my mentor from afar to my mentor in real life. And so, as with all of my friends and all the people I know, I'm fiercely protective of her privacy. So I won't share any details of what happened at her home that day during lunch.

What I will share is that we spent a few hours together, just the two of us. And I don't believe it was random or an accident. I do believe I'm supposed to help be of service in her life in some way. I still have no idea how. What I do know is that on that day, I was given the gift of seeing an example of the kind of human being I strive to be. That day, I got a front-row seat to the kind of strength I strive to have. I got to meet a real-life example of a woman who knows who she is. Who has overcome people-pleasing and doesn't apologize about doing only exactly what she wants to do. I got to see an example of multifaceted strength of character that will inspire me to continue becoming all I was born to be. For that, I will forever be grateful. And will forever do my best to pay it forward however I can.

As we said goodbye that day, Oprah gave me her cell phone number and her email address. We've since texted and emailed and she's even given me raw, tell-it-like-it-is honest feedback on a few of my daytime TV interviews and appearances. To this day, when I text her and I see those three dots that appear on my cell phone screen indicating someone is writing back to me, I still freak out. I still think it's the best thing in the world. Sometimes I even screenshot those three dots as they happen, just to remind myself that the moment is really happening. And I still can't believe it's happening. Every time.

Sometimes I look at the things that have happened to me in my life and think, *You just can't make this stuff up. It's like a movie — it can't be real,* and then other times I feel the health effects of hundred-hour workweeks for years and the battle scars of burnout and I think, *Yep, I worked my butt off for every bit of it.* But the truth is God placed dreams in my heart and what I did right was to listen, then decide to believe it was possible.

Ever since I was a little girl, I'd always had the dream on my heart to meet Oprah. And I decided to believe it was going to happen one day. When we have big dreams, one of the easiest things we can do is talk ourselves out of them. To start believing that miracles don't exist. To start daydreaming less and settling more. To decide that if we don't get our hopes up, we won't be let down. If this is you, maybe today is the day to decide to start dreaming again. Dreaming impossible dreams. Dreaming God-sized dreams. Because after all, in Oprah's own words, "You become what you believe."

*My kitchen table filled with squirrels in green frames,*
*the night before my lunch with Oprah.*

*My friends celebrating as they walked me to my car to drive to Oprah's house. If you look closely you'll see the baby oak tree in a green pot on the floor of my back seat.*

*Standing under the oak trees at Oprah's home.*

# SEVENTEEN:
## *BELIEVE* IN A POWER GREATER THAN YOURSELF

> When fear knocks, let faith
> answer the door.
> — ROBIN ROBERTS

Have you ever felt a presence greater and more powerful than yourself? This first happened to me while I was working as a TV reporter covering a story about a horse ranch in Oregon. I spent three days there and will never forget them. This was a horse ranch that welcomed in children and teens who had suffered unspeakable abuse, most of whom wouldn't speak about their traumatic pasts with adults. The ranch paired the kids with rescue horses, each of whom had also suffered abuse and neglect. After the workers at the ranch introduced a kid to a horse, they would step away and let them be. From a distance, I witnessed kids opening their hearts up for the first time and sharing the stories of their pain with their horses. There were kids with tears streaming down their faces as they embraced their horses, and it was as if the horse and the kid understood each other with an unspoken grace and complete unity. These kids who wouldn't speak with adults were actually talking aloud, in confidence, to their horses. There was one horse that had been paired with a teenage girl named Gloria. They had such a strong bond that when the horse lay down in the pasture, she would lie against him and rest her head on his belly. I had never seen anything like that in my life. Waves of feeling tuned in to a much bigger presence came over me, and tears started streaming down. God was there. Outdoors, on a horse ranch. That was the first time I realized that God doesn't need a church or a specific building to show up. God is love, and God is everywhere.

At the start of this book I promised to share with you the story behind the story. The one that doesn't get clicks for headlines. The true, real, love-it-or-hate-it journey about how I learned to believe in myself, overcome some deep pain, build a billion-dollar company, meet some of the most incredible people along the way, and build the best life I know how in the process. So leaving out this part of the story would be like leaving out the coffee from the latte. It's what I know for sure is the power inside of me.

When it comes to faith, I'm not here to change how you feel. And no matter how you feel, I'll invite you over to eat cookie dough out of a bowl together, drink wine out of coffee cups together, and lounge around in our pajamas or furry animal zip-up onesies, laughing our butts off. I will love you no matter what faith and prayer look like to you, or if neither are part of your life. But I would be robbing you of my truth if I didn't share with you the role that my faith has played in shaping my journey. For many years, I trusted only myself in the driver's seat, controlling the steering wheel. And I turned to God only when I got a flat tire and desperately needed a spare. For a long time I didn't trust Him to take the wheel, and on many occasions I didn't even believe He existed at all. Everything changed in my journey when I let go and trusted Him to take the wheel, and together we've driven to places beyond what I could have imagined.

I was raised in a Lutheran church; we attended services almost every Sunday. Maybe it was just me being an immature child, but nothing that the pastor said ever really resonated with me. I couldn't relate to it and I couldn't understand a lot of the words, or the way words were used back when the Bible was written. My parents made me sit through the full sermon every Sunday growing up, but I really can't remember a single one that I understood or that struck a chord in me. I usually just spent the time scanning the church pews for cute boys and counting down the minutes on my watch until the sermon ended.

Then, as the years passed, I started to doubt God exists. I shared with you how Dr. Z challenged me to challenge Him. She said, "What makes you think God can't handle doubt?" and encouraged me to tell Him I doubted Him and to ask Him to prove me wrong. This advice she gave me was some of the most powerful I have ever received. Since that day, there have been more examples than I can count where things transformed my journey and all but said out loud they were God. And a few of them actually did say it out loud. Here's what I mean.

Remember the QVC host who discovered my product at the big beauty expo and told the buyer at QVC to give me a chance? She had been at the network for seventeen years, and then, shortly after I launched IT Cosmetics on QVC, she left her job there. I stayed in touch with her over the next several years. One day, out of the blue, I gave her a call just to check in, and to let her know that now, many years later, we were the largest beauty brand in QVC's history. I thanked her for loving our concealer so much that she told the QVC buyer to give us a chance. She said, "Honey, your concealer is great, and I still wear it every day, but that's not why I showed it to the QVC buyer that day." She went on to say, "I was walking the huge show and God clearly told me to go up to you in that moment. He said I needed to go help that girl, and that's what I did. He told me to do it, and all I did was listen."

*Whoa.* Her response gave me goose bumps all over. I guess God was listening when I asked Him to clearly *show* me He exists. That day she gave our concealer to the QVC buyer changed the course of my life forever.

Another example happened one day when I received a FedEx envelope and inside was a letter from Pastor Victoria Osteen. At the time I had met her just once, briefly, backstage at a Night of Hope event that I attended, along with tens of thousands of others, to hear her and her husband, Pastor

Joel Osteen, speak. Many months later, to my surprise, I received a letter. It was a beautiful invitation asking if she could interview me onstage, as the featured guest at her annual Women's Conference at Lakewood Church. Over six thousand women would be in attendance. I didn't even know she remembered my name or that I had started a company called IT Cosmetics. We were still a very small company at the time, I didn't have public success of any kind, and I wasn't yet that well-known even in the beauty world. Plus, I had never made a donation to Lakewood Church. By email, we set up a time to talk on the phone. I asked Victoria why she was inviting me.

She said, "God put it on my heart to reach out to you and invite you to be my guest."

Here's the thing: Watching Pastors Victoria's and Joel's messages and sermons over the years on TV really helped me get through some of the toughest times at IT Cosmetics and in life. But I had never shared that publicly with anyone, and on top of it, I always felt this unspoken pressure to keep my views on faith private in the professional world. I felt an instant anxiety when she asked me to speak because I had never previously shared anything as personal as my faith in a public setting. I had so much respect for Victoria and for what an honor this was that I had to be honest with her. I mean, I was really, really honest. I told her how speaking on her stage at Lakewood Church was something I thought only "a really, really good or perfect Christian" should do, and that I wasn't sure I qualified.

She started to chuckle but kept listening to me with kindness.

I said, "Victoria, I have to tell you the truth: I've never even read the entire Bible. And I think the six thousand women who attend the conference would want to hear from someone who has. Someone who is a way better or more advanced Christian than I am."

"God put it on my heart to invite you for a reason. The women in my audience don't just want to hear from perfect Christians, they want to be inspired by all types of women," she said warmly.

Even though I had a bit of fear about it, that quickly shifted to a gut feeling that I was supposed to say yes. So, I agreed to do it. And when I stepped onto her stage, I was fully and authentically myself, for better or worse. I shared my journey around faith — including how I'd been doubting it all while still trying to be open to God showing up in different ways in my life.

I'll never forget the moment when I looked out into the audience at the midpoint of our onstage interview and saw several of the friends I had invited to the event sitting there with tears streaming down their faces. For many people, when they feel God's presence, tears often just flow. Not all of the friends I brought that day shared the same beliefs about faith that I do, but they were all emotionally moved. It was one of the most memorable experiences of my life, and especially in my journey toward growing my faith. I felt fully in every ounce of my being that day that God doesn't need us to show up perfect, He just needs us to show up. For Him. And He will do the rest.

I've learned time and time again, especially in my journey of building IT Cosmetics, the truth of those famous words from Oprah: *God can dream a bigger dream for us than we can for ourselves.* As a girl who encountered mountains of rejection and underestimation, mountains populated by people who didn't believe in me, I can barely get these next words out without getting choked up. In 2020, just after I completed my three-year commitment to L'Oréal and stepped away from my role in the company to begin the next chapter in my journey, IT Cosmetics officially became the NUMBER ONE luxury makeup company in the country, according to NPD data. This means that in the luxury makeup category, IT Cosmetics became larger than so many of the brands I've admired my whole life, like MAC, Lancôme, Estée Lauder, Chanel, and Clinique. When I was a Denny's waitress, I used to save up my tip money to buy MAC lipsticks and Lancôme eyeliners! And now this makeup company I started in my living room had taken over the number one spot! WHAT?! This little engine that could, started by a girl with a dream, had now surpassed them. And here's one thing I'm certain of. When people call me self-made, I know that's only partially true. I'm partly self-made, but I'm mostly God-made. I made the commitment to work harder than I could imagine and to stay in faith. God made everything else . . . the favor, the open doors, the closed doors, the serendipitous connections, the grace beyond comprehension.

As my journey of faith evolved, I started to get more and more tuned in to what felt right for me, and I became able to pay closer attention to when God is speaking to me. Not literally; I mean, I've never heard

God actually talk. But I would describe it kind of like this internal knowing. Like the still, small voice of your intuition and your instincts, the ones that are always right. I've felt His presence both inside churches I've attended, like Lakewood Church in Houston, Texas; Mosaic Church in Hollywood, California; and others. And I've felt His presence in the simplest of surroundings, in nature, or in the sparkle coming from another person's eyes. As I pay more and more attention, I've grown to believe that God is truly all around us and is there waiting for us to see Him and turn to Him.

I shared the story with you about how powerful God's presence was throughout our journey of partnering with a surrogate and having our daughter, Wonder. And how, though initially I was filled with fear, God gave me and Paulo such a feeling of peace when we met our surrogate and her husband and family for the first time. Through that journey, she and I truly felt like us bringing a child into the world together was divinely orchestrated.

A year after our daughter was born, we continued to be part of each other's lives. Then one day out of the blue, she reached out and said that if we would like to have another baby, she would love to do it with us again. And that she couldn't imagine doing it for anyone else. After I cried like a baby myself, Paulo and I said yes to us all trying to have another baby together. And a year later we did. Throughout the pregnancy ups and downs, we all had this peace that God was in control. We prayed together (especially that this time the doctor would actually make it to the hospital room in time for the birth!) and felt so blessed to be on this beautiful, unconventional journey together. And together, we welcomed our second child into this world, our baby boy named Wilder. He's so sweet, so cuddly, and has Michelin-tire-man-style leg and arm rolls for days!

There are still questions where I'm asking for strong guidance. After we sold the company we had spent years of our lives building, Paulo and I had to face the toll that it took on our marriage, which had been put on the back burner for more than a decade. Work addiction and busyness, like other forms of addiction, numb and separate us from ourselves. They end up separating us from actually feeling, living, and experiencing our own real, raw emotions. We realized that we'd each put all of our energy into the company, and we needed to begin the journey of discovering who we were again, as individuals and as a couple. We realize now that we truly lost touch with both while building IT. Every day, I ask God to help guide us on this path of rediscovery and healing.

Even now, as a parent, my inclination is often to prioritize work in all its forms over my own family. When I get a phone call from one of the many women I mentor, or an exciting speaking engagement where I know I can serve and make a great impact, or have a board meeting or an investment call, I am so quick to want to attend to those things first, at the expense of missing an important family event, even now, *still.* So I pray for guidance and correction and for God to give me strength around this too. And now that I am a parent, I'm in even more awe of the strength it takes to be one. Of course it comes filled with so many blessings and of course it's all worth it, but what I can say for sure is this: I've been CEO of a billion-dollar company, and I'm a mom. Being a mom is harder.

And speaking of parenting, I've learned time and time again that the more I ask God to show up for me, the more He does. And sometimes in the most powerful and unexpected ways. See, I still don't know who my father is. But I also do. Here's what I mean by that. This is so deeply personal, but maybe, like me, you don't know who your birth father is. Or maybe you don't like who your father is. Or maybe you don't have a good or loving father or mother. Or maybe you have a parent who has hurt you. Or who doesn't deserve to be your parent. Or there is some question mark or blank space in your life that you're not sure how to fill. Not knowing who my father is hurt me deeply for many, many years. And it was hard to meet my birth mom and learn that she couldn't help me find him. I thought, *What do you mean, you don't remember his name? How is that possible?* I spent years, even after I met her, searching online for him using every possible piece of info she could share with me. I went back to the UCSB library to search the yearbooks, just in case I could find any guys who even sort of looked like me. Anytime a guy on TV had features resembling mine, I would google his story to see if he'd gone to UCSB. Like the expression made popular by Troy Dunn goes, I felt like I would never have peace until I had all the pieces. I even submitted my saliva to those DNA relative matching companies like 23 and Me and Ancestry,

411

and still haven't found matches for my birth father or his immediate relatives. I spent countless nights searching online for him. Sometimes I still do.

One night it got so painful that I started sobbing. And praying. I prayed for God to take this obsession away from me because after all these years of searching, it was causing me too much pain. And then, it was as if God showed up for me and hit me over the head with a ton of bricks. All of a sudden it all made sense to me. I did know my father. God is my father. I might not know who my father on this earth is, but I know who my REAL father is. In that moment, I knew I wasn't forgotten. In that moment, I knew that God created me on purpose. And that while I was just a sweet baby girl given up for adoption . . . my creator, my REAL father, knew who I was. He had put his stamp on me: Marked for greatness. Marked valuable. Marked worthy. (And, by the way, he put that same stamp on you too!) I suddenly knew and felt all of this. And in that moment, I started to heal.

I still might not know all the parts that make me who I am, but I know WHOSE I am. I know who my real father is, and I know He made me *on* purpose, and filled me *with* purpose. I know I'm not perfect and I've made a lot of mistakes in my life, but I don't believe God is there to show up for perfect people. I believe God shows up for imperfect people who love and seek Him. And at last, while I still didn't have all the pieces, I finally had peace.

If you feel like I felt for many years, and you doubt God, or that a power greater than yourself exists, and if it's something you want to change in your life or that doesn't sit right with you, then if you're up for it, you might want to try what I tried. Tell God you're doubting that He exists and ask Him to prove you wrong. Then be open to seeing it in the most unexpected ways. Some big, and some so simple and small. And while it might not happen overnight, get ready to sit back and watch what happens in your life when you start looking for God to show up. And if it's the first time, or the first time in a long time, that you're opening yourself up to consider faith in your life, give yourself some grace. As Tony Robbins says, "Faith unused doesn't expand, it shrinks," and the great news is, no matter your starting point, you'll soon be walking into a season of expansion.

Opening your mind and heart to a power greater than yourself can look different for different people. Some people meditate or have a spiritual practice or pray quietly, or dance and pray out loud. I believe there's no right or wrong way to pray; the only right way is the way that's right for you. When something feels right, you might end up making it a regular practice. Almost every day I pray that God brings the right people into my life and has the wrong ones leave. Trusting this has helped ease the pain of employees leaving for competitors. And in every case, even though I worried I wouldn't know what to do without them, we ended up finding someone even stronger for their role. This could be a great prayer if you're in the dating world, or in the process of looking for new friends, or if you are in the process of taking inventory of the people you surround yourself with. "God, please bring the right people into my life, and have the wrong ones leave." It's such a simple prayer, but for me it has been one of the most powerful. Another one I love is "Let Your perfect will be done." Especially when things aren't going my way, I've learned how important it is to trust God's timing on both open and closed doors. The more I tune in to trusting Him, the stronger and more accurate my intuition gets.

> Quit waiting for a plan; just go love everybody.
>
> — BOB GOFF

If you're just starting your journey of growing faith in your life, or maybe restarting your journey, my best advice is that you will know it's right for you when it feels right. Remember, you can't fake authenticity. Don't be scared and don't worry you're going to mess it up. You might try reading different books or incorporating a spiritual practice into your life or exploring different churches. You will know in your soul if it feels right for you. But wherever you end up, I believe having faith in a power greater than ourselves — whether you call it God or love or Creator or the Universe; for me that name became Jesus — is the only way to truly feel connected as a human being to all of humanity, the only way to know that our life is divinely orchestrated. And I believe if we don't have a spiritual foundation to hang on to, we can too easily lose ourselves. If I hadn't discovered that in my life, none of my successes would have happened the way they did, and, more than that, I wouldn't feel the connection to life and to others (you) that I feel.

■ ■ ■ ■

Listen, I definitely don't have all the answers. The general definition of faith, *believing in something you can't see,* means that none of us do. But I just feel a deep knowing that God loves us exactly as we are and that we don't need to change anything about who we are to be loved by Him. I have more flaws than I can count. I have strong faith, but I also swear (some days like a sailor). Sometimes I get off track and go days, weeks, or even months without praying. Sometimes doubt over my faith still enters my mind. I haven't yet read the entire Bible. And yet I know in my soul that God loves me. In my heart, I believe God loves us whether we're young or old, gay or straight or anything in between. I believe He loves us no matter where we are on the gender spectrum. I believe He loves us despite how we feel about the latest political debate or where we fall on the most controversial issues. He is there ready to love us, no matter our past mistakes or whether we find Him in a building, on a nature trail, or in the sparkle of our baby's eyes.

If God wanted us to all be the same, or to

all fit some definition of perfect, He would have made us all the same and all perfect. But He didn't. I believe He made us all with the intention of living out a journey of discovery, of growth, of overcoming adversity, of learning to serve others, learning we are all connected, learning to lose our own judgments, learning to love each other unconditionally, and learning to trust in Him. Maybe you are like I was for a long time, and you feel like you're too flawed or too imperfect or have made too many mistakes to be worthy of having a relationship with God, or to be worthy of praying and asking God to show up for you in your life. If you feel this way, I want you to know you're not alone. And it's never too late. And here's the thing: I don't believe God just shows up for "perfect" people; I believe God delights most in showing up for imperfect people who love and seek Him.

*You're rejected. You're fired. Your body's not right. You're not the right fit. It's a NO. It's a NO. NO NO NO NO NOOOOOOOOOO!* These are the words that so many other people said to me. But those aren't the words God says about me. Or about you. Don't let anyone tell you who you are. Who you are is between you and God. Ask Him for strength on the days you feel overwhelmed with doubt or anxiety. And then remember that you were made with all the strength you need. Ask Him for love on the days you feel lonely. And remember that He made you lovable and fully worthy and deserving of abundant love. When you're feeling insecure about your body, ask Him for the confidence in it that He had when He created you. I believe He'll tell you that He made you perfectly, in just the right proportions, and that He sees the dimples on our thighs with as much pride as we see the dimples on children's faces.

I believe God is looking at you right now, saying, *Wow, she is beautiful. She is my perfect creation. I gave her all those things that she perceives as flaws, but I wish she knew that she is perfectly made in my image.* Like a proud father who delights in your talents and gifts, He sees every move you make as you move toward who He created you to be. In fact, I believe He's glancing down on you right now, beaming with pride, because YOU are the apple of His eye. I believe He's watching you read this book, watching you challenge yourself to grow into the woman He called you to be, and that He's got the biggest smile on His face the way parents do when they watch their baby take its first steps. I believe He'll tell you that He doesn't make mistakes. That He made us in His image. That He made us from, in, and of love.

See, you might have been underestimated time and time again by others, and even by yourself, but even in the moments when you say *I'm not enough,* I believe if you ask God right now He'll tell you He made you *more than enough,* and you have everything you need inside of you already. And no matter what faith looks like to you, these words have been life-changing for me anytime I've started to underestimate myself, or feel unqualified. If you often feel self-doubt or unqualified to go after your dream or your calling, these famous words could be life-changing for you too: "God doesn't call the qualified . . . He qualifies the called."

If you have a dream on your heart that you can't seem to shake, to me that's a calling. And if you have a calling, I believe "God doesn't call the qualified . . . He qualifies the called" means you are therefore already qualified. You were born with everything you need inside of you already. And I believe one of our greatest journeys in this life is to learn to believe that for ourselves.

# EIGHTEEN:
## *BELIEVE* YOU ARE ENOUGH . . .

The longest journey we take as human
beings is the eighteen inches from our
head to our heart.

— UNKNOWN

I have had Oprah's invitation to call her
personal cell phone number for almost three
years, yet I haven't called it a single time.
We've texted and emailed, but I've never
actually dialed her number. You're probably
thinking, *What! Why not? You're crazy!* Well,
want to know why? It took me a while to
understand the reason, but when I did, I
wasn't proud of it.

I haven't called Oprah because deep down
inside there are still parts of me that don't
think I'm truly enough and worthy. I still
can't fully receive it. And even though I
know in every ounce of my being that she,
or anyone else, would be so blessed to have
me as a close friend, even though I know

I'm a fiercely protective, loyal, kind, empathetic, generous, and incredible friend and the kind of person who genuinely wants the very best for others, there is still something deep down inside of me that isn't convinced I'm worthy enough to call her. I still don't feel like my vibration is high enough to be in the same space as hers. Clearly, it's an internal narrative I've somehow invented that I need to resolve. Because I know it's simply not true. Yet, while I know that, I don't yet fully embrace it. Not calling Oprah is just a symptom of a bigger issue. This deep feeling of not-enough-ness also plays out in other areas of my life, including my battle with weight and emotional eating. Sharing that I still struggle with the feeling of not-enough-ness is perhaps deeply surprising coming from a CEO and/or an author of a book about believing in yourself. While I've been able to overcome so many limiting beliefs in several areas of my life, some are still works in progress. And I want to share this in case you see your own story in mine. If you do, my hope is that we're both on the journey to heal. The journey to the true realization that we're enough as we are.

The best way I've ever heard this self-doubt and struggle with self-confidence described is that we all have a deep belief about our own value, and anytime we achieve something that's *above* what we think we deserve, we sabotage it. Similarly, anytime we are given something that's *less than* we believe we deserve, we find a way to improve it. Many teachers and thought leaders use this helpful analogy: Imagine it as if we all have our own automatic thermostat. Think about how a thermostat works — imagine a room in your home, with a thermostat that you set at 74 degrees. When the room gets too hot, let's say the temperature rises to 80 degrees, that thermostat kicks in and the AC goes on, lowering the room temperature back down to 74. And if the room gets too cool, let's say it falls to 69 degrees, the thermostat kicks in, the heat goes on, and the room warms back up to 74. That number you set on that thermostat keeps the temperature of the room exactly where you set it.

Now imagine that your own self-worth, or what you believe you deserve and are worthy of, is like your own internal thermostat. You've set it at a number, whether you realize it or not. That number is the level you've subconsciously landed on for your own worthiness. So, let's say, for example, you feel you're a 75 degree-er. Then something great is going on with you, like you're sticking to a healthy eating plan and getting in shape or getting an *A* on a school paper when you define yourself as a *C* student or seeing a guy who treats you super well. Let's say whatever's happening sets you flying high at 85 degrees, but you feel uncomfortable at that temperature because it's out of the norm of what you believe your worthiness is, so you are compelled to lower the situation back down to that 75 degrees of worthiness. You return to the unhealthy habits. You get a *C* on your next school paper. You decide the nice guy belongs in the friend zone.

The opposite is also true. Perhaps all chaos breaks loose in one area of your life, or you skip the gym for a few weeks when it's normally been a daily habit, or you drink much more than usual for a few days in a row, or you find yourself gossiping about someone and it doesn't feel good. In all of these cases you feel the temperature drop and know you're worthy of being better than that. So your thermostat kicks in. You stop doing the lower-temperature behavior. You correct the mistake, raising the temperature of your self-worth and life back up to where you think it belongs. Can you relate to any of this?

Identifying this inclination, coupled with all of the lessons and learnings I've shared with you in the stories of this book, has allowed me to raise my own self-worth many times. In many areas of my life, it's allowed me to increase and operate at a higher temperature, or vibration, permanently. And in the beautiful words of futurist, creativity expert, and author Erwin Raphael McManus, "It's less important to know who you are, than who you are becoming."

Keeping promises to myself, along with doing the hard work of being aware of and silencing my inner critic, has also been instrumental. You know, that voice of self-doubt inside our heads that basically lies to us all day long and tells us we're not enough. That voice that says things like "you're a bad mom" or "you're not smart enough" or "your body isn't beautiful enough" or "you don't deserve anyone better than him" or "if you leave, you'll end up all alone" or "you're not talented enough to ask for a promotion or a raise." If we don't stop the inner critic in time, we start to believe the lies. And once those lies take root as beliefs about ourselves, they can destroy our self-confidence and really affect all areas of our lives. For many of us, the relationship with our own inner critic is the most toxic relationship we'll ever be in. We need to take control of that voice. Our inner narrative, especially as it pertains to what we tell ourselves about ourselves, needs to be our biggest champion, because at the end of the day, we are who we tell ourselves we are.

When I think about my journey up to this point, I know this deep-rooted sense of not-enough-ness is why I've done things like stayed in some toxic relationships for far longer than I should have. And I worked so hard to change that. It's why in my past I kept certain friends around me, even though they would gossip or weren't always kind. I worked hard to up my own temperature and get new friends. Having set a low temperature in the area of abandonment is a way of understanding why I've been slow to fire toxic employees. I worked really hard to overcome and change that too.

I try to catch my thoughts in time and take control of them. Doing these things, coupled with a whole lot of grace, grit, and God, has allowed me to be open to receiving incredible things in my life. I changed my perspective on my rosacea. I went from being insecure about it to raising my own temperature and believing it was a gift I was given. I actually, truly, and fully believe my rosacea is beautiful. And a gift that could empower others. Changing what I believed about my rosacea, and getting inspired to change how other women see their own beauty, changed my entire life. It sparked the idea for my company, a makeup line that was quick and easy to use and looked like real skin on the days you felt like wearing it . . . and a makeup line with the bigger message that the real you is just as beautiful on the days you don't. And I truly believe this, and that's why it worked. Believing I was worthy of belonging on the shelves of Sephora and ULTA Beauty and on QVC is how I kept getting back up every time hearing another *no* knocked me down. Deciding and believing I was worthy of creating a billion-dollar company is a huge part of how I was able to do it.

But as the saying goes, *You didn't come this far to only come this far.* As I write this, I still have a long way to go. Every day is a work in progress as I strive to continue raising the temperature of my thermostat on my own journey of becoming the person God made me to be.

I still struggle daily to get that temperature higher in some areas of my life. It's why I've fallen off every healthy eating plan I started. It's why I turn to food every time I don't want to feel my own feelings. It's why I still struggle with loving and embracing my body. One of my many goals is to wear a bikini in public, strut my stuff while shaking my cellulite with pride, and not have it cause me an ounce of second thought. But I'm not fully there yet. And it makes me mad. I mean, how could I be the CEO of a brand that authentically inspires women and yet still have insecurities about putting on a bathing suit? I am the *last* person in the world who would *ever* judge or care or even notice what another person looks like in a swimsuit, yet I am judging myself for it, instead of focusing on the lessons of confidence I want to teach my daughter and how blessed I am to have a healthy body that's mobile. I mean, seriously, this has to stop! Life is too short!

I've learned the lesson that something's got to give, and I can know in my head all day long how ridiculous these things are, but I've learned that the only way to change them is to do the hard work of raising my own internal temperature to believe I am enough and worthy exactly as I am. The only way to change these things is to change what I believe to be true about each of them, and to do the work to triumph over my own inner critic. And I'm working very hard to do that. And I know I will succeed.

And as I gain a deeper understanding of how to change these limiting beliefs about myself, I promise I will continue to share what works for me in my journey.

While I haven't actually picked up the phone to call Oprah yet, I did text her (while praying like crazy) to let her know I wrote the first draft of my book, and I asked her if she would read it and give me her honest response. AND SHE SAID YES!!! (I can't even explain how many times I've reread her text. I might even blow it up into giant wall art . . . too much?) I had the manuscript delivered to her, and a few months later, she sent me her written feedback and notes. It was incredibly help-ful, and it gave me such peace to have her blessing on the stories I shared about her in this book. I was also so happy to learn that she found the countless frames of ballsy squirrels on my kitchen table super funny. So . . . here's where I'm at. One day I will actually *call* Oprah, and when I do, I hope I'm not surprised when she answers. But my ultimate goal is to arrive on that day knowing that even if she doesn't, no matter what, it has no impact on whether I believe that I am truly enough.

This book isn't a pure success story, but it's

the real story. I am a work in progress. And while I'm not yet the human being I want to be, I've come a long way, and keep striving toward becoming her every day.

Before you close this book, I'd like you to try something with me. First, take a few moments and think about all of the obstacles you've overcome to get where you're at right now. All of the hardships you've survived. The battles you've fought and the scars you have that tell your stories. Stories of love lost and gained, stories of pain and stories of blessings. Think about your victories, where you found strength to overcome fear, and where you chose love. Think about just how far you've come and how strong you are. Proof that you're a miracle in motion. Now, place your hand on your heart and thank it for beating for you all these years. Feel it beating for you right now and say thank you. Right now, at this very moment, it's showing up for you. Again and again. It's endured heartache for you during your lowest times and it's pumped fast for you during your highest. It continues to show up for you, giving you chance after chance to fill up yourself and the world with love. It's never failed you. It always shows up. Take a moment and say thank you to your heart that beats and to your soul that guides you. Next, look up to the sky with a big smile on your face. Then, still smiling, close your eyes. Visualize the feeling of complete power and utter joy when you channel true self-belief through your entire body. And just feel that for a few minutes. You can call this a meditation or a prayer, whatever feels right to you. Take a few minutes to get still and continue to give appreciation for how far you've come, for the challenges you've faced and the obstacles you've overcome victoriously. I believe the famous words "What you appreciate, appreciates," so appreciate YOU. You are a real-life miracle, and a living, breathing force for good. And the power has always been inside of you to believe — not only in yourself, but also in the power of your wildest dreams. God put those dreams in you, and He made you with everything you need to fulfill your calling. It's all in you. Truly imagine . . . what if you have everything it takes inside of you right now to accomplish your wildest dreams? And whether you do or don't, imagine what would happen if you believed it anyway?

So many people ask me how I started a business with an idea, with almost no money, in my living room, and grew it into a billion-dollar company. I worked really,

really hard and I didn't give up, but the most important thing I did . . . was believe that I could. I decided to believe that I could no matter what anyone else said. I decided to believe that I could no matter how many times the experts didn't. I decided to believe that I belong — in the beauty stores and in the beauty industry, on the magazine pages, in the CEO role, on TV, and in my own skin — and even though I was given away at birth, I decided to believe I was put on this earth on purpose and with purpose. Rejection comes in so many forms, and it almost always hurts when it happens, but I truly believe rejection is God's way of making us strong enough to one day be able to handle the weight of our biggest dreams coming true.

So I say it's time. It's time to believe in ourselves the way God believes in us. And the way we believe in our own babies as they are about to take their first steps. It's time to take that uninhibited faith and confidence and joy that we easily give to others and give it to ourselves.

It's truly an honor to share with you some of my life's greatest lessons in this book. Lessons I've learned, sometimes the hard way. To believe in the power of your own intuition. To believe that you're more powerful than your opposition, including mean girls, and that balance is a lie. To believe in the power of your own microphone, and in knowing how to use it, who to give it to, and who you need to turn down the volume on. To believe in the power of your WHY, and that your own authenticity is your superpower. To believe people when they show you who they truly are, believe in being brave, and believe that haters are just confused supporters. To believe in the power of living your values, and to value the power of asking for what you need. To believe that life isn't meant to do alone, and to know that where you come from doesn't determine where you're going. To believe in giving what you need most, then watching in awe as it comes to you in full force. To believe in miracles, believe you are more than enough, and of course believe in Oprah!!! To believe in the power of letting your light shine, and more than anything to believe that a power greater than yourself has already given you everything you need inside of you.

My prayer and challenge to you is to listen to what you know deep down inside to be true about who you really are, and who you were born to be. And then wholeheartedly, unapologetically, with big, bold, wild abandon and every part of your being, start believing fully in the power that's in, that's of, and that is YOU. We are all in this together, and it's an honor to share this life in community with you. I love you. You are worthy of your greatest hopes and wildest dreams and of all the unconditional love in the world. **Believe it.**

Love and blessings,
Your Sister (from another mister . . . although that technically could be TBD),
Jamie

# ACKNOWLEDGMENTS

The creation of this book wouldn't have been possible without the love, contribution, and encouragement of so many. Paulo, thank you for all of your support, especially on the days where I binge ate Lucky Charms, sobbing my eyes out, while writing my story for the first time ever. Thank you for being my partner in love and in life . . . wow, what a ride so far! To Wonder and Wilder, my prayer is that you grow up believing fully in the beautiful and authentic power that is you, exactly as God created you to be. Thank you to my friends and family, the ones mentioned in the stories in this book and the many, many more who are not, but who are equally to thank for being part of my story, my strength, my character, and my heart. I cherish you and am grateful to have the gift of doing life with you. Thank you for loving me. I love you.

This book is the result of many people

showing their belief in me through the most precious gift I could ask for: their time. I would specifically like to thank the following people for their mentorship, their leadership, their friendship, and their championship of me and my intention for this book to touch as many lives as possible: thank you, Brendon Burchard. I could write an entire book just on the ways you've shown up for me with your support, wisdom, and encouragement. Thank you, Oprah Winfrey, for the blessing of your time, your always-candid feedback, and your invaluable mentorship. A special thank-you to Bob and Maria Goff, Erwin and Kim McManus, Glennon Doyle, Robin Roberts, Victoria and Joel Osteen, David Bach, Sara Blakely, Chrissy Metz, Mel Robbins, Ellen De-Generes, John Maxwell, Tony and Sage Robbins, Dean and Lisa Graziosi, Jenna Kutcher, Jay Shetty, Jon Gordon, Joel Marion, Trent Shelton, Natalie Ellis, Danielle Canty, Jim Kwik, Randy Garn, Mel Abraham, Lisa and Tom Bilyeu, Craig Clemens, Sarah Anne Stewart, Christy Wright, Mally Roncal, Miles Adcox, Rory and AJ Vaden, Margaret Riley King, Lewis Howes, Russell Brunson, Lori Harder, Amy Porterfield, Gloria Williams, Donald Miller, Lisa Bevere, Alison Prince, Alli Webb,

Anthony Trucks, Pete Vargas, Prince EA, Evan Carmichael, and all of my amazing friends in The PR Beach Gang who have supported this book in ways I couldn't have imagined. And an extra special thank-you to my Wolfpack: Jacquie, Lia, Des, Dana, Denise, and Natasha. To the many, many more friends too numerous to list, who have helped support me in writing this book, thank you for sharing your encouragement, ideas, inspiration, contacts, advice, endorsements, prayers, and thank you most of all for your belief in me.

The creation and launch of this book was only made possible by a true dream team. Thank you to Dupree Miller, especially Jan, Nena, Lacy, and Shannon for approaching me many years ago to do a book. Thank you for believing, even then. Thank you, Sarah Witt and Holly Quillen, for wearing a million hats and for supporting me and this book in more ways than I can count. Thank you, Hilary Liftin, for your abundant talent and partnership. Thank you, Daniel Decker, for your advice and expertise.

Thank you to my editor, Lauren Spiegel, for your instincts, vision, leadership, talent, and partnership, and thank you to the entire team at Gallery Books and Simon & Schuster for your belief in me and this book, including Jen Bergstrom, Aimee Bell, Jen Long, Sally Marvin, Jessica Roth, Bianca Salvant, Eliza Hanson, Caroline Pallotta, Alysha Bullock, Davina Mock-Maniscalco, Mike Kwan, Lisa Litwack, John Vairo, Susan Fissell, Rebecca Strobel, Edward Klaris, and Chelsea McGuckin.

Thank you to my IT Cosmetics family. There are too many of you to name individually, but IT Cosmetics wouldn't have been possible without each one of you. There's not a day that goes by where I don't think of how blessed I am to have built a team far smarter and more talented than me, and with just as big of a heart. In the early years, so many of you left way more secure jobs to take a chance on this tiny company with big dreams to impact lives all around the world. And we did it! You did it! Thank you for your heart, your passion, your commitment, your talent, and for building something so much greater than ourselves. What started with a dream, and the name "IT," which stood for Innovative Technology, turned into meaning so much more for our millions of IT Girls and IT Guys around the world. A special thank-you to everyone in my and Paulo's family, for the years you walked into every store asking the manager if they carry IT Cosmetics, even when you knew they

438

didn't. Then asking them to start carrying IT! You are the original IT Team members, too! Thank you to Virginia Lima and Paulo's entire family for your love and support of our journey. And a fun fact and special thank-you to two special honorary IT Cosmetics family members, Ricardo Lima and Ilana Zylberman, it was while sitting around their kitchen table one evening while Paulo and I were crashing at their place while in NYC for a meeting because we couldn't afford a hotel room at the time, that Ilana came up with the name "IT." And from the moment she said it, we knew it was right.

A special thank-you to our IT team in Canada, and especially to Sonya Butler, who believed in me and Paulo and helped build IT in Canada from the very beginning. I'll never forget the very first time, many years in, when we did a million dollars in a day, and you couldn't stop crying. Best photo of you ever! Thank you to our team at The Shopping Channel Canada and our models, who are like family. You are my heart to this day, I love you.

Thank you to TSG Consumer Partners, especially Chuck, Blythe, and Diane, for believing in us when we were still running the business from our living room. I told you then that we'd be the most successful investment in the history of TSG. Thank you for believing in me and for your incredible partnership, and now lifelong friendship. Thank you to the Guthy-Renker team, and especially Bill and Greg for seeing our product vision long before it existed, and for your partnership and friendship. Thank you Bob Caudill and your incredible team. Thank you to L'Oréal for believing in our vision at IT Cosmetics and for helping spread our message of authentic and inclusive beauty globally. Thank you to all of the incredible teams at L'Oréal, both in the US and globally, for your passion and commitment to IT Cosmetics and our customers.

Thank you to our many partners and manufacturers who believed in us, even in the early years, especially Michael, Ian, and Sunny. Michael, thank you for making our very first product packaging samples for free, after I sketched them on the back of a piece of paper and explained this huge dream I had. Your belief in me, without any reason to have it, was true grace.

Thank you to our many amazing retail partners, who have helped get our products and message in the hands of women and men everywhere. Thank you to the entire team and incredibly talented hosts at QVC, and especially Allen Burke, Mike George, and Lisa Mason. Allen, you were always right when you said *NO,* and your *NO's* were the biggest blessings in hindsight. And you were also right when you said *YES.* Thank you for being right, each time. And thank you for your invaluable advice, mentorship, and friendship. Lisa, thank you for listening to that still small voice inside. Thank you to the team at ULTA Beauty, including Mary, Dave, Kecia, and Tara for believing in us, launching us into retail stores across the country, and for an incredible partnership. And thank you for the many events we've done together and the many tears we've shed together with customers as we share stories of confidence together. Thank you to the team at Sephora, including Artemis, Priya, and Alison for your belief in me and in IT Cosmetics. I still get butterflies every time I walk into a Sephora and see IT, and I still have to pinch myself to believe it. Thank you to the many other retailers and your teams for your love and support of IT Cosmetics and for touching the lives of our amazing customers each and every day.

Thank you to the many amazing people and friends who helped us build IT in the early years, both in Seattle and in Los

Angeles, before we could afford an actual office. David Van Maren, thank you for all of your support from the very beginning.

And, most importantly, as it pertains to the story of IT Cosmetics, thank you to the millions of IT customers, aka IT Family, who have bravely shared their stories and spread the word about IT Cosmetics. Thank you for sharing your product recommendations, your photos, your authentic beauty journey, and your heart. Thank you, most of all, for reminding each and every person that they are beautiful and that they belong, exactly as they are.

Thank you from the bottom of my heart to each and every person who has been part of my journey so far. And a final special thank-you to my mom Nina. Thank you for showing me an example of what a real-life superhero looks like. Thank you for the early morning pancake breakfasts at the diner before work and daycare. Thank you for always making me feel like I was your favorite person in the world. Thank you for loving me so well, that you're always the first person I want to call, in any situation my entire life, and still to this day. And, most of all, thank you for teaching me to believe all things are possible, a belief I now have the blessing of teaching Wonder and

Wilder and anyone else who will listen. I love you. Thank you for loving me. And for choosing me. I now get to choose you, too. And do and will every day. Forever.

# ABOUT THE AUTHOR

**Jamie Kern Lima** started IT Cosmetics in her living room and grew the company into the largest luxury makeup brand in the country. She sold the company to L'Oréal in a billion-dollar deal and became the first female CEO of a brand in its history. Her love of her customers and remarkable authenticity and belief eventually landed her on the *Forbes* America's Richest Self-Made Women list. Today, she's a mother of two and an active investor, speaker, and thought leader who is passionate about inspiring and elevating women. She's also an active philanthropist who has donated over $40 million in product and funds to help women face the effects of cancer with confidence. Learn more at JamieKern Lima.com

www.jamiekernlima.com | Instagram: @jamiekernlima